The B
for Vella

ALSO BY REG NEWELL

*Operation Goodtime and the Battle of the
Treasury Islands, 1943: The World War II Invasion
by United States and New Zealand Forces* (McFarland, 2012)

THE BATTLE FOR VELLA LAVELLA

The Allied Recapture
of Solomon Islands Territory,
August 15–September 9, 1943

REG NEWELL

McFarland & Company, Inc., Publishers
Jefferson, North Carolina

Library of Congress Cataloguing-in-Publication Data

Names: Newell, Reg, 1954– author.
Title: The battle for Vella Lavella : the Allied recapture of Solomon Islands territory, August 15–September 9, 1943 / Reg Newell.
Description: Jefferson, North Carolina : McFarland & Company, Inc., Publishers, 2016. | Includes bibliographical references and index.
Identifiers: LCCN 2015039571| ISBN 9780786473274 (softcover : acid free paper) | ISBN 9781476619842 (ebook)
Subjects: LCSH: World War, 1939–1945—Campaigns—Solomon Islands. | New Zealand—Armed Forces—History—World War, 1939–1945. | United States—Armed Forces—History—World War, 1939–1945. | World War, 1939–1945—Regimental histories— New Zealand. | World War, 1939–1945—Regimental histories— United States.
Classification: LCC D767.98 .N49 2016 | DDC 940.54/265931— dc23
LC record available at http://lccn.loc.gov/2015039571

British Library cataloguing data are available

Cover image: New Zealand soldiers disembarking at Barakoma (U.S. Signal Corps, Archives New Zealand/Te Rua Mahara o te Kāwanatanga, Wellington Office, WAII, 7 3)

Printed in the United States of America

McFarland & Company, Inc., Publishers
Box 611, Jefferson, North Carolina 28640
www.mcfarlandpub.com

To all those who fought in the struggle
for freedom in the Solomon Islands.

Acknowledgments

I would like to acknowledge the assistance of all those who contributed to this work, particularly the veterans who were on Vella Lavella: Gordon Graham, Lindsay Adams, Harry Bioletti, Lawrence Baldwin, Doug Ross, Jack Humphry, Ross Templeton, Denny Frangos, Frank Marks, and Jerome Hendrick.

I would also like to thank my typist, Kirsty Nolan, and above all my wife, Heather Newell, and son, Michael Newell, for their patience and support while I completed this work.

Table of Contents

Introduction

The Pacific war erupted on 7/8 December 1941 with the Japanese pulverizing the U.S. Pacific Fleet at Pearl Harbor and invading Malaya. For a period of six months thereafter the Japanese seemed virtually unstoppable, with the Japanese brushing aside Allied resistance and seizing Hong Kong, Malaya, Singapore, the Philippines and Dutch East Indies. That expansion came to an abrupt halt at a previously obscure island called Guadalcanal and an aptly named island called Midway.

The year 1943 would see the Allies in the Pacific begin to roll back the Japanese, and the threat to Australasia started to recede. The formerly peaceful islands of the Solomons became a battleground, and one of those was a place called Vella Lavella.

Vella Lavella. The name sounds pleasant and conjures up images of a Pacific island paradise. But the reality for those who encountered the island, located in the New Georgia group of the Solomon Islands, in 1943 was very different. The struggle for Vella Lavella involved intense, no-quarter air, land and sea combat. It began and ended with a series of naval battles as each side bitterly contested control of the waters around Vella Lavella. The Americans landed in August 1943 and secured a lodgment in the south of the island. They were followed in September by New Zealand soldiers. After a brutal struggle they succeeded in clearing the island of its Japanese defenders. It is doubtful if any of the American or Kiwi[1] soldiers had heard of Vella Lavella prior to their landing, but for those who fought on the island, their time on Vella Lavella would impact them for the rest of their lives.

Sadly, the actions of the Japanese, American, Fijian, Tongan, Solomon Islands and New Zealand soldiers who fought on Vella Lavella have sunk into the mists of history,[2] and today there is little, if any, recognition or remembrance of what occurred, particularly as the World War II generation passes

1

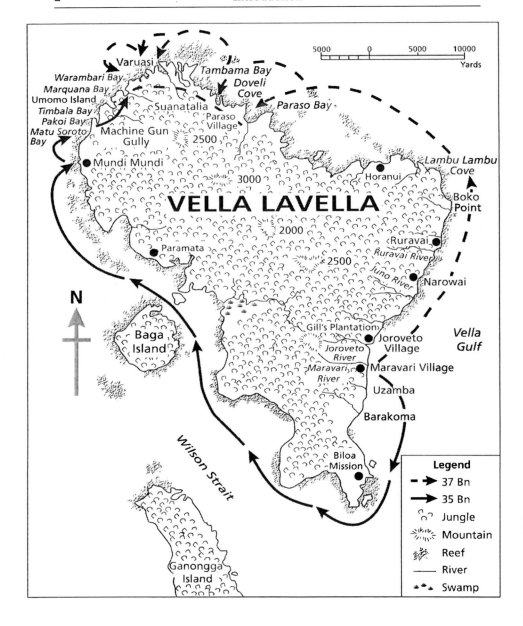

Vella Lavella, showing the movement of the 35th and 37th Battalion Combat Teams, 14 Brigade (Fran Whild).

away. The U.S. Army official history declares that "there was never any real ground combat on Vella Lavella because Japanese stragglers were mainly interested in escape rather than fighting."[3] It is the purpose of this book to refute that statement and to provide the combatants with the recognition they deserve. The impact of the war on the local people also needs recognition.

For the New Zealand infantrymen who fought on Vella Lavella, their experience was quite different from other battles fought by 3NZ Division. Combat was at close range and personal and often at the small unit level with limited fire support available. There was often not a superiority in Allied

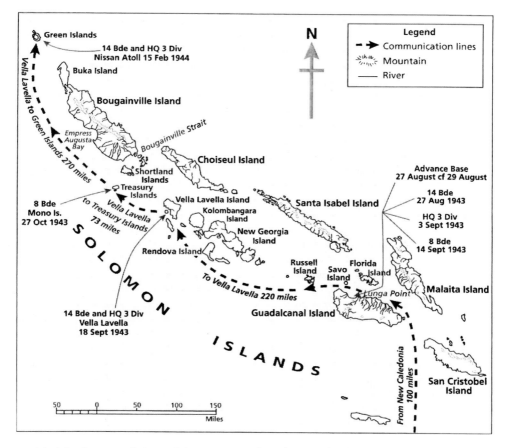

The Third Division's Area of Operations in the Solomon Islands, 1943–1944, showing 3NZ Division's long lines of communication and landing dates on Guadalcanal, Vella Lavella, the Treasury Islands and the Green Islands (adapted by Fran Whild from the 3NZ Division unofficial histories).

numbers, and on occasion soldiers from 14 Brigade found themselves out-numbered (and sometimes encircled) by determined Japanese defenders. The combat on Vella Lavella was very much a soldier's struggle.

At the time of this fighting the Kiwis were the northernmost Allied soldiers in the Solomons, and there was the ever-present threat of Japanese counterattack in force. There was also the threat of being strafed and bombed by Japanese aircraft. The fighting demanded high standards of the Kiwis' field and battle craft. The Japanese, for their part, were no pushovers and were determined to exact a high toll in New Zealand lives.

The struggle for Vella Lavella required sophisticated logistical and amphibious skills; for these reasons alone, it merits rescue from the veil of obscurity that has descended on it.

This book is an outgrowth of my interest in 3NZ Division and the research I undertook for my doctoral thesis. My original intention was to

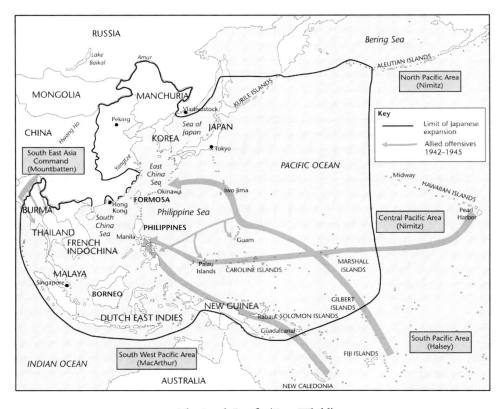

The South Pacific (Fran Whild).

focus purely on the New Zealand land battles of 14 Brigade, a story forgotten in New Zealand. However, as I began digging further into the Vella Lavella story, I began to appreciate that there were wider backstories—the fierce naval battles that raged around Vella Lavella and claimed (among others) the light cruiser USS *Helena*; the courageous Islanders and Coastwatchers such as Sub-Lieutenant Henry Josselyn and the Rev. Archie Silvester; the air battles that raged overhead, including the extraordinary story of Congressional Medal of Honor winner Kenneth Walsh, USMC; the efforts of the South Pacific Scouts and the 35th Infantry Regiment who invaded Vella Lavella; and the heroism of medic Rex Gregor.

One of the most melancholy experiences I had while researching this book was examining on the 35th Infantry Regiment (Cacti) Association website the photographs and biographical data of those soldiers killed on Vella Lavella. This brought home to me the personal cost of victory on Vella Lavella—children left fatherless, wives left widowed and parents who would never see their sons again. Freedom has a high price.

ONE

Ordeals of Fire and Water

Allied personnel who washed up on the shores of Vella Lavella in 1943 had to pass through both fire and water before reaching the island. For some, Vella Lavella would be a final resting place; for others, it was the hope of salvation.

Uncertain Sanctuary—USS Helena *and Vella Lavella*

Lieutenant Commander John L. Chew, USN, later blamed himself for breaking one of his rituals on board the ship and thereby creating bad luck. Like most sailors, he was deeply superstitious—he always wore the same pair of brown shoes and a flashproof jumper, and he carried his lucky hunting knife, lucky silver dollar and four-leaf clover. Above all, he never shaved before going into combat. On the night of 6 July 1943, Chew violated his routines and his ship's luck ran out.

His ship was the cruiser USS *Helena* (CL-50). One of the "Brooklyn" class of light cruisers, *Helena* was launched in 1939 and packed an awesome array of 15 six-inch guns and 8 five-inch guns. She was also fast, with a maximum speed of 33 knots.[1] There was, however, a price to be paid for weaponry and speed. As naval historian Richard Worth comments, "With its lavish weaponry and reasonable armor, the design had to lack something—structural strength."[2]

Nonetheless, *Helena* was a lucky ship. She was at Pearl Harbor on 7 December 1941, the morning of the devastating Japanese air attack, and took a Japanese torpedo. Prompt action by the crew in closing the watertight doors and carrying out damage control saved her. After repairs she re-entered the war in 1942, providing convoy escort in the vicious naval battles around Guadal-

7

canal. *Helena* used her surface radar very skillfully, and at the Battle of Cape Esperance on 11 October 1942 she sank the Japanese cruiser *Furutaka* and the destroyer *Fubuki*. She was also involved in the first Naval Battle of Guadalcanal on the night of 12 November 1942. *Helena* again used her radar to devastating effect and in return suffered only minor damage to her superstructure. After this *Helena* took part in the bombardment of Japanese positions in the New Georgia group.

On 4 July 1943, *Helena* was once more escorting troop transports in the Kula Gulf, and she bombarded Japanese positions. The unloading of troops was successfully carried out and *Helena* began steaming south. Chew, the assistant gunnery officer, anticipated that the ship was heading toward safety and a few days of well-earned rest. He began shaving. Events, however, were moving beyond his control.

Word was received that the Japanese were attempting to run a "Tokyo Express" (a reinforcement and supply convoy) to Major General Noboru Sasaki's troops on Munda. *Helena*, part of a group made up of three cruisers and four destroyers under the command of Rear Admiral Walden L. Ainsworth, USN, prepared to confront the Japanese. In the early morning hours of 6 July, *Helena* was at the mouth of the Kula Gulf in the northwest area of the New Georgia group. She was sailing at 25 knots and clouds hid the moon. At 0136 hours, her radar detected seven to nine Japanese ships coming out of the Kula Gulf near Kolombangara. *Helena*'s guns opened fire at 0157 and soon exhausted her supply of flashless ammunition. Her gun flashes outlined her structure and made the ship a perfect target. The Japanese were very skilled at night fighting and possessed a deadly secret weapon—the 24-inch Type 93 Long Lance torpedo of great reliability, accuracy and explosive power. Powered by oxygen and virtually wakeless, the Long Lance, with its considerable range, fitted perfectly into Japanese night-fighting doctrine. The Japanese preferred to use torpedoes rather than gunfire because this did not give away their position, and they were about to teach the American sailors a painful lesson in tactics.

At 0204 hours the first Long Lance torpedo struck, blowing off *Helena*'s bow. Within three minutes *Helena* was hit by a second and then a third torpedo. The second torpedo hit a vulnerable point, disabling the ship's machinery—the guns fell silent, all steerage power was gone and the lighting failed except for emergency lights. The third torpedo inflicted "maximum trauma on the ship's structure."[3] *Helena*'s fate was sealed.[4]

Captain Charles P. Cecil gave the order to abandon ship. *Helena* was dead in the water, broken into three sections and sinking. The crew began to go over the side. The stricken ship then jackknifed with the bow and the stern in the air. With a rumble the mid and stern sections of the ship slid downward, leaving the bow section still afloat.

Hundreds of sailors were in the shark-infested, oil-coated waters. Some had the good fortune to find rafts or bits of flotsam to cling to. The crew gathered in clusters, hoping that this would make them easier for rescuers to spot.

Japanese star shells illuminated the night and the battle raged around *Helena*'s wreckage, and then suddenly it seemed to have ended. The sailors hoped that their comrades would return to rescue them. At dawn their hopes seemed realized—the destroyers USS *Nicholas* and USS *Radford* appeared, lowered boats, dropped cargo nets over their sides and began taking on survivors. Ensign George Bausewine was floating on his back, calmly waiting his turn to be taken aboard. To his dismay, the destroyer took off, firing her guns. A Japanese ship had been sighted and had fired a torpedo. It seemed that battle was to recommence, but the Japanese ship withdrew. The American destroyers then left for Tulagi, having taken on board 745 of the *Helena*'s crew. The Japanese controlled the skies, and the destroyer captains wisely did not want to expose their ships to destruction from the air. The rescue effort had abruptly ended.

The destroyers had, however, left behind four boats that had been used in the rescue efforts. Captain Cecil organized three motor whaleboats, each towing a lifeboat, to sail to a small island near Rice Anchorage. They were rescued the next day.

That left a group of two hundred unfortunates, including Chew, most covered in fuel oil from the sunken ship and many with injuries. This group had been treading water, but circumstances provided a strange liferaft—the bow of their ship. Jutting twenty feet out of the water, it became a rallying point for the survivors. However, the bow was slowly sinking. Salvation then appeared in the form of a Navy Liberator plane, which dropped lifejackets and rubber lifeboats. One lifeboat failed to open, but Chew's group was able to inflate the other two. The problem was that each raft could only hold four men, so Chew put his most badly wounded in them.

The next planes to arrive were not friendly—they were Japanese Zeros. By this stage of the war no mercy was shown to helpless combatants. The Japanese routinely shot at Allied pilots in parachutes or in the water. By the same token, Allied planes had massacred shipwrecked Japanese survivors in the Battle of the Bismarck Sea. Chew did not expect any mercy. To his surprise, the Japanese planes made three passes, and then the lead plane's pilot waved, waggled his plane's wings and left. Chew believed that the Americans were so coated in fuel oil that the pilots had believed them to be Japanese sailors.

Fearing that the bow would attract further Japanese planes, Chew decided to strike out for Kolombangara. His group included fifty men and they had two rafts. They placed the wounded on board, with some paddling and others in the water clinging to the sides and attempting to propel their fragile refuge toward land.

Sadly, American search planes failed to spot the survivors and the injured began to die. The survivors were exhausted, and prospects seemed dim. Hallucinations set in—Ensign George Bausewine went underwater momentarily to find a bunk, and another man kept asking Bausewine for a cigarette. The rotation of men spending time on the raft paddling and in the water broke down on the morning of 8 July, when those on the raft refused to get back in the water. Chew was too exhausted to force them.

Chew could see land at what appeared to be a short distance away. It seemed like the last hope. He decided to try and swim for it with two others. They made little progress—Vella Lavella seemed as far off as ever, and they became separated. One of the men, Lieutenant Commander Warren Boles, an excellent swimmer, made landfall, found a coconut, drank its contents and then fell into an exhausted sleep. Chew, floating in the water and in semi-darkness, was utterly drained. Then he saw two Islanders paddling a canoe toward him. "You Melican?" they asked, and Chew replied, "You betcha." The Islanders then pulled him into the canoe and paddled for shore. On reaching land they asked Chew if he could walk. When Chew tried, he promptly collapsed.

Over a ten-mile stretch of beach between Paraso Bay and Lambu Cove, a rescue began to take place. Islanders in their canoes dashed in and out of the surf, pulling American sailors to safety. Other Islanders plucked Americans out of the open sea and onto shore. Chew's rubber boats were picked up and brought to the beach with other survivors.

However, the appearance of safety was illusory—Vella Lavella was a Japanese-held island and the sailors were in imminent danger from Japanese patrols. The Americans had by good fortune landed on the side of Vella Lavella opposite where the Japanese garrison was located.

Ken Schank, a machinists mate, survived the sinking but became constantly sick from having swallowed oil and seawater. When his group of sixty men reached Vella Lavella, Schank, half conscious and staggering, was met in the surf by Islanders and helped ashore. He had the good fortune to have kept his shoes. "In the protecting darkness natives pour coconut milk down parched throats. The men revive enough to comprehend broken English whispers from the natives: 'Japs that way—you go that way—hurry....'"[5]

Chew recalled:

> The natives took us about 2½ miles from the beach. It was a pleasant excursion for those of us in the litters who were merely too weak to walk, but tough going for the others. First, it was necessary to cross a thick swampy jungle, into which one sank up to the knees. Then we followed a very rough winding trail along the mountain side. The island had been occupied by the Japs for about a year and a half. When they first came, they killed 25 or 30 of the natives for no reason. This wanton murder fostered a deep hatred of the Japs, and the natives abandoned their villages along the beach and sought relative safety in the hills. Before Vella Lavella was invaded, the natives supported themselves largely by raising coconuts and selling them to island traders. They are also fishermen, and most villages had small garden plots. All of these had to be abandoned when they retreated to the bush.[6]

Some of the Americans found their saviors to be somewhat frightening. Frank Cellozzi, a Navy gunner's mate, endured five days on a raft before making landfall with his group on Vella Lavella. Their raft became stuck fast on one of the coral reefs ringing the island, and the shipwrecked sailors had to walk barefoot across 400 feet of razor-sharp coral rocks to get ashore, reducing their feet to a bloody pulp. When they reached land Cellozzi recalled, "Our first impression was of paradise—lush, rich jungle forest and cool green palm trees!" The Americans crawled into the jungle and fell fast asleep. They were completely helpless—done in by the rigors of their ordeal and lacking weapons. Cellozzi estimated that his weight had dropped from 150 pounds to 105 pounds.

> The next morning we heard some movement coming through the jungle. We figured it had to be Japanese jungle scouting troops. We knew we would be killed. Imagine our surprise when fifteen island natives emerged from the bush! For some short minutes, we wished we were back on their raft. We had heard that on some of these islands the natives were still cannibalistic. They appeared straight out of "National Geographic" wearing nothing but loin cloths with bones through their noses, wild-eyed, bushy haired and carrying spears. They seemed as surprised as we were.[7]

The Americans repeated over and over, "We no Jap—American." The Islanders shook hands with the sailors and "put their arms around [them] like old friends." The Americans were then hoisted onto the Islanders' backs and carried deep into the jungle, through mangrove swamps, jungle trails and rivers, for what seemed like miles. Eventually the group made camp for the night, and the sailors were fed by the Islanders—coconuts, tropical wild fruit and taro roots. They were taken the next day to a campsite, "sometimes led and sometimes carried by the friendly natives through the jungle, swamp and along a trail that climbed up into the hills."

The previous stresses on the Islanders' food stocks were now multiplied by the arrival of three groups of exhausted survivors totaling 165 men. The Islanders had been pushed into the interior by the Japanese, and their own supplies were meager. Nonetheless, they unstintingly supplied the exhausted and hungry sailors with food.

Chew found himself as the senior naval officer, with Major Bernard T. Kelly, USMC, as the head of a forty-two-man group of Marines. Chew became the self-appointed "mayor" of the little community, with Kelly as "chief of police" and head of "Kelly's Irregulars," his ragtag group of Marines. Although part of the U.S. Navy, Marine Corps personnel have their own particular military culture and identity that set them apart from their sailor counterparts. Kelly firmly stamped his discipline on both his own men and the sailors. The men were all in bad shape, some injured, most suffering from being covered in fuel oil and spending days in saltwater.[8] They had only a few pistols, limited ammunition and minimal capacity to defend themselves against Japanese troops with a reputation for slaughtering prisoners. Their survival depended on help from the Islanders and some amazingly colorful and exotic characters.

One was a Chinese trader, Sam Chung. He was one of thirty-five Chinese who had fled into the interior when the Japanese arrived. He made his home, some two and a half miles from Lambu Lambu, available to the exhausted Americans. Chung's family vacated the house, a small bungalow made of bamboo with a galvanized iron roof. Islanders soon created a lean-to.

Another was Sub-Lieutenant Robert Firth, an Australian Coastwatcher. Firth and his English companion, Sub-Lieutenant Henry Josselyn, were based on Vella Lavella and had covertly reported Japanese shipping and aerial activity and kept watch on the Japanese garrison at Iringila. Japanese barge traffic had increased, and so had Japanese patrols on the island. Josselyn had left their camp at the village of Joupalando on an errand, leaving Firth in charge. To Firth's surprise, a breathless Islander ran up to him saying that there were "plenty Americans" on the beach on the east coast of Vella Lavella. The Islander showed Firth a pair of U.S. dog tags. Suspicious that this might be a Japanese trick to entrap the Coastwatchers, Firth radioed to the American base on Guadalcanal, gave them the details of the name and number on the dog tags and waited for a response. It was not long in coming—Guadalcanal confirmed that the dog tags belonged to a machinists mate on the *Helena*. Firth sent for

Josselyn, and when he arrived they agreed they had to act fast. The survivors had landed in Paraso Bay and in the vicinity of Lambu Lambu village. The Japanese maintained outposts near both areas, so urgent action was needed to pick up survivors and clear away any evidence of their arrival. Once detected, the Japanese could be counted on for a swift and brutal response.

Two messengers were sent off. One came to "Bamboo," the chief of Mundau, a village at the back of Boro, in the area where the survivors were landing. The second went to one of the most significant personalities to figure in the fate of the shipwrecked Americans: a balding, round-faced man of the cloth, the Rev. Archie Silvester. Silvester was a New Zealand Methodist missionary who had stayed with his congregation despite the Japanese invasion. The "Bish" (Bishop) or "Tanula" was a man of considerable charisma. Silvester immediately began organizing the Islanders to assist the Americans. He arranged for the Islanders to provide labor to build shelters for the Americans and to provide food from their meager supplies. James Layton, a pharmacists mate first class, observed Silvester in action:

> The one man to whom we all owed so much was Sylvester [*sic*]. I had almost daily contact with him and in my opinion he was quite a man. He was a major player in organizing the natives to rescue many of our shipmates from certain death at sea and getting them safely into camp. He took care of our food, shelter, medicine and security. But more than that he gave the spiritual aid that held us together.[9]

The Christian religion was a common bond between the people from a hunting-gathering society and those from one of the most advanced twentieth-century industrial societies. Cellozzi recalled the interaction:

> That night Reverend Silvester held a service for the survivors and the natives. We sang with them and smoked their handmade cigars. Such fellowship! As the evening progressed we became louder and louder. We were all laughing and had our arms around each other. Apparently the cigars were a relaxant herbal leaf that produced a drugged effect.
>
> It was unbelievable to be with these people of the past. Their earlobes were cut and weighted and hung halfway to their shoulders; spiked bones pierced their noses. They couldn't seem to do enough for us, and a deep bond grew between us all. We saw no women or children. We learned they were hidden from the Japanese due to the ravaging and raping from prior confrontations.[10]

Deale Cochran also recalled the effect of religion and how the Reverend Silvester had organized a meeting with the sailors and the Islanders:

> It started out as a prayer meeting to thank God for our blessings to this point and to ask for deliverance, but by the time it ended it was as memorable a service as any of us would ever witness. We sang some of the old favorite hymns like "The Old Rugged Cross," "Rock of Ages" and "Onward Christian Soldiers." The *Helena*

men remembered words as best they could but the natives were outstanding. Singing in their native tongue their deep voices boomed out above ours, a different sound, beautiful, burning that moment into our memories. There were no atheists at that service or others like it. More of these wonderful services would be held, usually in the late afternoons, on days when Reverend Sylvester [*sic*] was not preoccupied with his Coastwatcher duties.[11]

For Josselyn, Firth and Silvester, the priority was getting the shipwrecked sailors off the beaches and concealing rafts and any evidence that they had landed on the island. Three different groups of sailors were spirited to secure locations in the interior of the island. The Islanders disposed of any rafts.

As time went by, things became more organized at the encampment at Sam Chung's house. Food, cooking, care of the sick and wounded, and basic sanitation had to be arranged. The sailors were given tasks such as digging and cleaning latrines, patrolling the campsite, supplying fresh water and foraging for food.

Because they were on a Japanese-held island, the sailors had to be particularly careful about lighting fires, noise and anything else that might attract the attention of the Japanese.

Chew observed:

> Usually we were not much concerned about a Japanese attack at night. We did not believe that they would go into the jungles then in search of us, as they were probably afraid to go out among the natives in the darkness. They had reason to fear them, for the standard native weapon was a long sharp knife, similar to a machete. Each native always carried one of these knives with him and held it suspended from the little finger of the right hand. I have heard that the little fingers of many of the islanders were permanently curved from this often odd custom.[12]

However, it was almost inevitable that some contact with the Japanese would occur. Cellozzi recalled:

> We did have a number of close encounters with Japanese patrols. One day a four man patrol came close to the camp. Our native scouts intercepted and killed three of them. The fourth was taken alive, which posed an even greater problem for us. We had no facilities for handling prisoners. It was up to Commander Chew to decide what to do with him. We simply could not have a prisoner on our hands.[13]

Strictly speaking, the Japanese soldier, having been delivered into Allied hands, was a prisoner of war and therefore entitled to the protection of the 1929 Geneva Convention. However, Japan had never ratified that document, and Japan's treatment of Allied prisoners of war varied between the abysmal and the barbaric. Chew faced an agonizing decision. He could not let the Japanese soldier go, because this would alert the Japanese to the sailors' presence, and it would also certainly bring down reprisals on the Islanders for killing Japanese soldiers and harboring Allied personnel. Nor could he simply keep the Japanese soldier a prisoner—he lacked the means to keep him secure. The soldier would also be a drain on the limited food supplies. Chew put the problem to his "Mayoral Council" and then resolved the issue by ordering that the soldier be executed as humanely as possible. The execution was carried out by one of the Islanders, who struck the prisoner a sharp blow to the back of the head, resulting in instant death. It is one thing to kill an enemy in the heat of battle; it is another thing to kill in cold blood. Interestingly, the gruesome task was left to an Islander. War is an untidy business and throws up uncomfortable ethical dilemmas. Often there are no easy answers.

It seemed that the Japanese response to their missing patrol was not long in coming. Several days later twenty heavily armed Japanese soldiers landed from a barge at Lambu Lambu Cove and began to climb the track to Sam Chung's house and the American camp. Kelly's Irregulars were armed with a motley collection of weaponry and limited ammunition. It seemed that it would be a one-sided fight, but Kelly decided to try and ambush the Japanese. The Japanese drew closer and combat was imminent when one of those miraculous events of war happened. In a stroke of incredible good fortune, several Corsair planes appeared and began to strafe the Japanese barge. Seeing black smoke rising, the Japanese soldiers rushed back to the beach.

It had been a close run thing, and the shipwrecked survivors and their hosts knew that their days were numbered. The Japanese garrison had increased to between three hundred and four hundred troops, and outposts had been set up near the American camps at Paraso Bay.

Josselyn made contact with Guadalcanal and asked for assistance. An awful dilemma confronted the U.S. Navy. Vella Lavella was behind Japanese lines. Would further ships and men be risked to retrieve the survivors? Despite the immense danger, Rear Admiral Richmond Kelly Turner made the decision to attempt the rescue. Morale was the key consideration—American sailors could not be abandoned. The problem was how the rescue would be accomplished. The sheer number of survivors meant that multiple ships would be needed. Fortunately, Turner had the resources in the form of two APD fast destroyer-transports, USS *Dent* and *Waters*. These destroyers had been developed before the war as troop transports for raiders. Now they would come into their own as rescue craft. They were ideal—they were fast and camouflaged in mottled green, with crews were skilled in amphibious operations. The downside was that they were lightly armed and would be operating in enemy waters. This meant that they would need an escort of destroyers. The operation was a formidable undertaking involving sending the rescue force into close proximity of Japanese air and naval bases. The force had to remain undetected on its approach and would have to navigate through barely charted waters. Then there would be the difficult task of establishing communication between the rescue ships and the Coastwatchers.

There were three dispersed groups of Americans on Vella Lavella—104 with Chew, 50 with Bauswine and a further 11 with Chief Warrant Officer William Dupay. The logistics of rescue made it impossible to concentrate all of the survivors in one place, so Josselyn decided to do two evacuations: one at Paraso Bay and the second at Lambu Lambu. Josselyn planned on joining Bausewine's and Dupay's groups together and leading them to Paraso Bay, where he would signal to the American rescue ships. He would then board the ship and guide it to the rendezvous at Lambu Lambu Cove. Meanwhile, Silvester and the Islanders were to guide Chew's group to the rendezvous point.

To add an extra complication, the Islanders delivered up another Japanese POW, a shot-down Zero pilot. The consensus was to execute him, but in this case the prisoner was docile and allowed to live. Also to be evacuated was a shot-down P-38 pilot, Lt Eli Ciunguin. He had arrived prior to the sailors.

The plan was to carry out the evacuations on 12 July at 2 a.m. However, the Japanese destroyed that plan by sending a Tokyo Express "down the Slot," triggering the naval Battle of Kolombangara and forcing a postponement. Time ticked by agonizingly for the survivors as the evacuations continued to be delayed. Finally, it was decided to undertake the rescue on 15 July.

Dupay's group, including the blindfolded Zero pilot, went to their beach on the evening of 15 July. Some 12 miles down the coast Chew's group began their agonizing progress to their beach. Carrying stretchers and including walking sick and wounded, the group had to travel in daylight to get to their rendezvous point. Sam Chung and fifteen local Chinese also seized the risky opportunity to get off the island.

The site for the rendezvous with their rescuers was an old dock used by traders about a mile up the Lambu Lambu River. Chew sent Warren Boles in a canoe to meet the rescuers and bring them in. He was in a canoe rowed by an Islander with no English. However, Silvester had arranged for the Islanders to be positioned at every turn in the river to act as guides.

The waiting got to all concerned. If dawn came, the Americans and their hosts would be exposed to Japanese attack.

At Paraso Bay Bausewine's group also had a long night. Josselyn set off in a canoe with Bill Dupay and three Islanders to make contact with the rescuers. They spent two hours offshore in total darkness. At 2 a.m. they saw the shape of ships approaching and, taking a risk, Josselyn flashed out a series of R's in Morse code, the recognition signal.

The commodore of the two APDs, Commander John D. Sweeney, had been given the codename "PLUTO." Because of their shallower draft, the two APDs had to shed their escorting destroyers—USS *Taylor* signaled, "PLUTO, you're on your own. Good luck." *Dent* and *Waters* inched slowly toward shore until they could make out the shapes of trees. A signalman told Sweeney, "Captain, there's a light." Sweeney peered over the side of the bridge and saw a figure below in a canoe, who yelled, "I am the gunner of the *Helena*." The sailor was Bill Dupay, and he had taken the risk that the ships were American. Dupay and Josselyn then boarded the *Dent*.

Both APDs lowered three landing craft into the water and, with Josselyn acting as pilot, set off through the coral reefs to rescue Bausewine's group. Once this had been done, Josselyn clambered onto the bridge of the *Dent* and delivered a piece of news that chilled Sweeney: only half of the ship-wrecked sailors had been picked up; the rest were at Lambu Lambu, and time was running short—daylight was coming in only a few hours. Undaunted, the APDs, once again guided by Josselyn, set off. At about 4 a.m. *Dent* nosed into Lambu Lambu Cove and a light was seen flashing the number 50, *Helena's* number. *Dent* gave an answering flash and stopped her engines. Warren Boles did not see the answering flash, however, and he grew increasingly concerned. It was all wrong—the rescue ships were supposed to be coming from a different direction. Deciding it was "do or die," Boles continued flashing his torch.

Soon he heard the sound of landing craft engines and then, to Boles' surprise, a voice with a British accent yelling, "Hello there!" Josselyn was in the first landing craft. Boles, despite being in truly wretched physical condition (his leg was injured, and he had an infected gash on his left arm), clambered aboard the landing craft and acted as pilot. The six landing craft traveling in a column found the mouth of the Lambu Lambu River and, with the help of the Islanders acting as channel markers, made their way to the trading post dock. The dock could only take one landing craft at a time, and the fear was that any moment the Japanese would strike. A Chinese baby began to cry, ratcheting up the tension.

As the shipwrecked sailors departed, the men shook hands with the Islanders, handing over cash and knives to them. Kelly's Irregulars also handed over their motley collection of firearms.

Jim Layton, a pharmacist's mate, said goodbye to Silvester. "I was standing alongside Silvester and I was begging him to go with us," he recalled. "He had tears in his eyes." But it was not the reverend's time to leave the island yet. "I can't leave," Silvester replied. "I may be able to help someone else like I helped you guys."[14]

As senior officer, Chew was the last to go. He gave his thanks to Josselyn, struggling to express his gratitude. He reached into his pocket and handed to Silvester one of his most prized possessions—his lucky silver dollar.

The landing craft departed; Josselyn and Silvester gave a final wave and, with the Islanders, merged back into the jungle. The landing craft were hoisted aboard the APDs, and, together with their escorting destroyers, they sped off at 25 knots. Sweeney had completed the rescue none too soon. At daylight American fighters appeared overhead as the rescue fleet surged toward Tulagi and safety. The U.S. Navy had pulled off one of the most impressive rescues of World War II.

The sailors of the U.S. Navy had just had their first introduction to Vella Lavella. They would not be the only unexpected guests the Islanders would host.[15]

The Zeros, the Kiwi Who Lost His Teeth and the Islanders—Ganley's Ordeal (Sgt. Trevor Ganley, No. 3 Squadron, RNZAF)

Chance and circumstance in war can mean the difference between life and death. For Sergeant Trevor Ganley, an RNZAF wireless operator/air gunner, bad luck and bad timing would result in a lifetime connection with Vella Lavella. His unit, No. 3 Squadron, RNZAF, operated twin-engine Lockheed Mark III Hudson Patrol Bombers from an airstrip on Guadalcanal. Regular, unescorted reconnaissance sweeps were made by these lightly armed bombers as far north as the Shortland Islands, just to the south of Bougainville.

On 24 July 1943, Ganley's plane departed on such a mission. Shortly after becoming airborne, the Identification Friend or Foe device was tested and found to be faulty; as a consequence, for safety reasons 300 gallons of aviation fuel had to be dumped before landing, and then the aircraft returned to base. A hasty change of aircraft took place, and the aircrew again took off on their mission. They had, however, been critically delayed, and this would have fatal consequences.

The crew of the Hudson NZ 2021 consisted of the captain, Flight Lieutenant William G.C. Allison; a second pilot, Pilot Officer Frank B. Kerr; the navigator, Ronald G. Douglas; and two gunners, Trevor Ganley and Sergeant James H. Johnson. They also had an unusual passenger: Colonel C.N.F. Bengough, who was acting British resident commissioner for the Solomon Islands and part of the Solomon Islands Defence Force. Bengough would have been very familiar with the area over which the Hudson would pass.

At 1500 hours the Hudson was bounced by 8 Zero fighter planes. Up to that point the patrol had been uneventful. The Hudson was under a low cloud climbing toward the sun, and the skilled Japanese fighters achieved surprise. The first that the crew knew was the impact of the Japanese cannon shells striking the Hudson's wings. Fire broke out inside the plane and rapidly spread to engulf equipment and the parachutes stored along the sides of the fuselage. Pilot Officer Kerr, although wounded in the back, tried in vain to extinguish the flames.

One of the Zeros attacked from the rear of the Hudson and one hundred feet above, but Ganley opened fire at four hundred yards; the Zero broke off the attack at one hundred yards and rolled away smoking badly. The other Zeros were, however, attacking from other quarters. Ganley fired his gun at the Japanese fighters but received shrapnel wounds on his forehead from a shell splintering against the armor-plated shield of his turret, as well as wounds to his left middle forefinger, left forearm and hip. Col. Bengough staunched the flow of blood from Ganley's forehead but was subsequently hit and killed. Ganley's turret was then hit by a Japanese shell, which disabled the electrical system and rendered the gun useless. The fire was raging in the fuselage of the plane, so Ganley tried fighting the flames. He then moved to the plane's belly gun and fired a few bursts at the fighters to deter them. The Japanese, however, quickly realized that they had knocked out the rear turret and moved in for the kill.

Ganley and Kerr fought the flames with limited success and with the fire extinguishers. Almost exhausted, Flight Lieutenant Allison decided to ditch the Hudson in the sea while it was still possible to make a controlled landing. Allison succeeded in putting the burning, stricken aircraft down on the sea about two miles northeast of Baga Island. Douglas, Ganley and Kerr were badly wounded, but despite this all of the crew got into the Mae West lifejackets and were able to leave the sinking plane. A dinghy was inflated and floating near the plane. Douglas, who was badly wounded in his leg, and Ganley swam toward the dinghy while Allison, Kerr and Johnson floated away.

At this point the Zeros returned and began strafing runs, shooting up the helpless aircrew as they struggled in the water. Over ten minutes the Zeros made repeated attacks. As each attack occurred, Ganley dove under the dinghy, and although the dinghy was hit, miraculously Ganley was not.

When the Zeros departed Ganley discovered, to his horror, that he was the only survivor. The other members of the crew were floating some distance away, lifeless. Ganley was alone, wounded and bleeding in shark-infested waters. The dinghy was punctured, so Ganley began the two-mile swim to Baga Island. However, his problems with the Japanese were by no means over. He later recalled:

> When I was only fifty yards from shore during my long swim I noticed a barge some two miles out to sea, it seemed to be heading away from Baga Island, but when I had reached the shore I lay down as I was pretty exhausted, to my surprise I heard motors. Looking up I saw the barge coming around a point not sixty yards away. I sprinted for the jungle as fast as my legs would take me. They had not seen me as they were busy erecting branches for camouflage. This barge had come to evacuate some sailors from a ship sunk by Allied airmen.[16]

The Zeros that had intercepted the Hudson may have been acting as fighter cover for this barge. The Hudson had been at the wrong place at the wrong time.

Ganley took stock of his situation. He had left his revolver in the Hudson, and the only items he had were a mechanical pencil and a mosquito head net. The mechanical pencil was put to good use in puncturing coconuts. The mosquito head net also proved invaluable. Nets had been given to Ganley and the other crew members by Allison only a week before and had been placed in the pockets of their Mae Wests. Ganley did have one huge disadvantage—during the attack he had somehow lost his false teeth! Also of concern was that he had lost his flying boots in his swim to the island. That night, Ganley covered his head with the net and tried to sleep but found his rest disturbed by hermit crabs attracted by his wounds. He shrugged them off with revulsion.

The next morning Ganley tore apart his Mae West jacket and wrapped the material around his feet to give them some protection from the sharp coral. He began walking in a northeasterly direction in the mistaken belief that the land he could see in the distance was joined to the land he was on. When he discovered he was on an island, he retraced his steps to his original landing place and cracked open some coconuts. He then walked around the island in a westerly direction and had some amazing good luck: he found a spring of drinkable water, an empty Islander hut, and a deflated rubber one-man dinghy of the type used by American fighter pilots. There was, however, no sign of life. Ganley examined the dinghy, and, to his delight, he found a quantity of concentrated chocolate and a bottle of water.

Over the next week, surviving on the chocolate, bottled water and coconuts, Ganley explored the island. He found that he was completely alone. He tried unsuccessfully to build a raft from salvaged empty barrels that had washed up on the beaches.

On his seventh day on the island, Ganley's hopes soared. He witnessed a big dogfight taking place in the sky above him and saw an Allied plane crash into the sea. Ganley hoped that a "Dumbo," a PBY-5A Catalina seaplane, would come to look for the downed pilot. His hopes were dashed when this did not happen.

Ganley decided that his best hope of getting off the island was to salvage the American dinghy. He unscrewed the valves of the dinghy and drained the water. Fortunately, he found only a small puncture under the carbon dioxide bottle, which he removed using pliers found on the dinghy. He also discovered that the dinghy contained a repair outfit; using this, he was able to successfully repair the raft. Ganley carried the dinghy about five miles to the coast facing Vella Lavella. Spending his last night on Baga Island in an old copra shed, Ganley prepared for the next stage of his journey.

The following morning, using a bamboo pole as a paddle, Ganley began the daunting task of rowing to Vella Lavella. The Japanese were not, however, done with him yet. A Val Aichi Type 99 Divebomber suddenly appeared from the south at a low altitude and spotted him. As it flew overhead, the pilot dipped the plane's wings and flew on, leaving Ganley unmolested. Ganley believed that the Japanese pilot had mistaken him for a downed Japanese flier.

There were other eyes that were watching Ganley and observing the actions of the Val. These observers had big concerns as to Ganley's allegiance.

An Islander, Kisine Zoro, was keeping an eye on the coast. Kevin Zoro later recalled his father's actions:

> At dawn he spotted something paddling about two hundred meters away and so he waited. And when Trevor Ganley came ashore just ten meters away from the shore he put his hands up, that's his British sign so when he knew he's not an enemy my father carried him off the rubber boat and he go and fetch help, a couple of men, they came and take him off to the actual place he was hiding. And that is the place where they nursed him.[17]

Ganley recalled that on struggling ashore he was met by an unarmed Islander, but other Islanders armed with primitive weapons were covering him from the jungle. Ganley tried to reassure the Islanders in pidgin English that he was not Japanese. From the viewpoint of the Islanders, it would have been difficult to distinguish between olive-skinned Japanese pilots wearing aviator uniforms and sunburnt Allied fliers wearing similar uniforms. A mistake could have had fatal consequences, and their caution was well merited. It was only after the arrival of a "Teacher Boy" who was able to talk to Ganley in perfect English that it was conclusively established that he was an Allied flier.

A messenger was dispatched to the local Coastwatcher, informing him of Ganley's arrival. Ganley, meanwhile, had the luxury of bathing in a tub provided by the Islanders and was nursed and fed. Ganley later recalled:

> Then waiting till dark and in what seemed about an eight oared canoe paddled me to a place called Kila Kila, a distance of some ten miles and how they paddle as silent as a ghost. They seemed to know where every Jap was situated. I suggested that Gordon McMohan [one of the Islanders whom Ganley first encountered and who spoke perfect English] accompany us as one of the paddlers which was promptly accepted, the reason being to act as an interpreter.
>
> When we arrived at Kila Kila Lt. Josselyn had sent a runner with sulpha drugs and other medical supplies which were promptly applied. My finger which at that time was completely black, I didn't quite know what was the trouble with it. The next day Lt. Firth arrived at one o'clock. After administering further first aid which included plastering my feet with tape and applying a pair of sandshoes, we started ou[r] long trek through the middle of the island. Lt. Firth offered to have me carried by the natives but I declined in favour of walking after seeing the trail and its narrow confines through the jungle. That night we slept at what was called the halfway house and there I had my first real meal for nearly a fortnight. Lt. Firth slept on the salvaged rubber boat. We arrived at the hideout sometime the next afternoon.[18]

The "first aid" that Ganley referred to had consisted of Firth utilizing brandy as a form of anesthetic and using a razor as a surgical knife to remove shrapnel from Ganley's finger. One can only wonder at Ganley's powers of endurance as, despite his evident pain, he trekked uphill inland to the sanctuary provided by the Coastwatchers and Islanders.

On arriving at Josselyn's camp, Ganley met Josselyn; two Australians, Lt. Bob Firth and Tom Mungoven; and an American, Red Cunningham. Ganley marveled at the strange circumstances that had led to these individuals being the only white people on the island (excepting the Reverend Silvester at Maravari). He remembered:

> The hide out was most interesting. Lt. Josselyn had things very carefully planned. A ladder was erected some 60ft up a tree with a platform on top, from this tree ran a field telephone to his hut some 40 yards away. Natives maintained watch day and night from this position and all enemy movements were promptly radioed to the proper quarters. I stayed with this courageous quartet for a month and everyday

natives brought in the movements of the Japanese on the Island and the way Lt. Josselyn extracted these by using Pidgeon [*sic*] English was a treat to watch.[19]

Ganley, for his part, earned his keep by assisting the Coastwatchers and teaching them aircraft recognition. More often than not, aircraft were heard but not actually seen, and the ability to recognize aircraft by sound was useful for the Coastwatchers. Ganley also witnessed the naval battle off Vella Lavella on 18 August 1943.

Ganley recalled his departure:

Towards the end of July, news came by radio that a P.T. boat would be picking me up at Parramatta at one o'clock on the morning 30th August. The day before Lt. Josselyn loaned me a .45 and with two natives I started my journey back. We arrived at the shore just on dark, waiting till completely dark we paddled to Parramatta. Just on one o'clock we waited just off shore for the signal from the P.T. boat three short reds. We heard the engines before seeing the reds but waiting for the signal before paddling out. After dropping some stores and returning Lt. Josselyn's .45 and his wrist watch to the natives also loaned to me, I went on patrol with the P.T. boats to Bougainville before returning to Rendova Island arriving there about 8 a.m. the next day. I was flown by S.C.A.T. from Munda to Guadalcanal the next day. That day will live in my memory forever, the excitement at meeting all the squadron boys again was terrific.

Ganley returned to flying operations. For his courage, he was awarded the Distinguished Flying Medal. He survived the war and died in 1997 at the age of eighty.

Two

The Battleground—Vella Lavella: The "Euphonious Island" and the Islanders[1]

Vella Lavella is located in the northernmost part of the New Georgia group, one of a chain of islands in the Solomon Islands in the South Pacific. Rather like an inverted triangle, Vella Lavella is positioned roughly forty miles northwest of Munda Point, New Georgia, and is separated from Kolombangara Island fourteen miles to the northwest by Vella Gulf. Vella Lavella presented formidable obstacles for anyone foolish or desperate enough to fight there.

Some twenty-six miles long in a northwest-to-southeast direction and twelve miles at its widest point, the island is covered in heavy dense jungle that limits visibility to only a few yards. Of volcanic origin with some raised coral, the center of the island is dominated by hills, which rise to a maximum elevation of 2,651 feet. Streams and rivers flow from these hills to the sea. Hot thermal mud pools are located at the Ulo River area, near the village of Simbiland in the north of Vella Lavella. The coastal area, which is relatively flat, varies in depth from one hundred yards to one mile. Beyond coconut plantations, the island had no economic value in the pre-war period; consequently, it was undeveloped, lacking even roads. A basic native track along which men could move with difficulty in single file[2] followed the coastline, but the interior remained largely inaccessible. The island is fringed with coral reefs that contain few openings. Even sea travel for modern craft is fraught with danger. For the Americans the real value of Vella Lavella lay in its southern area, which was relatively well drained and held the possibility of development for airfields.

The resources that Vella Lavella had in abundance which would be useful for Allied engineers were the coral, which could be crushed and used for road surfacing, and the plentiful supply of millable timber.

The Islanders' main village was at Barakoma in the southeast of the island.[3] The Islanders are Melanesians, a dark-skinned people. It is important to appreciate that Vella Lavella was not an empty desert over which the Japanese and Allies contended. For the Islanders, the Japanese invasion was a disaster that resulted in devastation to their crops and villages, as well as extreme disruption to their society and, for some of the Islanders, death and maiming. War came to them without invitation. Francine Tozaka, a young girl at the time, recalled that the Japanese destroyed things so that the people ran away and lived in the bush.[4] A small number of Chinese traders, including Sam Chung, were resident on the island and hid from the Japanese.

Vella Lavella was part of the Gizo District of the British Solomon Islands Protectorate. British influence and the activities of missionaries would be crucial in securing the Islanders' allegiance to the Allied cause. The Rev. Archie W.E. Silvester, a New Zealand missionary, had been resident on the island in the prewar period. Some locations on Vella Lavella were named by the New Zealand missionaries after places in New Zealand, such as "Paramata." There was in that sense a close connection between the people of Vella Lavella and New Zealand, and it was fitting that the liberation of the island would be completed by New Zealanders.

Like most Pacific islands, Vella Lavella has the odor of decay as vegetation rots in the humid climate. Mildew attacks anything damp. A New Zealand soldier, Frank Rennie, observed, "The island teems with small life—ants by the million, millipedes, slugs, crabs, lizards and iguana, some so big they are sometimes taken for the crocodiles which abound in the rivers and unusually the sea."[5] To that list Rennie could have added flies and rodents.[6] Of particular revulsion to Allied soldiers were the large, luncheon-plate-sized land crabs that inhabited Vella Lavella. At night, in huge numbers, they traversed the beaches and jungle, completely oblivious to the fact that their island was being fought over. The crabs would often fall into foxholes, only to be picked up and thrown out with gusto. For Rex Gregor, a U.S.N.R. pharmacist's mate, the black gnats that settled on wounds and infections were of particular horror.

The only open spaces were the coconut plantations, and even these were overgrown.[7] The close, dense vegetation and limited avenues of approach would act as a huge force enhancer for the Japanese defenders.

A New Zealand official history described the island as follows:

> The jungle is the most difficult and pestilential country in which to wage war. Visibility ends only a few yards away in a barrier of thick, fleshy leaves, writhing vines and creepers, shrubs and tree trunks as this mass of vegetation fights upwards to the sun. Large trees, whose massive trunks sprawl out like flying buttresses several feet above

the ground, are matted together with stout vines and a horrible variety of climbing palm which has nasty barbed fronds, the whole forming an impenetrable canopy overhead. Only a few tired rays of sunshine filter through to rich earth which is never dry and never free from the heavy odor of decay. The moist, warm atmosphere produces a crop of mildew overnight on anything damp. Growth is so swift that a rain of leaves falls continuously though the trees are all evergreens. By day the jungle is comparatively quiet except for the chatter of parrots and parakeets and the harsh grating of myriads of cicadas, one variety of which makes a piercing noise like a small but particularly busy sawmill. These insects, as though working to a signal, begin and end their crude orchestra in a flash. One moment the air is vibrating with their shrill din; the next all is silent. But when night falls, as it does swiftly with the setting sun, the jungle comes to life and bedlam reigns until dawn. The noise is incredible. Millions of frogs, one resembling a tiny brown leaf, croak and whistle; night birds chatter and screech; the cicadas maintain their incessant chirping and rasping.

Among dead and dying leaves underfoot the jungle seethes with insect life. Every creeping and crawling thing finds a home there, from crabs, millipedes and myriads of ants of various sizes and colours to bright green, blue, and brown lizards, including one fellow some feet in length rather like a prehistoric dragon in miniature. By day brilliant butterflies with inches of wing-spread hover among the trees like large snippets of coloured paper; spiders, swinging their strong webs among the undergrowth, are almost as brightly decorated. At night fireflies flicker like tiny street lamps in the velvet gloom, and the phosphorescent light from chips of one particular tree is so strong that a newspaper may be read in its glow. To this exotic land thunderstorms of great violence bring frequent torrents of rain, adding to the discomfort and depression which are born of a feeling of imprisonment under a canopy of leafy growth. In the plantation areas, of course, there is more freedom and space, though fallen nuts have taken root and grown in thickets to a height of several feet during the war years.[8]

The jungle of the Solomon Islands, with its heavy precipitation, humid temperatures and luxuriant growth, is one of the worst places on the planet for a modern industrialized army to wage war. The limited visibility, restriction on movement and torpor-inducing heat all combine to make the use of infantry support weapons extremely difficult.

Infantry squads, platoons and companies grope slowly through jungles at reduced distances between elements with little or no direct assistance from adjacent units, because visual contact and natural fields of fire for flat trajectory weapons seldom exceed a few yards.... Tense searches that culminate in fleeting fire fights at point blank range characterize up close and personal combat.... Armed conflict under such circumstances emphasizes needs for simple centralized plans, standing operating procedures (SOPs) that anticipate unexpected contingencies, decentralized execution, and above all astute junior leaders.[9]

On top of all that, the "wrap-around rain forests intensify latent tendencies towards claustrophobia and paranoia, since belligerents can neither see nor hear well under the best case conditions."[10] This phenomena is heightened at night, with pitch-black darkness accentuated by the unfamiliar sounds of birds and animals that encourage green troops to fire wildly and increase the risk of fratricide.

The humidity of the jungle rots and rusts military equipment very quickly, requiring intensive maintenance of essential items such as rifles. To add to the misery, "jungles are filled with animate and inanimate objects that bite, sting and stick, a host of micro-organisms that are harmful to humans, fungus infections that troops affectionately call 'jungle rot' and steamy atmosphere that encourages profuse perspiration, body rashes and heat exhaustion."[11] Malaria is prevalent on the island.

Strangely, given the island's unhealthy climate and deadly flora and fauna, Vella Lavella and its raw beauty did have its admirers—Private Frank Marks of the 35th U.S. Infantry Regiment recalled that

> after the combat we experienced on Guadalcanal, being on Vella Lavella was almost like a vacation. Of all the places we went and territory we saw, Vella Lavella was tops. I would have been satisfied if they had dropped me off and let me live the rest of my life at the lagoon where the Mission was located. It was like what most people would envision a tropical paradise to be. If I could afford to, I would like to go back.[12]

Marks believed his positive view of the island stemmed from the fact that he had volunteered for military service, whereas many of his comrades were conscripted: "80 percent of our men were there because they had been drafted and they hated every minute of it. They were patriotic and did what they had to do, but that was the extent of it." As regards the weather, Marks conceded, "Yes, at times it was hot and muggy and we experienced a lot of rain. But it wasn't that much different from Hawaii."[13]

Nor was Marks alone in his view of Vella Lavella. Dan Harper, a ground crewman-gunner for a "Dauntless" divebomber squadron based on the island, thought "Vella Lavella was great, a beautiful little island." He fondly recalled the hikes he undertook into the interior, albeit armed with a rifle: "It was idyllic ... beautiful. I loved it. If I'd had another daughter, I'd probably have named her Vella."[14]

Marks and Harper were in a distinct minority, however. Most who served on Vella Lavella were only too glad to leave its shores. One of those was Jerome J. Hendrick, a soldier with the 35th U.S. Infantry Regiment and a veteran of the fighting on Guadalcanal, Vella Lavella and later the Philippines. After the war he described Vella Lavella as "the worst, most intense, frightening combat, worse than Guadalcanal. Vella Lavella was an absolute hell hole. I never want to see that place again."[15]

THREE

The Opposing Forces

The forces involved in the struggle for Vella Lavella were of a varied and sometimes exotic nature. In many ways, they represent the forces fighting for the South Pacific in microcosm.

The Americans

THE 35TH INFANTRY REGIMENT, "THE CACTI," 25TH INFANTRY DIVISION, U.S. ARMY

The 35th Infantry Regiment, U.S. Army, was formed in 1916 at Douglas, Arizona—hence the cactus in the regimental coat of arms and the reference to the Regiment as "The Cacti." In the inter-war period the Regiment was stationed in Hawaii. In September 1941 it was attached to the newly formed 25th Infantry Division ("Tropic Lightning") based in Hawaii. In November 1942 the Division was sent to Guadalcanal and took part in the elimination of Japanese resistance, particularly around Mt. Austen and the Gifu Stronghold. At this time, the Regiment was introduced to the brutal complexities of jungle warfare and the difficulties of eliminating Japanese bunkers and pillboxes. When the desperate Japanese defenders realized that they had no hope, they undertook a mass banzai attack on 25 January 1943 and were cut down by rifle, machine-gun and mortar fire. After the Japanese withdrawal from Guadalcanal, the Regiment undertook garrison duty.

Jerome J. Hendrick, with Company K, 35th Infantry Regiment, remembered the condition of his unit at the end of the Guadalcanal campaign:

> We were all sick with malaria and parasites when we were sent back to the beach at Guadalcanal. We'd had it. I weighed about 150 pounds, just skin and bones and

we sat around for about a month. They wanted us to offload supplies, but nobody was interested in that, so we avoided everything we could and just tried to eat and get well.

We thought we were going to Kolombangara and we dreaded that. There were 50,000 Japs on that island but it was pretty obvious we weren't combat ready so we took it easy.... Then they said part of the Division was going to New Caledonia but we were attached to a group to attack Vella Lavella. I'd never heard of it.[1]

As the American push into New Georgia became bogged down, the 27th and 161st Regimental Combat Teams of the 25th Infantry Division were deployed to aid in the drive on Munda. As division reserve, the 35th Infantry Regiment was earmarked to join the 25th Division in August and take part in the seizure of Rendova Island. However, the Regimental Combat Teams had the situation in hand and plans were altered. The Regiment was therefore available for operations on Vella Lavella. The men of the Regiment were acclimatized to the tropics, trained, familiar with jungle warfare and one of the most experienced parts of the 25th Division.

The 35th used the concept of the Regimental Combat Team. This was an infantry unit augmented with smaller units such as artillery, medical, reconnaissance and signals, and so on, in order to carry out a particular task. Such combat teams were generally of short duration and disbanded once the mission had been accomplished.

On 1 August 1943 the Regiment undertook practice landings for the invasion of Vella Lavella. The attitude of the soldiers of the 35th to the Japanese was summed up by Frank Marks: "At that time we knew they were our enemy and as such had to be annihilated. I don't think any of the men in our company ever considered taking prisoners."[2]

1 MARINE AMPHIBIOUS CORPS

One Marine Amphibious Corps, also known as "One Mac," embodied the USMC knowledge and expertise in amphibious operations. The USMC in the interwar period had worked out amphibious warfare doctrine and how assaults could be made against enemy shores. Although the Marines were not directly involved in the initial amphibious landings on Vella Lavella, they had considerable influence on how operations were carried out. A small provisional USMC force from the 3rd Marine Division, consisting of two rifle companies, an AA platoon, a motor transport section and various supporting elements, was landed on Ruravai Beach on 25 September 1943.

The Seabees (Naval Construction Battalions)

One of the problems that the protagonists in the South Pacific faced was that there were little in the way of ports, loading and unloading facilities and heavy equipment. Logistics was crucial in the battle for the Solomons in order to keep the troops fed, supplied with weapons and equipment, and healthy. The Americans had a secret weapon in the form of their Naval Construction Battalions, or "Seabees." The men of these units were to perform prodigious feats of construction ranging from building airfields to creating port facilities. The 58th NCB, 77th NCB and 6th Special NCB would all take part in the struggle for Vella Lavella. The Seabees tended to be older men who in civilian life had been employed in heavy construction work. It was a joke among American soldiers that "you should never be rude to a Seabee—he could be your father." The ingenuity of the Seabees in both construction work and pilfering supplies was legendary.

Military Intelligence Service— Japanese Language Specialists

One of the more unusual American units on Vella Lavella was from the Military Intelligence Service; this group specialized in Japanese translation and interrogation of Japanese prisoners. The unit was commanded by Major John Alfred Burden, a Japanese language officer, and made up of Nisei, second-generation Japanese Americans, who, motivated by patriotism, had agreed to offer their services to the American military. These individuals faced greater than normal dangers. On Vella Lavella misunderstandings almost proved fatal. One night one of the Nisei, Tateshi Miyasaki, had stripped to the waist and was in the process of cooking his rice dinner when he was suddenly confronted by three tense New Zealand soldiers with their rifles aimed at him. He cried out, "I'm an American, don't shoot." John Burden desperately yelled, "He's O.K. He's one of my boys," and tragedy was averted.[3]

The MIS would perform extremely useful work in translating captured Japanese documents, interrogating Japanese prisoners and broadcasting surrender appeals.

The Coastwatchers and the Islanders

One of the most critical intelligence assets that the Allies had in the struggle for the Solomon Islands was the Coastwatchers. The Coastwatching system was set up by the Royal Australian Navy in the pre-war period with the intention of gathering intelligence on the movement of enemy troops, vessels and planes. Linked by radios and tied into the civilian radio network, the intelligence reports provided extremely useful information for the Allies. The Coastwatchers were a polyglot mixture of British, Australian, and New Zealand personnel (as well as at least one American). The Coastwatchers had a primary role as intelligence gatherers and were not supposed to fight. They adopted the Walt Disney cartoon character Ferdinand, the pacifist bull, as their symbol. Invariably, however, the Coastwatchers occasionally had to rely on the local people to fight and protect them from Japanese forces intent on eliminating them. It helped that many of the Coastwatchers were district officers and part of the pre-war British or Australian colonial administration.[4] They therefore knew the local people and had their trust and support. The added benefit was that they were seen as a continuation of the colonial administration and evidence that King George had not abandoned his subjects.

The Coastwatchers were equipped with teleradios that could transmit either voice messages or Morse code. Reports were made by radio on secret frequencies, and the Japanese strove to locate the position of radios. Without

Vella Lavella Islanders in canoes (photographer unknown; author's collection).

the support of the locals in providing portage and protection, the Coastwatchers would have achieved little.

The Coastwatchers were given military rank in the forlorn hope that if they were captured by the Japanese, they would not be tortured and shot as spies. The dangers can be gauged by the fact that thirty-eight Coastwatchers lost their lives.[5]

Henry Josselyn had been an assistant district officer in the Solomon Islands before the war. He had tried unsuccessfully to enlist in the armed forces in 1939. After the attack on Pearl Harbor, he volunteered to be a Coastwatcher on Vella Lavella even though he had not previously been there. He was, however, an old Solomon's hand and experienced with the ways of the Islanders, and his application was accepted.

Josselyn selected as a companion an Australian, John Keenan. Keenan had been a patrol officer on Bougainville. Josselyn and Keenan were delivered to Vella Lavella by the American submarine USS *Grampas* on 14 October 1942. The pair had to paddle through the darkness and collapsed in exhaustion on the shore. Two days later they set up their transmitter on a hill near the Mundi Mundi River. To their chagrin, when they tried to transmit their radio would not work. The only option seemed to be to contact a New Zealand Coastwatcher, Donald Kennedy, who was based at Segi, some 150 miles away. Up to this point Josselyn and Keenan had not had any contact with the locals. They chanced upon two Islander canoes and hailed them. One contained Silas Lezatuni, who was the chief of Paramata Village. He was astonished that the Coastwatchers had been on Vella Lavella for ten days without the locals being aware of their presence. Nonetheless, he was very helpful and provided information about a Japanese outpost with a radio at Iringila, not very far away. The other piece of information was that

Sub-Lt. H. Josselyn, Coastwatcher (photographer unknown; courtesy Archives New Zealand/Te Rua Mahara o te Kāwanatanga, Wellington Office, WAII, 7 3, Official Photograph Album).

the Rev. Archie Silvester ("Wattie Silvester") was at Bilua on the southern end of the island.

Josselyn decided to leave Keenan behind to set up an observation post while he made the 150-mile journey to Kennedy to get the radio fixed. However, first Josselyn went to Biloa to see Silvester, who had been on Vella Lavella since 1935 and had set up a model mission station. The mission had been established in 1902, and the missionaries had to deal with medical work as well as education and religious instruction. Malaria, measles and mumps were the major medical problems. Silvester's wife Moyna and baby daughter had been evacuated after the bombing of Pearl Harbor, but he had decided to stay.[6] The Islanders were fiercely loyal to Silvester. To Josselyn's surprise, he discovered that Silvester was accompanied by a slightly built thirty-six-year-old New Zealand nurse, Merle Farland. She had arrived in 1938 and had run the mission hospital. The Japanese invasion had not deterred her because she was the only medical person left, and the responsibility weighed on her.

Although Silvester was a missionary, he was nonetheless part of the Coastwatching network run by Donald Kennedy. Silvester recorded shipping and aircraft movements and had Islanders keep watch on neighboring islands. He had a short-wave radio that he used to receive messages, but he could not transmit, forcing him to send messages to Kennedy by canoe.

Josselyn explained about his busted radio, and Silvester arranged for Islanders to take him through 130 miles of Japanese-held waters to Kennedy. Josselyn set off on 30 October, traveling at night and going from village to village, where he received a fresh set of paddlers. After a fraught journey, Josselyn arrived at Segi on 2 November 1942. Kennedy resolved matters by giving Josselyn his radio, indicating that he would use a set salvaged from a crashed Japanese bomber. Josselyn then made his way back to Vella Lavella by means of a launch loaned to him by Kennedy. By 14 November he was back in Biloa. Silvester had organized a gathering of local chiefs to discuss intelligence work. They agreed to help, and a series of posts were set up along the coast to watch for and report on Japanese activities and any downed aircrew members. (It was one of these posts that spotted Ganley.)

Keenan established a radio station at Deneo, three miles inland from Mundi Mundi. Below the radio post lay the Japanese observation post at Iringila, where the Japanese were easy to observe.

The benefits of the Coastwatching system rapidly became apparent. On 18 November 1942, a B-17F Flying Fortress piloted by Major Allan J. Sewart took part in a raid on Bougainville. The raid was intercepted by Japanese fighters, which carried out slashing head-on firing passes against the big bombers, a weak point in the early model Flying Fortresses. These attacks killed Sewart and mortally wounded his co-pilot, 1st Lieutenant Jack Lee. The observer, Colonel Saunders, commander of the 11th Bombardment Group, took over the controls. On fire and with only two engines, the crippled bomber began to lose altitude. Saunders ditched the plane in the sea off Baga Island. He and the navigator, Lieutenant Nelson Levi, managed to get into life rafts and rowed to the beach. They met Islanders in a canoe but were unable to communicate with them. The Islanders left and returned with Jack Keenan. After darkness fell, the two airmen were moved by canoe to Paramata Village and were fed and rested at Silas Lezatuni's house. Josselyn and Kennan radioed Guadalcanal and made arrangements for the aircrew to be picked up. Merle Farland heard of the wounded men and traveled across Vella Lavella to tend to them. However, no sooner had she arrived at Paramata Village than the sounds of a PBY-5A Catalina seaplane and its escorting fighters were heard. The airmen were bundled into the seaplane and returned to Allied lines.[7]

Because Kennedy was so shorthanded on Segi, he suggested to Merle Farland that she relieve him. Farland accepted the challenge and traveled by canoe to Segi. She successfully operated the radio but, in doing so, drew the attention of the Australian authorities to her existence behind Japanese lines. They insisted that she be removed, and, despite her protests, she was picked up by a Catalina on 21 December and flown to Guadalcanal. There her presence spawned the rumor that the missing aviatrix Amelia Earhart had been found.

John Keenan was moved to Coastwatching duties on Bougainville. He was replaced by an Australian, Sub-Lieutenant Robert Firth.

Josselyn and his network of helpers continued reporting on Japanese activities and rescuing Allied aircrew. They were in a good position to assist the shipwrecked sailors of the USS *Helena*. The importance of the Islanders' support for the Allied cause is difficult to overstate. There was, however, one threat to the close relationship between the Coastwatchers and the Islanders. According to Coastwatcher Dick Horton:

> One most unfortunate aspect of the preparations to move forward into Vella Lavella was the bombing and strafing of friendly villages by Allied pilots who were unfamiliar with the area. All the Coastwatchers suffered from this and there were strong protests from Josselyn and Firth on Vella Lavella, Waddell and Seton on Choiseul and Evans on Kolombangara, for it was essential to retain the goodwill of the people and it was made very clear to Allied headquarters that unless the pilots were very much more careful, there was a grave risk not only of alienating loyal islanders but also of drying up the sources of intelligence on which the Coastwatchers and through them the Allies relied so much. Thereafter pilots on missions taking them over unfamiliar ground were required first to fly reconnaissance and

only then to set out on their bombing missions and this did much to check indiscriminate bombing and strafing.[8]

Not every Allied airman who was shot down on Vella Lavella was saved. Lt. (J.G.) Anderson and his crew flew one of the special black-painted, night-attack Catalina flying boats of VP-54. On 16 July 1943, the starboard engine of their Catalina caught fire, and the seaplane went down off the coast of Vella Lavella. The crew had several close encounters with Japanese patrols and one man (Evans) was killed. The crew members were then found by Islanders, who took them to a Coastwatcher and to safety.[9]

The Kiwis—14 Brigade, 3NZ Division

The New Zealanders who would take part in the battle for Vella Lavella were from 14 Brigade of 3NZ Division. This brigade consisted of the 30th, 35th and 37th Battalions backed by supporting units. The men of 3NZ Division were essentially "citizen soldiers," civilians who had no prior military experience and were in the army only for the duration of the war. Very few in the Division were professional soldiers, and even less had combat experience. None had experience in tropical warfare and fighting the Japanese. Vella Lavella would be a true initiation to battle.

The 3NZ Division had been formed from the cadre of units that had garrisoned Fiji in 1941. The garrison had returned to New Zealand in 1942, and a two-brigade division had been created. Efforts to develop a third brigade on New Caledonia, 15 Brigade, proved abortive, and its men were used to reinforce the two remaining brigades, 8 and 14 Brigade. The commander of 3NZ Division, Major General Harold Eric Barrowclough, aged 49, a decorated combat veteran of the First World War, the Greek Campaign and the Desert War, had ensured that his men were thoroughly trained and equipped. Since he had been appointed by the New Zealand government to undertake offensive operations, he was keen to get his men into action.

Barrowclough got on well with Admiral William Halsey and the American commanders. His problem was that due to the binary nature of his Division, it could not be used to replace a full American division in the front lines. Barrowclough was also aware that New Zealand's manpower reserves were at an all-time low, its military-age male population providing men for the RAF and the Bomber Offensive in Europe, as well as the naval war, including the Merchant Marine and especially the needs of 2NZ Division in the Mediterranean for replacements and reinforcements. The swirling battles of the

Desert War required fresh troops. Compounding matters, the RNZAF was determined to build up its strength in the Pacific. Essential agricultural industries producing food for Britain and forces in the South Pacific also impinged on manpower resources. Barrowclough knew that no reinforcements were likely to be made available to him, even if his Division suffered significant casualties.

Barrowclough can be credited with introducing to the New Zealand Army the innovation of the Battalion Combat Team (BCT), a self-contained all-arms battle unit, similar to the American Regimental Combat Team. Barrowclough had fought in the Desert War in North Africa and was very impressed by the way the Germans used a combined-arms style of fighting. He argued that the New Zealand Army should adopt a similar structure. When he became commander of 3NZ Division, he had a chance to implement his ideas. The advantage of Battalion Combat Teams was that the infantrymen received the support of dedicated artillery, as well as medical and logistical support. But as would become evident after the battle, the downside was that this approach spawned an unwieldy command structure. In later battles the concept was not utilized. Because of his divisional command responsibilities, Barrowclough was very dependent upon his subordinate commanders: "In general, Barrowclough believed that a commander should lay down an overall approach to be taken in an operation and then leave it to his staff to work out the details."[10]

The 14 Brigade was led by Brigadier Leslie Potter, a career soldier. Potter was an unusual personality and, in the words of Frank Rennie, a junior officer, "didn't radiate charm, warmth or inspiration."[11] Rennie assessed Potter's command style as being brusque, introspective and exercising command through authority.[12] Another junior officer, Lindsay Adams, found Potter's mannerism of looking past you when talking to you unsettling. He had mixed feelings about Potter, whom he saw as militarily capable and who "was loyal to those who served him well whatever their status." However, Adams found him an enigmatic personality who took strong likes and dislikes and "cultivated his reputation for ruthlessness."[13] There was tension between Barrowclough and Potter. Barrowclough had been a Territorial officer and was proud of that fact. Potter had been a Regular officer in the Permanent Force. The Regulars tended to look down on the Territorials as amateurs. Adams believed that "Potter was jealous of Barrowclough and thought he could do better."[14] The comment was also made that "Potter may have been an excellent soldier but he never commanded love or adulation."[15]

The battalion commanders would play an important role in the battle for Vella Lavella. They set the tone for their units in terms of leadership and training. The 35th Battalion was commanded by Lt. Colonel Cyril Frederick Seaward, DSO, MC, a London-born, fifty-eight-year-old veteran of World War I who assumed command of the Battalion in March 1942. Seaward had spent five years with the 1st New Zealand Expedi-

Top: Major General Harold Eric Barrowclough, 1943 (photographer unknown; courtesy Alexander Turnbull Library, Wellington, New Zealand, reference number H-346/7/43). *Bottom:* Brigadier Leslie Potter in the Pacific, 1944 (photographer unknown; courtesy Alexander Turnbull Library, Wellington, New Zealand, reference number DA-00175).

Colonel Seaward and New Zealand officers of 35th BCT at Pakoi Bay. (L to R) Lt. L. McMillan, Lt. Colonel C.F. Seaward, Capt. A.J. Robertson and 2nd Lt. C. D. Griffiths (photographer unknown; courtesy Archives New Zealand/Te Rua Mahara o te Kāwanatanga, Wellington Office, WAII, 7 3, Official Photograph Album).

tionary Force in World War I and later, at the war's end, continued his involvement with the military by serving for thirteen years with the Territorial Force. His civilian occupation had been working as a company manager with Dominion Motors.[16] Adams noted that Seaward did not have a grip on what was going on as the battle progressed: "Seaward was too old and did not know what was happening. His battalion commanders would have meetings to decide what should be done."[17] This would have tragic consequences as the battle progressed. Combat is a very unforgiving audit of command abilities.

The 37th Battalion was led by Lt. Colonel Arthur Harris Linsel Sugden, a forty-two-year-old regular soldier who had taken command of the Battalion in December 1941 while it was part of the Fiji garrison. Sugden had joined the New Zealand Army at the age of seventeen in 1919, in the aftermath of World War I. He was sent to the Royal Military College, Duntroon, Australia, as an officer cadet. However, his military career seemed blighted when, as part of fiscal retrenchments, the New Zealand government discharged the Duntroon cadets from the New Zealand Army in 1922. Sugden's career was rescued by his appointment to the New Zealand Staff Corps in 1925. Thereafter he served on attachment with the British Indian Army, and in the 1930s he was posted to the United Kingdom to study developments in infantry weapons. On his return to New Zealand he held various staff appointments. Ironically, his specialist knowledge meant that he was not sent overseas at the outbreak of World War II because it was felt that he could best be utilized in New Zealand. He was posted to the New Zealand Tank Brigade in 1941 and then to 3NZ Division as a battalion commander.[18]

When Sugden was appointed to command the newly formed 37th Battalion, he had a huge advantage: He was allowed to pick his officers, and since he had previously been commandant of the Army School, he had good knowledge of military personnel. Inevitably, the officers he chose included a number of World War I veterans, some of whom would later prove unfit for tropical service. The officers who would lead the men on Vella Lavella were predominantly younger men who had been through officer training courses, and many had been taught by Sugden. The 37th Battalion, therefore, was very much Sugden's battalion.

The commander of 30th Battalion, Lt. Colonel Frederick Charles Cornwall, was in many respects unusual. He had been born in Manchester, England, and was aged 51 in 1943. He had risen from the ranks, having enlisted as an NCO in the New Zealand Expeditionary Force in 1914, and had fought in Egypt, Gallipoli and the Western Front. He was promoted to second lieutenant in 1917. He had distinguished himself at Passchendaele in 1917, where he was awarded the Military Cross for successfully leading an assault on a German pillbox. He was also wounded in the upper left arm by a gunshot wound during the pillbox assault and had to convalesce.

In the inter-war years he was placed on the Reserve of Officers, and it was only the outbreak of World War II and the NZ Army's chronic shortage of officers that reignited his military career. There were, however, issues as to his medical fitness, age and rank. By arguing his case, he was able to re-enter the army and received promotion to the rank of temporary captain. This was followed by advancement to major and finally lieutenant colonel in April 1943. He took command of 30th Battalion in September 1943. Cornwall had limited command experience, had not been actively involved in the Territorial Army in the inter-war years, and was considered overage.[19]

Potter's men welcomed the prospect of action. They had performed garrison duties of a hum-drum nature and trained intensively. In particular, the troops had painstakingly learned the skills required for amphibious assault. For example, in August 1943, the 37th Battalion undertook embarkation and disembarkation drills using the troopship USS *President Jackson*. Mustering in correct waves, net drills and boat drills became familiar skills, although the Battalion War Diary noted that there was "too much delay in moving from beach under cover."[20] Climbing the rope ladders slung over the side of the troop transport in full webbing, weapons and packs was another challenge the troops mastered, although, as one noted, "It was a stiff pull up the side. We were huddled into cramped berths in the holds." There was a "hot and heavy atmosphere of the berthing quarters. Unfortunately, *President Jackson* was not fitted out with an adequate ventilating system."[21]

The 3NZ Division was equipped with British-style weaponry ranging from the excellent .303 Lee Enfield Rifle and the Bren Light Machine Gun to the versatile twenty-five-pounder field gun. The only weapon common to both Americans and Kiwis was the Thompson Sub-Machine Gun. The consequence of this incompatible weaponry was that 3NZ Division was an American quartermaster's nightmare. Ordnance had to come from New Zealand.

The Kiwis were provided with American field rations, some items of which they held in high esteem, although they hated others. A "K Ration" was the basic type and was considered sufficient for one day. It included canned meat (and often induced a lifelong detestation of Spam and chili con carne), biscuits, coffee, lemonade powder, Bovril (a popular meat extract), sugar and chocolate. An emergency "C Ration" usually contained three 12-ounce tins of meat and one of biscuits, coffee, sugar and hard candy. The "D Ration" consisted of fortified chocolate and was generally popular.

The attitude of the Kiwis toward the Japanese varied. For Doug Ross, an officer in the 37th Battalion, there was much hatred of the Japanese due to stories of how badly Allied POWs had been mistreated, the Japanese disregard of the Geneva Convention regarding prisoners of war and the American experience on Guadalcanal. The Japanese were regarded as a greater evil than the Germans: "We knew how hard it was to take them prisoner and that they regarded surrender as a disgrace."[22] According to Harry Bioletti, an officer in 30th Battalion, his greatest fear was being captured by the Japanese, who had a reputation for butchering prisoners.

The brutality of the Japanese posed a dilemma for Allied medical workers. It was known that the Japanese did not respect the Red Cross. If medics carried weapons, they lost the protection of the 1929 Geneva Convention. If they did not, they invited death. The New Zealand Army resolved this conundrum by granting permission to the soldiers of the New Zealand Medical

Corps to carry weapons if they wished. Stretcher bearers going into the jungle were to be escorted by soldiers of the Army Service Corps equipped with Thompson Sub-Machine Guns. Red Cross symbols on ambulances were also painted over.

The Fijians—"Guerrillas, Commandos and Scouts"

When war broke out in 1939, a New Zealand officer weighed up the martial ability of the Fijian soldiers by commenting that they were good parade-ground soldiers but would not be able to face the withering fire of machine gun bullets.[23] His comments were no doubt molded by his experience of the grim conditions of the Western Front during World War I. However, the war in the South Pacific would be unlike the trench warfare of the previous conflict. It would be jungle warfare where stealth and the ability to locate one's enemy and strike first would be decisive. The Fijians were to prove masters at this—indeed, they were so valuable to their American allies that Halsey would not allow them to be withdrawn from this theater in order to bolster up the ranks of 3NZ Division.

Fiji had initially been inadequately garrisoned. New Zealand had sent men to protect the islands, but its manpower resources were very limited. It was decided to mobilize the local Fijian population, and thought was initially given to setting up armed guerrillas in the event of Japanese invasion. Out of these efforts Fijian Commando units were formed, generally led by European New Zealand officers and NCOs of 3NZ Division. The officers were able to tap into a formidable Fijian martial tradition. Recruits came from their villages having never handled any weapon other than a cane knife or an ax. However, they had a superb sense of discipline and an "unbounded zest for soldiering."[24] Training was intense, and the Commandos' worth was soon established on Guadalcanal as they scouted for the Americans. However, the Americans disliked the word "commando" and dubbed the Fijian unit "South Pacific Scouts," which they felt was a more realistic description of their role.[25] Further combat experience was gained on Munda, New Georgia.

The Scouts, however, were more than simply Fijians and New Zealanders. There were thirty Tongans (including 2nd Lieutenant Henry Taliai) and about twenty-four Solomon Islanders, causing Captain (later promoted to Major) Charlie Tripp to refer to his men as "The International Brigade."[26] Tripp asked the Americans for the opportunity to let the Scouts "get into the thick stuff," pointing out that his men had acute eyesight and hearing

Private P. Waquawai of 1st Commando Fiji Guerrillas (South Pacific Scouts), waiting in ambush (photographer unknown; courtesy Archives New Zealand/Te Rua Mahara o te Kāwanatanga, Wellington Office, WAII, 7 3, Official Photograph Album).

and were able to cross the most difficult terrain with heavy loads.[27] The Americans obliged, and the Scouts took part in the hard slog across mosquito-infested swamps and dense jungle in the drive on Munda, New Georgia. A highlight was the defense of the Zenana beachhead, where seventy-five Scouts and a scratch force of thirty American non-combat troops held off a force of two hundred Japanese troops.[28] The Scouts earned high praise—General Beightler, 37th Division, U.S. Army, commented, "The South Pacific Scouts furnished distant reconnaissance patrols which worked well into enemy territory, often at great hazard, and further furnished battle guides in some instances who actually led front line units in assaults on enemy positions."[29]

The Scouts' jungle patrols were highly dangerous and had to be carried out with stealth and care. They also required considerable trust and faith between the New Zealand officers and the Fijian NCOs and men. Orders could not be given in the jungle by shouting, and command and control were difficult. The men had to know what to do, and they had to be led by example. This required a style of command very different from normal military units.[30]

The leader who could ensure the welfare of his soldiers and was able to obtain their confidence "had almost hypnotic power over his men."[31] Officers also had to eschew emblems of rank because of the danger of Japanese snipers.

Their efforts on Munda earned the Fijians the respect of the Americans. There was a ready willingness to ask for information and advice. On the other side of the coin, the Americans were unstinting in their material and logistical support of the Scouts, "without which the unit could have achieved nothing."[32] The Fijians were natural bushmen and warriors. They did, however, have one drawback: they lacked the skills to use navigational equipment and were reliant on their New Zealand officers and NCOs when in unfamiliar country.

The primary role of the Scouts was to provide intelligence. They were too small in number to be used to attack Japanese positions, and only when they considerably outnumbered the Japanese or could achieve surprise and melt away were attacks initiated. One Kiwi sergeant who was awarded the American Legion of Merit, Sgt. N.B. MacKenzie, commented that "he had scarcely fired a shot until he left the fighting area to return to the beachhead."[33]

Aggressive patrolling in enemy-held territory required conquering fear and being very self-contained. These singular qualities set the Scouts apart from other Allied soldiers.

The Japanese

The Japanese on Vella Lavella were a mixture of Imperial Japanese Army forces, Imperial Japanese Special Naval Landing Force troops, Imperial Japanese Navy personnel (including sailors who had been shipwrecked on Vella Lavella), and downed Japanese aircrews. Allied intelligence reported that the morale of army personnel seemed low, and they remained in close proximity to their headquarters. The navy personnel were deployed forward and did most of the fighting.

Japanese plans to retain a grip on New Georgia and launch a counterattack fell apart on the night of 6-7 August 1943. Two mixed battalions from the Japanese 6th and 38th Divisions were dispatched to Kolombangara on IJN destroyers. USN destroyers destroyed three of the four Japanese destroyers in Vella Gulf. Some three hundred Japanese survivors swam or drifted to the safety of Vella Lavella. Some were then taken off by barge to the Shortland Islands, while others died of their wounds.[34]

The Japanese defenders were ill supplied but made up for that in determination. They were averse to either giving or taking quarter. To be taken prisoner meant social disgrace to oneself and one's family. The Japanese soldiers were the product of a highly regimented system that stressed veneration of the Emperor, Japanese racial superiority, and the importance of group solidarity and individual self-sacrifice. A bastardized form of Bushido, the ancient warrior code, heightened a Japanese propensity for atrocity. In training, emphasis was placed on the offensive spirit, and even outnumbered, isolated troops were expected to develop counter-attacks and seize moral ascendancy over their enemies.[35] To the Japanese there were no such things as non-combatants; unarmed corpsmen or medical workers wearing the Red Cross insignia simply provided easier targets. The brutal discipline of the Japanese military and its ferocity ensured that the war would be one without mercy.

The Japanese were armed with rifles, sub-machine guns, light and heavy machine guns, light Type 89 50mm mortars (mistakenly called "knee mortars" due to a mistranslation of captured documents by Allied linguists), and grenades. Although it was reported that they had no artillery,[36] the Japanese were later found to be equipped with 75mm mountain guns, heavy mortars and 20mm guns.

Food dumps were established, which varied in size. The Japanese had no transportation apart from handcarts. Medical supplies were sparse and medical services elementary.

Japanese air superiority meant that attempts were made to supply their troops from the air. Brightly colored red-and-white-striped parachutes were used to deliver rice, "knee mortars" and ammunition. Often these landed among Allied lines or in the sea.

The main Japanese positions were at Horoniu and Boko. The estimate of Japanese forces was 290 army and 100 naval personnel who landed at Horoniu on 19 August. There were approximately 190 army and 120 navy survivors from the Battle of Vella Gulf on 6–7 August.[37] There were also remnants from other Japanese garrisons. Estimates ranged from five hundred to seven hundred in total.

There was no coordinated defense because the Japanese overall commander never arrived.[38] In any case, the discord between the Imperial Japanese Army and Navy was legendary and would have hindered an effective defense.

The Japanese attitude toward the local population was brutal and quickly alienated the Islanders. If any had been wavering in their support of the Allies, Japanese ill treatment would have pushed them into the Allied camp. Japanese destroyers had shelled coastal villages on Vella Lavella, driving the villagers inland and fostering an intense hatred of the invaders. The Japanese shelling was likely retribution for the presence of Coastwatchers and the loss of Japanese shipping.

A Coastwatcher, D.C. Horton, wrote:

> The Japanese did not help by their exceptionally stupid behaviour towards the Islanders and their possessions. Perhaps the most foolish thing they did was to destroy the native gardens they found. In the primitive conditions of the Solomons each family would make its own garden by the very laborious method of burning off the jungle, cutting down the large trees and then clearing the land and planting such crops as sweet potatoes, yams, taro etc by the use of pointed digging sticks so that by careful husbandry there was food for the whole family and only enough for each day was taken at any one time. But this meant nothing to the Japanese who would wantonly destroy a whole year's work in one visit to a garden. Nothing infuriated the Islanders more, and when in addition the Japanese smashed their canoes and desecrated their churches it was small wonder that the Islanders took their revenge whenever they could.[39]

FOUR

The Strategic Situation
in the South Pacific, 1943

In January 1943 the grinding, attritional battle of Guadalcanal came to an end. American forces had stopped the Japanese juggernaut in its tracks, and the Japanese had tasted the bitter dregs of comprehensive defeat in the South Pacific. For the Americans, the question became one of what to do next. In theory America was committed to a "Germany first" strategy, whereby the Germans were the primary enemy. This implied that operations against Japan would be of a defensive, holding nature. However, the Japanese strike south had proven to be too threatening and had seemed poised to take Australasia. For the first six months after Pearl Harbor, America poured double the amount of resources into the Pacific as was sent to Europe. With the buildup of men and resources in the South Pacific and memories of Pearl Harbor still fresh, the temptation to take the offensive against the Japanese proved irresistible. The first American offensive in World War II secured the island of Guadalcanal, but the Japanese held islands to the north and still posed a significant threat to the Allied position in the South Pacific.

Of particular concern was the Japanese base at Rabaul in New Britain. Developed as a major air, ground and naval base, it was the centerpiece of Japanese operations in the South Pacific. As long as it remained unsuppressed, it threatened the Allied position, both defensive and offensive, in the South Pacific. The campaign to neutralize Rabaul came to be known as "Operation Cartwheel."

The key problem that the Allies faced was a critical shortage of aircraft carriers and shipping, especially the specialized landing craft necessary for amphibious operations. This necessitated a reliance on land-based airpower and limited Allied advances to the radius of Allied fighter-cover.[1] The Allies had also learned from the fighting on Guadalcanal that the Japanese were a tenacious and unpredictable foe.

The Japanese strategy had been to seize the resource-rich areas of Southeast Asia and to create a series of interlocking bastions held together by air, land and sea forces. They had reckoned that the superior Yamato spirit of the Japanese would prevail against the effete Allied forces, and that the cost in blood would be so high that the populations of the Allied countries would insist their governments agree to a negotiated peace, leaving the Japanese in possession of the lands and resources they had seized. The Japanese calculated that they could hold the defensive perimeter in depth and that the Americans would emasculate themselves in assaulting Japanese defensive positions backed by powerful Japanese air and naval forces.

It appeared initially that the Americans would fall into the Japanese trap. In June 1943 the Americans decided to capitalize on their Guadalcanal victory by moving northward up the Solomon Islands ladder and into the New Georgia group. They hoped that New Georgia could be seized rapidly but instead encountered solid, determined Japanese resistance. The defenders maximized their advantage in the hilly, close jungle terrain by setting up near-invisible, mutually supporting log and coral machine gun nests and strongpoints. These positions were well constructed and camouflaged, and they proved well-nigh impossible to destroy by shellfire short of a direct hit by high explosives. The Japanese had to be burned and blasted out.

Compounding matters, the Americans threw into the battle barely trained National Guard troops unaccustomed to jungle warfare. Predictably, the Americans adapted quickly but suffered huge casualties from Japanese fire and disease. The lesson was painfully learned that frontal assaults and slugging matches against well-fortified Japanese defenders were prohibitively costly and time consuming.

American historians Jeter A. Isley and Philip Crowl noted the paradox that "Americans controlled the sea and air, yet it required over a month of fighting and the employment of over 30,000 army and marine troops, outnumbering the Japanese more than five to one before the Munda airfield was finally seized in early August 1943."[2] To the dismay of the Americans, their units on New Georgia became rapidly eviscerated. Casualties were so horrible that the combat power of some units was burned out. There were limited numbers of American troops[3] in the South Pacific, and these could not be squandered on frontal assaults. A new strategy was needed.

The American commander (COMSOPAC), Admiral William ("Bull") Halsey, USN, initiated the "island hopping" strategy in the South Pacific, whereby the Japanese strong points would be leapfrogged, isolated and left to wither on the vine.[4] New amphibious shipping had become available, enabling amphibious strikes. "At little risk and with greater economy of means, sea-air power is then able to harass the isolated enemy, shatter his morale, and leave him to die unsupplied and ineffectual, far behind the zone of combat. Unlike warfare on continental land masses, enemy groups isolated on islands by amphibious warfare have no opportunity to engage in partisan or guerrilla tactics."[5] The American intention was to exploit their technological superiority, particularly their skilled naval and army engineers, by building airfields and docks, thereby projecting air and naval power and choking off the supply routes of the Japanese defenders. The Americans took advantage of one of the key areas of Japanese vulnerability—their supply lines.

By 1943 the Japanese faced an acute shortage of merchant shipping. Their merchant fleet had initially been small, and the problem was worsened by the increasingly effective U.S. submarine campaign. The Japanese response was to create *Daihatsu*,[6] cheap, easily built motorized barges packing considerable weaponry, sometimes including anti-tank guns. These wooden barges were used to create a supply line to Japanese outposts. The barges required staging posts because they traveled in short stages, moving at night and concealing themselves in inlets during the day. One of these staging posts was set up on Vella Lavella. Although far from perfect, the barges provided a workable Japanese supply system. The *Daihatsu* were a premium target for U.S. P.T. boats, and the Americans were keen to slash the Japanese supply lines.

One Japanese advantage was that their airpower was still an extremely potent weapon, and Japanese air superiority could often be taken for granted. The Japanese aircraft, particularly the nimble, well-armed Mitsubishi A6M Zero, were of excellent quality, and until Allied attritional efforts began to take their toll the quality of Japanese aircrews was high. Japanese airfields were plentiful, and closest to Vella Lavella was one a mere sixty miles away at Ballale on Bougainville. As an American artilleryman noted, "The nearest friendly airbase was in the Russell Islands, 200 miles southeast. The soldier and the seadog soon learned that aircraft identification was easy—all planes seemed to display the red meatball."[7]

Vella Lavella lies at the topmost end of the New Georgia group, and the decision was made to invade it using American troops and then begin airfield and naval construction. In some respects it was simply the completion of a grinding, attritional campaign, but in other respects it represented a new beginning with an innovative strategy that would become standard in the Pacific War. Whereas previously the Americans had seized islands with airfields, on this occasion they seized an island without airfields (which would be built later).

The Japanese had heavily fortified and garrisoned Kolombangara Island, north of Munda and fifty miles southeast of Vella Lavella, in the expectation that the Americans would attack it. The main Japanese base on Kolombangara was at Vila. However, Vila was too swampy for development as an airbase, which lessened the incentive to launch an attack into the teeth of Japanese resistance.[8] It made sense to bypass and isolate this tough nut: "The enemy could have made an Allied frontal assault on Vila a most costly business, for the place was studded with pillboxes, trenches, machine gun emplacements and coastal guns."[9] In contrast, Vella Lavella was relatively undefended; the Japanese had run out of time to fortify it. For the Americans, Vella Lavella held another advantage—fighters from Munda and Segi Point airfields could provide some air cover. Given the relative absence of Japanese, the Americans focused on bypassing the Japanese defenders on Kolombangara by landing at Barakoma Bay on the eastern coast of Vella Lavella. Halsey made the decision to cancel the intended invasion of Kolombangara and instead take Vella Lavella. This was a significant shift in plans.[10]

However, at that point Halsey ran into a problem that had the potential to derail his plans. Early in the Pacific War there arose the issue of whether there would be one supreme commander who would direct strategy. Neither the U.S. Army nor the U.S. Navy was ready to concede supreme command to the other. A compromise of sorts had been worked out whereby the Pacific was divided into command zones, with the South Pacific being under the aegis of the U.S. Navy and Admiral Chester Nimitz, and the Southwest Pacific being under the U.S. Army and General Douglas MacArthur. Admiral William Halsey had been appointed Commander of the South Pacific Area (COMSOPAC), and because the northern part of the Solomon Islands was in MacArthur's patch, and Halsey was responsible for the naval aspects of Cartwheel in the Solomons, Halsey found himself having to deal with the egotistical MacArthur. Fortunately, both men were able to work well together. MacArthur's primary focus was New Guinea and the neutralization of the Japanese base at Rabaul, which threatened his flank. Having been humiliated in his defense of the Philippines in 1941–1942, and having given his pledge to return to the Philippines as a liberator, MacArthur had powerful reasons to object to any plans that did not align with his own. As Halsey's biographer, E.B. Potter, commented, "Halsey could bypass Kolombangara but there was no bypassing General MacArthur."[11]

Halsey appreciated that he had to sell MacArthur on the idea of the bypass, and he anticipated opposition from him. Halsey sent Vice Admiral Fitch, the number two man in the South Pacific, as his emissary. Fitch feared that he would have a difficult job, and so he put together a collection of senior naval officers who he anticipated would be able to answer any of MacArthur's potential questions. On arrival in Brisbane, Fitch and his companions were shown into MacArthur's office. Fitch made an introductory statement but was then interrupted by MacArthur, who proceeded to lecture them on the strategy of the war in Europe. After fifteen minutes MacArthur dismissed them with a smile and "thank you gentlemen." Thunderstruck, Fitch then appreciated the error he had made: he had been warned that if presented with an audience, MacArthur could not resist giving a lecture. Fitch desperately tried to arrange another appointment. Eventually he secured a brief interview. This time, MacArthur simply nodded and said, "Work it out with General Sutherland [MacArthur's chief of staff]. I agree with anything you and Halsey want to do."[12] Halsey had his approval.

On 12 July 1943, Halsey sent an advance warning of the change in plans to both Rear Admiral Theodore S. Wilkinson, whom he had selected to lead the invasion, and Admiral Fitch, who would command the aerial aspects: "Bypass Vila area and allow to wither on the vine. Seize Vella Lavella and establish fighter field there on."[13]

In hindsight, it is easy to overlook how truly audacious and risky the bypass was. It had not been tried in the South Pacific before, and there was no certainty it would work, especially in the face of hostile Japanese airpower.

Beadle's Reconnaissance

From an Allied perspective, there was a critical vacuum of intelligence regarding Vella Lavella. Although limited information about Vella Lavella could be gleaned from such sources as plantation managers, missionaries and Coastwatchers, what was lacking was hard technical geographical data about possible airfield and landing beach sites. General Harmon, U.S. Army, decided it was necessary to send his engineer, Colonel Frank W. Beadle, U.S. Army, to investigate. Beadle was put in command of a reconnaissance party of six U.S. Army, U.S. Navy and USMC officers. Their mission was to focus on the southern coastal area of Barakoma and the Biloa Mission. The reasons for this focus were that it was closest to Munda; the native population was pro–Allies; a New Zealand Methodist missionary, the Rev. Archie W.E. Silvester, and a Coastwatcher, Sub-Lieutenant Henry Josselyn, RANVR, were resident there; and also the area seemed to hold the best prospects.

Beadle's party departed Rendova on the night of 21-22 July 1943 and traveled by P.T. boat to Barakoma. There they were greeted by the Reverend Silvester and Sub-Lieutenant Josselyn. For the following six days, Beadle's patrol, accompanied by Silvester, Josselyn and Islanders, explored the southern area of Vella Lavella without encountering any Japanese. They did encounter the crew of a downed PBY5A Catalina and returned with them by P.T. boat on 28 July.[14] On returning to Rendova on 28 July, Beadle recommended that a landing be made in the area south of the Barakoma River and that, prior to landing, a group be sent to mark the channels, beach landing area, dispersal points and defense positions. Barakoma was the preferred landing site because "of good drainage, safe approaches, suitable beaches and bivouac areas."

The Battle of Vella Gulf—6–7 August 1943

The Japanese expectation was that the Americans would do the expected, rational, thing and move progressively up the Solomons chain island by island. They attempted to counter this action by building up their defenses in the Upper Solomons. As they did so, the need for supply of their troops grew.

As part of their supply effort, the IJN sent four Japanese destroyers, *Hagikaze, Arishi, Kawakaze* and *Shigure*, all crowded with troops, to Kolombangara on the night of 6–7 August 1943. The force was commanded by a torpedo expert, Captain Sugiura Kaju. Sugiura had a good reputation and was experienced. The Japanese felt confident in their night-fighting superiority, an assumption borne out in the naval battles in the South Pacific. They welcomed the prospect of a night action and the opportunity to use their Long Lance torpedoes.

On this occasion the Americans were only too willing to oblige. Tipped off by Allied intelligence in the form of an Ultra intercept[15] that the Japanese would undertake a "Tokyo Express" operation, the Americans set a trap. Commander Frederick Moosbrugger, USN, had several advantages: his Task Group 31.2 was fully trained in radar-controlled night attacks, his skippers were familiar with his battle plans and his destroyers were not impeded by having to accompany cruisers.[16] The Americans detected the Japanese convoy near Buka at 1630 hours on 6 August,[17] and six American destroyers—USS *Dunlap, Craven, Maurey, Lang, Sterrett* and *Stack*—moved to intercept the Japanese. What followed was a pure destroyer-on-destroyer fight.

Moosbrugger had positioned his force close to the dark shoreline of Kolombangara. This and rain squalls made it very difficult for the Japanese to see his ships. The Americans divided into two groups of three apiece and, using their radar, were able to spot the Japanese. Closing to 6,000 yards, three of the American destroyers launched their torpedoes at 23.43 hours. *Shigure*, captained by one of the luckiest Japanese destroyer commanders of the Pacific War, Captain Tameichi Hara, was an older destroyer in need of a refit and lagged behind. The torpedoes were launched before any American gun had opened fire—this was the type of tactic the Japanese had employed so successfully in the past. The Americans would show that they were apt pupils. The *Shigure*'s lookout spotted the American ships and eight torpedoes were launched in return. As she did so, her sister ship *Arishi* was hit in the engine room, while *Kawakaze* was hit in the magazine; the *Hagikaze* was also hit. The *Shigure* was struck by a dud torpedo that failed to explode but damaged the rudder.[18] Three of the Japanese destroyers were set on fire and sunk. The fortunate *Shigure* managed to comb the tracks of the American torpedoes. The fact that *Shigure* lagged behind had saved it. Conscious of the fact that his was the only Japanese warship left and outnumbered, and also conscious of the fact that he had 250 troops and deck cargo on board *Shigure*, Captain Hara made smoke and prudently fled northward.[19]

The Americans successfully evaded the Japanese torpedoes, reformed their formations and headed south. The commanding officer of *Lang* observed "the sea was literally covered with Japs so thick that their bodies were seen to be thrown up in the phosphorescent wake of the vessel. From all sides the survivors lifted a cry that sounded like 'kow-we, kow-we' chanted in unison with considerable volume. It was a weird unearthly sound punctuated by shrieks of mortal terror." When the American ship tried to rescue the survivors, someone in the water blew a whistle and the Japanese swam away from their would-be rescuers.[20]

The Americans had gotten the drop on their Japanese opponents and in the ensuing clash, rare in the early destroyer battles, pulled off a successful ambush. As the naval historian Mark Stille notes:

> The battle of Vella Gulf was a total victory for the Americans. Mossbrugger had a solid plan and used his weapons flawlessly. He took advantage of local conditions to exploit his advantage in radar. This marked the first time in the war that Japanese destroyers had been beaten in a night action. It was also the first time in the Solomons campaign that American destroyers had independently engaged the Japanese. The results of the new doctrine and reliance on torpedo attacks were immediate and dramatic.[21]

For the Japanese, it was a singular disaster—fifty tons of equipment, three destroyers and over a thousand men had been lost.[22] Worse, the feeling of superiority that the Japanese destroyer men had regarding their American counterparts had evaporated. As Captain Hara commented, "Never before had I seen such marksmanship by the enemy. We had been taking altogether too casual a view of his torpedo technique."[23] The defeat also marked the last time that Japanese destroyers would attempt to supply Vila. Barges would subsequently be used for this task.

The outcome of the naval battle would have some unforeseen consequences for Allied planning. Shipwrecked Japanese soon began to arrive on Vella Lavella. Petty Officer Tokugawa survived two days in the water until the currents delivered him to the shores of Vella Lavella. There he found himself in the company of some two hundred Japanese survivors of the sea battle.[24]

The Advance Party

Rear Admiral Theodore S. Wilkinson, USN, accepted Beadle's recommendations and ordered the creation of an advance party. This group of fourteen officers and men commanded by Captain G.C. Kriner, USN, prepared to leave Rendova by P.T. boat when an unexpected complication arose. On 11 August Josselyn sent a radio message stating that forty Japanese crewmen, survivors from the Battle of Vella Lavella Gulf (6–7 August 1943), had been captured by Islanders. A Comairsopac Intelligence report noted, "Forty Japanese had landed on SE Coast of Vella Lavella by 12 August. They were unarmed and were taken prisoners by Allied scouts on the island." It also remarked, "They came from Vila because of the food shortage and the terrific bombing."[25]

Harmon, no doubt realizing the intelligence treasure trove this might provide, arranged for the advance party to be strengthened in order to deal with the Japanese prisoners. An additional group of twenty-six men from E and G Companies, 103rd U.S. Infantry, was provided.

The advance party's passage from Rendova was far from smooth. Although leaving at 1730 hours from Rendova on the night of 12–13 August, the group of four P.T. boats was discovered by Japanese planes and bombed and strafed. One of the P.T. boats was hit by Japanese planes and had four wounded. When the P.T. boats arrived off Barakoma in the dark of night, the Americans discovered, to their chagrin, that their rubber boats were not able to be inflated from the provided carbon dioxide containers. The situation was remedied when Islanders paddled out in their canoes and brought the Americans safely to shore.

The situation on their arrival seemed to be deteriorating. There were in fact no prisoners, but there were said to be forty Japanese at Biloa and another 100 five miles to the north of Barakoma. It was also reported that there were several hundred Japanese "refugees" from Kolombangara and naval survivors on Vella Lavella armed with "grenades, clubs and a few firearms."[26] Captain Kriner requested urgent reinforcements. These arrived in P.T. boats after dawn on 14 August in the form of seventy-two soldiers from F Company, 103rd Infantry. Fighter cover for the PT boats was provided by four RNZAF P-40s from No. 16 Fighter Squadron from 0700 to 0930 hours on 14 August. No Japanese fighter attacks occurred and the reinforcements arrived safely. This time the rubber rafts were able to be inflated, and the soldiers paddled the three hundred yards to the beach.

There was a clear disconnect between the two mission objectives: the beach-marking team required stealth to do its work, but the prisoner retrieval team was likely to draw Japanese attention. Ultimately, the beach-marking team was able to complete its mission satisfactorily and the prisoner retrieval team was successful in capturing seven Japanese sailors. In the meantime, F Company, 103rd Infantry, set up a defensive perimeter fortuitously facilitating the eventual American landing.[27]

A member of 58th Naval Construction Battalion recalled:

On August 11, 1943, the 58th prepared to embark from Guadalcanal for the landing on Vella Lavella. An advance party went ahead to survey the site for the air strip and mark the beach for the landing. This party was composed of the Skipper, CDR. Lewis, Lt. Reynolds, Lt. Currie, W.O. Smith, W. Moss, and F.J. Dowling. CCM. The scouting party boarded P.T. boats at Guadalcanal on the afternoon of August 11 for the overnight run up to Vella Lavella. It was a rough trip and not only did the party suffer PT sickness but were spotted by Jap planes who bombed and strafed them for nearly two hours. Lt. Reynolds said afterwards, there was nothing else for us to do but lie under the torpedo tubes and pray. After a while of praying that the bombs would not hit us, we thought better of it and decided that the bombs were not as bad as the sea sickness. The party sneaked ashore just before daylight on August 12. The island was alive with Japanese patrols but they evaded them and began surveying the landing and air-strip sites. However, they did encounter some Japanese, who were wiped out to the man. The men were looking forward to the 15th, when the first detachment of the battalion was due to land, because the Japanese patrols were becoming larger.[28]

Plans for Invasion

Halsey issued his orders for the invasion of Vella Lavella on 11 August 1943. By this time the U.S. Navy had considerable experience in the intricacies of amphibious operations, and their planning reflected this. As he had during the New Georgia invasion, Halsey created the Northern Force, designated as Task Force 31, under the command of the highly competent Rear Admiral Theodore Stark "Ping"[29] Wilkinson, an expert in amphibious operations, with the objective of capturing Vella Lavella. In conjunction with this, General Griswold's New Georgia Occupation Force would strike at Arundel, and New Georgia–based fighter aircraft would provide cover. South Pacific Aircraft, designated as Task Force 33, would interdict enemy airfields on Bougainville and the Shortland Islands. Naval support was to be provided by three naval task forces. The American policy, bewildering to outsiders, was to first create task forces for specific jobs and then, on completion, disband them. This provided considerable flexibility in planning and operations. In all, Halsey was able to bring considerable strength to bear for the invasion. Halsey planned that 15 August 1943 would be D-Day.

Rear Admiral Wilkinson carried out his own detailed planning and issued Operations Order No. A12-43. He defined his objective as follows: "Commencing on Dog Day this force will seize the vicinity of BARAKOMA, VELLA LAVELLA, capture or destroy enemy forces encountered, and will construct an airfield; in order to develop VELLA LAVELLA as a base for further offensive operations."[30] Wilkinson merely intended to seize the southern portion of Vella Lavella. The clearance of Japanese forces from the island could wait. Ever present was the threat from IJN forces based at Rabaul.

Wilkinson divided the Northern Force into three echelons, consisting of an invasion group (the main body) and two other echelons. Wilkinson then subdivided the main body into three subgroups: The Advance Transport Group (Captain J.J. Ryan, Commander Destroyer Squadron 23) consisted of six APDs escorted by the destroyers USS *Nicholas*, *O'Bannon*, *Taylor*, *Cony* and *Pringle*. The Second Transport Group (Captain W.R. Cooke, Commander Destroyer Squadron 22) consisted of twelve LCIs escorted by USS *Waller*, *Saufley*, *Philip* and *Renshaw*. The Third Transport Group (Captain G.B. Carter, Commander LST Flotilla Five) consisted of Landing Ship, Tanks (LSTs) 354, 395, and 399, escorted by USS *Conway*, *Eaton*, and Submarine Chasers 760 and 761. The choreography of invasion meant that the slowest craft, the LSTs, would leave early in the morning, the six Landing Craft Infantry some five hours later, and the speedy APDs would leave eight hours after that. The different arrival times at Barakoma (0610, 0710 and 0800) were designed to allow each group full use of the beaches before the next group arrived. Given the threat from Japanese airpower, getting the craft unloaded and away in the most efficient manner was critical for success.

P.T. boats from Rendova and Lever Harbour were designated to screen the movements of the highly vulnerable ships by setting up picket lines to the west, south and northeast of Vella Lavella during the night of 14–15 August, retiring to their bases by daylight on the morning of 15 August.[31] Naval gunfire support was not thought to be needed, but Wilkinson designated two destroyers to provide this if necessary. Fighter direction had evolved hugely and two fighter director groups were placed aboard two destroyers.

According to the debarkation plan, it was intended that the ships of Transport Division 22 would at 0610 receive the signal "Land the Landing Force" and commence debarkation. Twelve boats in three waves would act as an assault group to seize the beachhead and cover the next waves of troops.[32]

A map was prepared of the transport area and beaches designating Beaches A, B, and C. Each was marked with a colored flag. The map showed a coral shelf and "nigger heads" (coral outcroppings), and it indicated that "underwater obstructions will be marked by spar, beacon or native canoe mounting yellow flag."[33] Despite having what looked like a comprehensive landing map, problems would arise. Amphibious operations are among the most complex and unforgiving of military operations.

Wilkinson's timetable was tight—he intended to land the force within twelve hours. The APDs would unload the troops into LCVPs, which would deliver the troops to the shore and return for more. Sixty minutes were allowed for this, and then the LCIs would land, followed one hour later by the LSTs.

It was intended that after the initial invasion, the second echelon would beach at Barakoma on D-Day plus 2, stay overnight and then return to Guadalcanal. The third echelon would arrive on D-Day plus 5, and it would consist of three LSTs escorted by three destroyers. Again it would beach, stay overnight and then return to Guadalcanal.

The huge LSTs loomed large in the invasion planning. These specialized craft had bow ramps that enabled the delivery of trucks and heavy equipment straight onto a beach. The LST had the ability, once unloaded, to retract and sail away. The quip was made that "an LST is the only ship in the world of 4,000 tons or over that is continuously rammed onto and off of coral, sand and mud."[34] They were in short supply, and the loss of or damage to them could potentially derail later operations. They had to be treated like gold.

The Northern Landing Force comprised 5,888 men of the 35th Regimental Combat Team of the 25th Infantry Division, the 4th Marine Defense Battalion, 25th Reconnaissance Troop and also a naval base group.[35]

The landing force was to be commanded by Brigadier General Robert B. McClure of the 25th Division. McClure was a 47-year-old professional soldier and veteran of the Western Front. He had been appointed to command the Division in 1942 and led it during the battles for Guadalcanal and New Georgia. Following American amphibious doctrine, McClure was to be under Wilkinson's command until such time as the beachhead was secure, and then command would revert to General Griswold.

Planning was done hurriedly, which had its consequences. As Lt. Col. W.H. Allen observed:

Brigadier General Robert B. McClure, U.S. Army (photographer unknown; *Marines in the Central Solomons*, p. 131).

> Information available to the artillery prior to the landing was meager: essentially only a few poorly lithographed copies of a 1/20,000 uncontrolled mosaic. Shown on the mosaic was the shoreline: inland nothing but solid jungle, broken only by occasional white patches of cloud, usually where information was most wanted....
> Stereo photos of the landing area, if any were available, never percolated down to the artillery battalion, which during the brief "planning phase" of the operation, was in the Russell Islands, 75 miles from the Northern Landing Force headquarters at Guadalcanal.[36]

The loading of the LSTs with supplies and equipment began on 12 August and was completed by the following day. A practice disembarkation was carried out successfully, and then the soldiers were re-embarked.

By 14 August the troops and equipment had been combat loaded aboard the ships, and the echelons sailed for Barakoma. One reinforced battalion of the 35th Combat Team embarked from the Russell Islands, but the rest left from Guadalcanal.[37] The night was cloudless with a brilliant moon, and even though there were Japanese air raids on Guadalcanal, the Russell Islands and New Georgia, the convoy's luck held.[38] The night voyage was uneventful, and, as planned, the LCIs passed the slower LSTs north of Rendova, and both groups were in turn overtaken by the faster APDs.

FIVE

The Initial American Invasion, 15 August 1943

H-Hour

Amphibious landings, even unopposed ones, are extremely complex affairs, requiring close cooperation between land and sea forces. Unloading troops and vital supplies requires considerable skill and insight into cargo handling and troop deployment.

As planned, the APDs carrying the 1st and 2nd Battalions of the 35th Infantry arrived off Barakoma at daybreak (0610 hours) on 15 August 1943; after deploying their landing craft, the heavily loaded troops climbed down rope cargo nets into the waiting boats. Since the beachheads were secure, there was no need for a preliminary naval bombardment. Overhead fighter aircraft from Munda and Segi Point provided aerial protection. Things proceeded like clockwork, with the 2nd Battalion landing and pushing inland to the Biloa Mission and the 1st Battalion pushing in a northerly direction to the Barakoma River. The precious APDs, along with their escorts, then left rapidly at 0730 hours for the safety of Guadalcanal. The destroyer USS *Cony*, with Wilkinson on board, remained on station together with *Pringle*.

Frank Marks, a private with Fox Company, 2nd Battalion, 35th Infantry Regiment, recalled his grisly introduction to Vella Lavella:

> When we landed on Vella Lavella there were no ground forces present for us to fight. Fox Company was assigned to head for the Baracomba [*sic*] Mission on the south end of the island. As we made our way along the beach, the shoreline was covered [with] the bloated bodies of dead Japanese soldiers. This was the result of our Navy and Air Force sinking Jap ships that were trying to bring reinforcements to the island of New Georgia. Shortly after we landed and while others were

58

being unloaded we came under air attacks from the Japanese. These attacks went off and on for several days. Fortunately, none of our ships were sunk and our casualties were minimal.[1]

For Marks the unpleasant experience of being bombed and strafed by Japanese planes was nothing new. He had experienced such attacks on Guadalcanal and took them in his stride. However, for Private James C. Cook, also of the 35th Infantry Regiment, the arrival on Vella Lavella was one to remember. His unit had captured three Japanese prisoners, and everything seemed calm until Japanese planes arrived. The distance from the beach to the safety of the jungle was some three hundred yards. When the bombing and the strafing began, Cook's platoon dashed for the jungle, with Cook's lieutenant vainly pleading for his men to catch the Japanese prisoners.[2]

The 3rd Battalion encountered much more difficulty. The Second Transport Group, the LCIs, arrived on schedule at 0715 but found difficulties with coral reefs blocking the northern area, forcing four LCIs to heave to offshore. It was then discovered that the three beaches could only accommodate eight instead of twelve LCIs. This could have had deadly consequences for the vulnerable LCIs. In addition, a wrongly interpreted visual message from the beach party delayed the completion of unloading the last four LCIs until about 0900.[3]

To add to the congestion, the Third Transport Group arrived on time at 0800 and had to wait for the LCIs to clear the beaches. On the fighter director's destroyer the radar showed blips of incoming aircraft at 0747 and at 0751 hours. Visual contact was made at 0758, and a minute later Japanese dive-bombers began attacking the screening destroyers. The *Conway* and *Eaton* began laying down smokescreens.

The two sub-chasers, SC-760 and SC-761, had been deployed in Gizo Strait as flank protection for the invaders. Not being large targets, they did not initially attract Japanese attention. Then two planes began an attack on SC-761. J. Henry Doscher recalled, "As we wildly zigzagged in Gizo Strait, firing our 40mm gun, two small bombs landed about 100 to 200 yards on the starboard bow. We did not notice any damage to these two planes from our guns, and SC-761 experienced no damage."[4]

The Combat Air Patrol and the ships' anti-aircraft guns engaged the attackers, but some Japanese planes broke through. Following the Japanese warrior ethic that it was beneath their dignity to attack non-warships, the pilots focused their attention on the destroyers. *Cony* was attacked at 0801 hours and, despite high-speed maneuvering, narrowly escaped being hit by bombs, two of which landed within fifty yards of the ship. The other destroyers also experienced near misses. So, too, did the vulnerable, immobile LCIs and the slow LSTs. Some casualties were also suffered from strafing.

The main impact of the air attacks was that they delayed the unloading of the beached LCIs, and it was not until 0915 hours that they were able to clear the beachhead. The three LSTs of the Third Transport Group were then able to beach and unload their cargoes. This was not without its difficulties, however. Lt. Col. W.H. Allen recalled,

> When at 0915 the LST eased up to the shore, the ramp lacked several yards of touching firm footing. Eventually an engineer dozer from an LST farther down the shore clanked up and, with the aid of strong artillery backs, made a ramp of stones over which unloading could proceed. (Causeways were then unknown.) The next problem was that, once ashore, vehicles could find no place to unload in the jungle that grew to the water's edge. Here again the indispensable bulldozer went to work to clear out a turnaround loop that wove among the giant trees. As soon as the truck prime movers towed the 105s ashore, the firing batteries began to wrestle with the 30 days of rations, drums of gasoline, and the five units of ammunition stacked to the roof of the LST's tank deck. Engineer shore parties were a luxury unknown to early South Pacific expeditions.[5]

Conway and *Eaton* were left to screen the LSTs. But the Japanese pilots were not deterred. Further Japanese planes arrived at 1227 hours—eleven bombers and forty-eight fighters. This time the LSTs were attacked, but the targets were successful in bringing down several Japanese planes. At 1724 hours, forty-five fighters and eight bombers attacked without success. The bombing and strafing resulted in twelve dead and forty wounded, but, almost miraculously, no significant damage was suffered by the shipping. Sadly, some soldiers—such as Sgt. Edward Pristosh, PFC Joseph Tatsey III, PFC Elmer Griffin, and Private John W. Horvath of Item Co., 35th Infantry; Tech 5 Louis Kovacs, Charlie Co.; Private Doyle McClain of HHC Co.; Private Joseph Monaco of Able Co.; PFC John Pursell of Alpha Co.; and Corporal Charles R. Watkins of Mike Co.—were killed during the landing, some not even making the shore and their bodies not being recovered.

By 1800 hours the Third Transport Group had completed most of its unloading. There seemed little point in leaving the exposed, vulnerable ships on the beaches without Allied fighter cover. The order was given to retire. However, the LSTs would not have a comfortable passage back to Guadalcanal. Japanese planes dropped colored flares and float lights; this was followed by six horizontal bombing attacks. The escorts made smoke as a way of protecting their charges. After a harrowing passage, the Third Transport Group arrived safely at Guadalcanal on 16 August.[6]

The 58th Naval Construction Battalion (NCB) landed after the 35th

Infantry Regiment, and although their landing was unopposed, Japanese airstrikes interrupted unloading operations. Large bulldozers were the first items off the ships and were set to work clearing beach exits and roadways and creating access to supply dumps.[7] Repeated bombing and strafing continued over the course of the day and into the night. The following day saw further Japanese air attacks.[8]

The 58th NCB Cruisebook records:

On the morning of the 14th, the convoy shoved off and, at dawn of the 15th, it approached the beach at Vella Lavella. We began to unload the cargo from the ships at Barakoma Village. The boys with the "BAR's" were acting as guards, and the unloading proceeded very swiftly as we had practiced it many times back on the "Canal." As the ramps of the LST's came down, men and vehicles rolled out, as most of our equipment was on six wheelers, and bumped into the jungles. Bulldozers were sent ashore and soon coconut and palm trees came crashing down and pushed over with yards of coral to form ramps to the ships. Meanwhile, long lines of men waist deep in water passed boxes of supplies and equipment, for on LCI's all cargo must be man-handled. We all worked feverishly because we knew it was only a matter of a shorter space of time before the Japanese planes would be on us as the whole landing operation could be observed from enemy lookouts on Kolombangara only thirteen miles across the water. Quite suddenly, the alarm was sounded and all hell broke loose. Every one took off for the boondocks or the ships. High in the sky, planes zoomed and droned, their machine guns spitting leaden death. The first attack lasted five minutes and seemed hours, then it began again, through some miracle, none of the gang were hurt. When the attack was over, we completed the unloading and moved up a hill to dig in for the night as best we could in foxholes. There were so many attacks during all of the day and the night that it was a continual "Condition Red."

Lt. Col. Allen remembered that

Nightfall found the first echelon of the landing force ashore in an area some 600 yards wide by 300 deep. The howitzers pointed seaward, the only direction in which they had a field of fire, and the 90mm AA guns and radar of the Marine Defense Battalion remained parked, as they, too, had no field of fire. In the light of the full moon, enemy planes droned all night over the island, searching with lights, here and there laying an egg, then impudently rat-tat-tatting with their tail guns. Fortunately, the jungle provided a screen, and with the LSTs having left, planes had difficulty locating the troops, who held their fire. A piece of luck spared C Battery—at daylight they saw a 500-pound dud that had plunked into their bivouac during the night.

The next morning disclosed some damage. An AA radar was riddled with bullets and some stores had been hit. The principal damage the artillery suffered was to two truck lockers brought along by officers in violation of instructions. The offenders received scant sympathy as they gazed at the tattered fragments of their woolen uniforms, fluttering from tree limbs high above the ground. (The reader may wonder why woolen uniforms were carried to the Solomons—they were brought by the entire division, which had been en route to Australia when it was diverted in late 1942 to Guadalcanal to relieve the Marines.)[9]

The invasion, carried out in the face of Japanese airpower, had been immensely successful. Allied airpower had played a considerable role in this achievement.[10]

At the time of the American landing on 15 August 1943, Japanese strength on Vella Lavella was estimated at five hundred to one thousand men, comprising elements of 6 Japanese Division, 38 Japanese Division, survivors of naval actions, survivors of destroyed Japanese barges and evacuees from Kolombangara and surrounding islands.[11]

The Air War—15 August 1943

The Japanese reaction to the landings on Vella Lavella on 15 August 1943 was to make a maximum effort to hit the amphibious forces with airpower. Some 149 fighters, 25 Val dive-bombers, 11 Kate torpedo bombers and 24 Betty bombers[12] were directed to Vella Lavella. The pilots came from the IJN aircraft carrier *Junyo* and Air Group 204. Some twenty-one sorties were made against Barakoma.[13]

They would be opposed by a mixed force of USAAF, USMC and RNZAF fighters: the 44th USAAF Fighter Squadron, USMC squadrons VMF-123 and VMF-124, and RNZAF No. 16 Squadron based at Segi and Munda. The payoff of the seizure of the expensively obtained airfield on Munda was that fighter aircraft were able to linger over Barakoma for longer periods than those based at the more distant Guadalcanal and Segi airfields.

Walsh's War

One of the defenders of the shipping on 15 August was Lieutenant Kenneth Ambrose Walsh of the USMC fighter squadron, VMF-124. Walsh had distinguished himself as a very capable flier of the newly introduced (October 1942) F4U Corsair and had rapidly acquired ace status. By mid–August the squadron was based at the newly captured airfield on Munda.

On 15 August Walsh was part of a five-member Corsair Combat Air Patrol over the invasion beaches and shipping. The fighter director gave warning of incoming bogeys. Walsh was low on oxygen, so he and his wingman stayed low and his section leader climbed for high altitude. Walsh turned to attack the incoming Vals and their escorting Zero fighters. The enemy force outnumbered his by six to one, but this did not deter Walsh. He repeatedly attacked the Japanese aircraft and downed two dive-bombers and one fighter. A Zero scored hits on Walsh's Corsair. Walsh recalled, "He got on my tail and hit me with cannon shells, one of the rounds exploding in my starboard wing tank—fortunately the wing didn't blow off."[14] Walsh took desperate evasion action to shake off the attacking Zero but suddenly experienced vertigo and his plane began to loop wildly.

> I was spinning around doing 400–500 kts, and as I came out of the cloud I realized that I was commencing an outside loop, inverted going down at 45 degrees. I barely missed the rim of an extinct volcano and with one aileron gone, I just managed to roll the aeroplane back into level flight!

With difficulty, Walsh regained control of his plane and landed safely at Munda. The plane was so badly shot up it was later scrapped and used for spare parts. Walsh discovered that a 20mm shell had cut the hydraulic lines in one wing and hit the main spar. By rights he should never have made it home.

Walsh would face even greater odds later and win the Medal of Honor for his actions on 30 August 1943, in battling against fifty Japanese aircraft. He was forced to ditch off Vella Lavella, and a Higgins boat rescued him. Walsh became the first Corsair ace to receive the Medal of Honor.

The RNZAF Contribution

The New Zealand fighter squadrons flew the P-40 Kittyhawk. The American-supplied P-40s were of the older variety and, while heavy and rugged in construction, were easily outmaneuvered by the nimble Zero. In the opinion of Squadron Leader Bob Spurdle, RNZAF, they had the flying characteristics of a brick.[15] However, an appreciation of the limitations of their aircraft and good flying tactics and discipline meant that the New Zealanders could at least hold their own against the Japanese.

On 15 August 1943, sixteen fighters of No. 16 Fighter Squadron, RNZAF, equipped with P-40 Kittyhawks, staged out of Segi to patrol Munda and Vella Lavella and cover Allied shipping.[16] Thirty-two sorties were flown, but most were uneventful with no contact. A section of four P-40s led by Flight Lieutenant J.R. Day at 0800 hours came across Japanese aircraft attacking shipping and downed four of them. Day recorded:

> One of my section called that there were Bogeys about but there was so much talk over the air that I could not get [the] Bogeys' position. We then jettisoned belly

tanks. I saw one bandit in a dive at approximately nine o'clock and 3000 feet to 4000 feet below. I dived down on him, coming out dead astern, when I found the enemy aircraft to be a Zeke. At about four hundred to five hundred yards, I opened fire, continuing the burst up to within about two hundred yards. Although no smoke appeared, he immediately burst into flames from the cockpit. He started in a gentle diving turn to the right, increasing the dive. I lost sight of him about one hundred feet above the trees, when he was going straight down, approximately five miles north-west of the south-east tip of Vella Lavella.

At that time, I noticed a Val attacking a destroyer, so I immediately turned to attack this Val, which broke towards the north-west. I was then at right angles to the Val, so I carried out a full beam attack, altering to a quarter attack as I closed in. I opened fire at about 300 yards, allowing three rings deflection. The Val flew straight through my fire when pieces were flying from his wing and canopy. I then broke away to make another pass, but observed a machine starting an attack on me from behind and above. I broke down to about one hundred feet above the sea and, as fuel was very low, I returned to Segi, landing at 0845 hours.[17]

Another section of four P-40s, flying thousands of feet above Day's section, was hit by Japanese aircraft attacking out of the sun. One P-40 flown by Pilot Officer D.L. Jones was hit and crash-landed at Munda.[18] At the end of the day, fifteen of the sixteen RNZAF P-40s returned to their base on Guadalcanal.

In a typical example of over-claiming kills, the Allies claimed thirty-four Japanese planes shot down, whereas the reality was that nine fighters and eight Vals had been lost. Nor were the Japanese immune to this temptation—their pilots claimed twenty-nine Allied aircraft shot down, whereas the Allies actually lost six aircraft, four Corsairs and two P-40s.[19]

In all, twelve Americans were killed and forty wounded by the Japanese air attacks on the day of the invasion. However, the Americans had landed some 4,600 troops, 2,300 tons of gear and equipment, and fifteen days' worth of supplies.[20] The 35th RCT had set up a defensive perimeter, field artillery was sited and the 4th Marine Defense Battalion had installed 90mm anti-aircraft guns and searchlights. The AA defenses were able to provide a warm welcome to the last Japanese aerial raiders of the day.

While the invasion was successful, the unloading process had been disrupted by the coral reefs and air attacks. The materiel of war had been unloaded, but much of it was scattered across the beach and it would take time to cache and store properly.

Subsequent Echelons

In the initial planning it had been intended that subsequent echelons would be beached just before dark, unloaded during the night and well clear of the beaches before daybreak, thereby limiting the exposure of the precious shipping to Japanese air assaults. However, this plan proved impracticable due to Japanese night attacks, particularly on shipping in the narrow waters of the Gizo Strait, which severely restricted maneuverability. Plans were modified so that shipping, either going to or coming from Vella Lavella, would be clear of Gizo Strait during daylight hours. This entailed the ships beaching during daylight and being reliant on fighter cover for protection. The use of smoke to cover "slow ill armed convoys" was approved.[21] The combination of high-speed maneuvers and smoke may have lessened damage to the task group from air attack, but it increased the danger of collision. Admiral Carney, Halsey's chief of staff, stated, "The hazard must be accepted."

The Second Echelon of the Northern Force, consisting of LSTs 339, 396 and 460, screened by destroyers and a sub-chaser, arrived off Barakoma on 17 August and beached at 1625 hours. The American fighter cover had to return to Munda, and at 1850 and 1910 hours the vulnerable ships were hit by Japanese aerial attacks. The ships had not fully unloaded, but McClure ordered the ships to put back to sea. The LSTs suffered an air attack lasting 2 hours and 17 minutes as they sailed into the Gizo Strait.

The escorting destroyers laid down smoke to screen the LSTs. Japanese attacks seemed directed at the destroyers, but their swift evasive maneuvers made them difficult targets. *Waller* and *Philip* collided at one point; fortunately, they sustained only superficial damage and were able to continue with their screening role. No action was therefore taken against the captains of *Waller* and *Philip*.[22]

Valuable lessons had been learned, particularly with the offloading of the vulnerable LSTs. Wilkinson reported:

> It was found that an LST, loaded with four hundred tons of loose cargo and twenty loaded 2½ ton trucks could be unloaded in five to six hours with a working party of 250 men and additional trucks from the beach. In later echelons each LST was assigned 20 trucks for this purpose, empty trucks returning to GUADALCANAL with the LST.[23]

Wilkinson also noted that "the usual reluctance of shore unloading details to return promptly to their tasks as soon as an air raid was completed was overcome during the later echelons. This was reflected in the dispatch with which ships were unloaded."[24] In this, Wilkinson was probably not taking into account the greater effectiveness of air cover and AA defenses. The loss of LSTs would continue, and few could blame unloading parties for apprehensiveness during air raids.

At one point, LST-396, loaded with aviation gasoline and 155mm artillery shells, caught fire and had to be abandoned. The cause of the fire was attributed to an underwater explosion, the likely result of a Japanese submarine's torpedo. Although the ship burned and sank, only one crew member was killed.[25] In large part the low casualty rate was due to the courage of Coxswain Benjamin Brumbleboe. Despite flames and explosions, Brumbleboe lowered a boat and then picked up survivors, repeatedly venturing close to the ship's side to rescue people in an area where heavy wreckage and flaming debris thrown out by the explosions were constantly falling.[26] He received the Navy and Marine Corps Medal for his actions.

The other two LSTs reached Barakoma on 18 August, where they endured another two air attacks while unloading their cargoes. Fighter cover was unavailable due to bad weather at Allied airfields. The LSTs fled to the relative safety of Guadalcanal. The stress on the ships' crews must have been immense. Closed up at General Quarters for a thirty-six-hour period and under repeated air assaults, nerves must have been stretched taut.

It was not only the ships that felt the sting of Japanese airpower. Robert Kennington of the 35th Infantry Regiment recalled the unpleasantness of being strafed:

> Just before we were ready to jump off the boats at Vella Lavella, Japanese fighter planes flying out of Bougainville hit us. We were supposed to get air cover but it was twenty minutes late. We jumped into the water over our head, carrying our packs and rifles. The jungle was right at the beach so I got my squad under a tree as soon as possible. I laid my squad behind a little tree that seemed about ten inches in diameter. The Japs kept up the attack, dropping bombs and strafing. They came in so close you could shoot them in a slingshot. They flew in, one right after another. Strafing planes cut the limbs and leaves off trees all around us. We huddled down and could see the smoke coming from the guns mounted in the wings and bombs drop on the beach. We were lucky that day, or maybe the Japs were losing their touch because casualties were light. But it scared the hell out of everybody.[27]

The Third Echelon (led by Captain Carter), made up of LSTs 354, 395 and 398, escorted by destroyers and sub-chaser SC-505, had a hard passage through the Gizo Strait on 21 August. The convoy was repeatedly subjected to torpedo, bombing and strafing attacks. USS *Pringle* suffered two dead and several wounded with "slight material damage."[28] The LSTs beached at 0700 hours on 21 August and began unloading as rapidly as they could. The destroyers withdrew from the beach area on the grounds that the LSTs had their own anti-aircraft weapons and 90mm anti-aircraft guns had been established on shore. SC-505 was left behind to guard the LSTs against possible submarine attack. Risks have to be taken in war, and Wilkinson later candidly acknowledged that this action "deprives the SC of the benefits of the destroyer's anti-aircraft fire, but is done in order to remove the larger and more valuable combatant vessels from the usual air attack following close upon the arrival of the convoy." He concluded by noting, "Heavy air-cover is provided during the unloading period but it is expected that some dive-bombers may get through."[29]

For their part, the LSTs had their own formidable weaponry. LST-354, for example, had three 37mm guns, four 40mm guns, eighteen 20mm guns, nine .50-inch machine guns and one 3-inch dual-purpose gun. The wisecrack that LST stood for "Large Slow Target" had an uncomfortable ring of truth to it, nonetheless. For the invasion of Vella Lavella, the anti-aircraft arsenal was supplemented by the placement of U.S. Army AA units on the main deck, a practice that would have tragic consequences later for the New Zealanders. The captain of LST-395 commented that the men from 35 Combat Team, "although not experienced with 40 mm guns ... steadied well on the targets and behaved throughout as if they were fighting their own ship in the landings at Vella Lavella ... their action provided invaluable protection during heavy air attack."[30]

At 1010 hours Val dive-bombers appeared high over Barakoma and the AA batteries swung into action. The beached LSTs were sitting ducks, but instead six of the Vals concentrated their attacks on a sub-chaser, SC 505, which had been patrolling offshore. Five bombs were dropped, landing twenty to forty feet from the ship. The Vals all strafed the sub-chaser. One near miss "caused the ship to heel over to a 65 degree angle. Water flooded the deck to a depth of 24 inches." The attack "caused extensive damage to the sound gear and the electrical system," and one man received a shrapnel injury while other crew members suffered minor injuries "as a result of being thrown about the ship."[31] SC-505 was a lucky ship.

A second wave of twenty Vals appeared at 1515 hours, and this time they attacked the beached LSTs. Some fifty bombs were dropped but were near misses. Nonetheless, four men were killed and eleven wounded. The heavy fire from the AA guns and weapons undoubtedly put the aim of the Japanese pilots off. Some Japanese planes were shot down. Fighter cover, even though it did not succeed in engaging the Japanese aircraft, probably hastened their departure. First Lieutenant William D. Armstrong, flying a Corsair, was on patrol over Vella Lavella and short on fuel. He was returning to Munda when he heard of the Japanese air attack. Despite being on his own, he attacked the Japanese and downed a fighter. For this he would later receive the Distinguished Flying Cross.

The escorting destroyers returned at 1600 hours, and at 1615 the LSTs retracted from the beach and the convoy headed for Guadalcanal. It arrived there the following afternoon.

A member of 58th NCB recalled:

> The third wave landed on August 22nd. This bunch really got the business for by now the Japanese really had us spotted and knew what we were about to do. In the early morning about 1000 came over and bombed us at about 800 feet. At top speed, screaming eerily over the jungle the Jap bombers flew to the attack. The ship's gunners returned their fire, but still the planes came in and released their loads of destruction. In a formation of six, one suddenly wavers and to the cheers of the gang, it bursts into a bright pyre of flames as the gunners found their mark. The other five however broke through and plastered us. They didn't miss the target at this range and of the fifteen bombs that fell not one was less than a hundred yards from the ships. It was a literal rain of death when the bombers pulled out of their shrieking plunge, not a man on the ship's deck was left standing. The guns were either blasted to scrap or choked with coral dust. While the smoke and dust of the explosions still blanketed the ships, the gang on the beach and below the decks swarmed aboard to clean up. They found the decks littered with coral boulders, wounded and dead shipmates.[32]

The Fourth Echelon (under Captain Cooke) proved to be a sign of changes to come. LSTs 339, 397 and 399, screened by the destroyers *Saufley*, *Renshaw* and *Cony*, together with the sub-chaser SC-733, arrived off Barakoma at 0820 hours on 26 August 1943. The LSTs rapidly unloaded and left for Guadalcanal at 1530 hours without being attacked from the air.

The Fifth Echelon (also led by Captain Cooke) was similarly lucky. LSTs 341, 353 and 398, escorted by the destroyers *Saufley*, *Renshaw*, *Cony*, *Dent* and *Talbot*, left Guadalcanal in the early morning hours of 30 August 1943. The *Dent* and *Talbot* each carried 175 men consisting of a platoon of South Pacific Scouts and replacements for the 35th Infantry. Off Rendova at 0200 hours on 31 August, the convoy was joined by five LCIs carrying the 1st Battalion, 145th Infantry. Radar blips indicated Japanese aircraft were nearby, but only one attack was made on *Dent*, which was at the rear of the convoy. No damage was suffered.

APDs of the Fifth Echelon arrived off Barakoma on 31 August and speedily off-loaded their troops and supplies. Having completed their task, they retired by 0730 hours. The LSTs and LCIs arrived at 0800, and by 0900 hours the LCIs were headed for Rendova escorted by three destroyers. As the convoy was forming up, nine Japanese dive-bombers struck, targeting the destroyers. Two men on USS *Cony* were injured, and both *Cony* and *Saufley* sustained minor damage. The ships of the Fifth Echelon headed for Guadalcanal.[33]

The resupply effort had succeeded—the U.S. forces on Vella Lavella had about 40 days' worth of rations, five units of fire, and thirty days' worth of fuel.

The two convoys on 26 August and 31 August were luckier due to more effective fighter cover and better weather. On 26 August RNZAF fighter aircraft from Munda carried out patrols over the landing area. No contacts were made with Japanese aircraft. The Marine Defence Battalion had also established its anti-aircraft guns. In the week of 23–26 August, Japanese aerial activity was restricted to small-scale attacks on Vella Lavella. The focus of the airwar in the Solomons was shifting in the Allies' favor as Allied airpower pounded Japanese airfields, particularly in southern Bougainville.[34]

Radar was still in its infancy, but it nonetheless provided the defenders with valuable warning of incoming Japanese air raids. In the initial phase of operations, radar coverage was provided by fighter director officers aboard

An LST being prepared for discharge, 20 September 1943 (U.S. Signal Corps; courtesy Archives New Zealand/Te Rua Mahara o te Kāwanatanga, Wellington Office, WAII, 7 3, Official Photograph Album).

destroyers, who attempted to control air cover. However, the geography of Vella Lavella hindered them, as the mountainous terrain interfered with radar reception. Vella Lavella was split into two areas—on the west side, the defenders had to rely on visual sightings and radar reports from stations based on Munda, while the east side had better radar cover.[35] It was not possible to control fighter operations from Barakoma due to its poor radar coverage.

In his report Rear Admiral Wilkinson summed up the air cover situation:

> Adequate and most efficient air cover was supplied over BARAKOMA during all days when a convoy was present. Due to shortage of fighter squadrons in this area and other requirements for air cover, as on striking missions a continuous day-by-day coverage in protection of the BARAKOMA position could not be supplied by Commander Air, SOLOMONS.... While this exposed the position to somewhat greater hazard and damage from air attack, the efficiency of the AA batteries and the discipline of the troops prevented serious loss of life or material.[36]

Put another way, the invasion of Vella Lavella had been a calculated gamble that Japanese airpower would not destroy the invasion force or the Allied garrison. The shipping—particularly the specialized amphibious vessels—were not put at hazard lightly. Once ashore, the troops would be able to take cover and avoid catastrophic attack, and were therefore a lesser consideration.

The invasion of Vella Lavella was almost textbook—Wilkinson's Task Force 31, between 15 August and 3 September, delivered 6,505 men and 8,626 tons of supplies, vehicles and equipment to Vella Lavella, allowing the American forces ashore to consolidate their grip on the island.

The landings on Vella Lavella had clearly been successful. On 3 September, Wilkinson, as amphibious commander, relinquished command of the forces onshore, which then passed to General Griswold, U.S. Army.[37]

On the night of the American landing on 15 August, Admiral Kusaka had suggested to General Imamura that a battalion carry out a counter-landing. Imamura's response was that sending such a small force would be "like pouring water on a hot stone." Transport difficulties were also a factor. Moreover, Imperial Headquarters had directed that Japanese forces fall back slowly. The chief Japanese response to the American landing was to be from their airpower.[38] The Japanese set up a barge staging post at Horoniu Village on the northeast coast of Vella Lavella and an outpost at Ganongga, an island to the south.

Rather than simply providing defensive cover over Vella Lavella, the Allied airforces concentrated on suppressing Japanese airpower. An RNZAF Operational Narrative recorded, "For several days after the initial landing on

Vella Lavella the Allied airforces were principally engaged in striking at enemy air bases at Raketa Bay, Vila and Kahili and in attacking barges and staging points."[39]

To secure the island, it was vital to build an airfield. A member of 58th NCB also recalled, "After the landings we set about to build a campsite and establish an airfield previously surveyed by our advance party. Slow progress was made because we were constantly under 'Condition Red' because of the lack of air protection in the first few days."[40]

Supply efforts had to continue in order to consolidate the Americans' grip on Vella Lavella. This meant exposing shipping to Japanese air attacks.

The Invaders Consolidate

The invaders took up defensive positions in the southern part of the island from Biloa Mission to the Barakoma River in the west. Patrols were sent out from this perimeter with the harrowing task of locating Japanese resistance. Generally, these patrols did not make contact with the enemy.

Frank Marks, 2nd Battalion, 35th Infantry Regiment, reached the Barakoma Mission:

> As soon as we reached the Mission, that was situated on the shore of a lagoon, we set up our perimeter and awaited further orders. The day after we landed the Marines sent a unit of Black Marine anti-aircraft gunners who set up in the hills right above us. Boy, were they good. Their first 3 kills were Marine Corsairs that had come to give us some protection against the Japs that were bombing and strafing us. There was a lot of jubilation when they finally dropped a Jap Zero.

Marks and his comrades soon found that the mission station offered recreational opportunities:

> The Mission consisted of a school building and a storage building whose structure was typical native construction. Along the side of the school building lay an overturned whaler boat that had several bullet holes in its bottom. One of the men from the 1st Squad, 1st Platoon found several pairs of oars under the boat. Ten of us decided to see if we could row the boat from the Mission across the lagoon to the other side where we had seen two buildings. Without letting anyone know what we were doing, or where we were going, we put the boat in the water and headed for the other side of the lagoon. In order to make it across we had to have six men rowing while the other four bailed like mad to keep us afloat. When we reached shore we found a house and an outbuilding. The house was wired for electricity. In the shed we found a generator which was powered by a gas-operated motor that looked like a motor from a Model A Ford. Before we could explore any

further the Japs honored us with another air raid. We immediately headed back to the Mission and our unit. Before we made shore the air raid was over and our company began counting noses. Of course there were ten of us listed as missing. When we hit shore, boy did we ever catch hell from our platoon leader and C.O.[41]

The attitude of the Americans to their Japanese foe had been largely shaped by the Japanese attack on the U.S. fleet at Pearl Harbor on 7 December 1941. Marks reflected, "At that time we knew they were our enemy and as such they had to be annihilated. I don't think any of the men in our company ever considered taking prisoners."[42]

As John Dower recorded in his book *War Without Mercy*,[43] one of the more malevolent aspects of war is the dehumanization of the enemy, leading to the desecration of enemy bodies. "Harvesting gold teeth" from the bodies of enemy dead was a feature of the Pacific War. Frank Marks observed one of the corporals in the 35th Infantry Regiment

going along the shore examining the dead Japs for gold teeth. He did this by peeling their lips back and if he found one he used the butt of his bayonet to knock them out. Those he found he would put in an empty Bull Durham sack he always carried. His squad followed him around on his search and because he was a seasoned vet and all the men in his squad were new to combat, they followed him around like he was a God. How he could touch those bloated, stinking bodies is more than I could do.[44]

A call was made for experienced men to volunteer to join a new unit called "Merrill's Marauders" to fight in Burma. Several men volunteered and left the Regiment.[45]

A few days after these men left the company we received about 20 more new men as replacements. Boy, did they get sick when they had to sit and eat their rations next to the bodies of the dead cattle and Japs that were in or near our area. I remember one man by the name of Chamberlain. From the minute he got to our company he began crying that he didn't belong in a combat area and had been marked "limited service" and told he would be a non-combatant. He kept crying about this continuously until the company received orders to move out. He was then sent to the rear echelon and we never heard from him again.

There was some excitement in Frank Marks' unit when a Japanese plane was hit by anti-aircraft fire and the pilot bailed out over the southern side of the lagoon.

The Regiment sent several landing barges to us and we proceeded to the south side of the lagoon. The company lined up our platoons across the south arm of land by the lagoon and we were put at arm's length apart. We proceeded to go from the east end to the west to see if we could rout out any Japs. The only thing we routed out was a couple of cows and some pigs that had been left there and had become wild.[46]

Additional American forces were landed, and McClure began to think in a more aggressive manner. A report was received that Japanese forces were in the Kokolope Bay area in the northeastern part of the island. He issued orders to the 1st Battalion, 35th Infantry, to clear the area of Japanese with the intention of establishing a radar site at Sirumbai Point on the northeast coast, about twenty miles north of the American perimeter. Japanese fliers had managed to evade radar detection by hugging the ground and coming in from the north. There could be no effective defense until radar could be established to pick them up.

On 30 August the battalion set off up the east coast along a narrow track. Company G, 65th Engineering Battalion, was ordered to construct a road behind them. By 4 September the infantry had reached Lambu Lambu Cove, but the Islanders warned them that there were many Japanese in the Boko Mission area. Led by Island guides, A Company, followed by C Company, headed for the Boko Mission. A Company's lead elements reached a point where the track forked in three different directions. Patrols were dispatched down each fork, and those on the left and center killed several Japanese who were in the process of digging defenses. As Lt. Col. Allen observes, "Examination of the enemy dead and captured arms showed that the battalion had to fight healthy, well equipped, well organized enemy soldiers rather than starving stragglers."[47] One of the Japanese dead was an officer who had a sketch map of the defenses in the Boko Mission–Kokolope Bay area. This was sent back for translation and analysis.

In fighting on 4 September 1943, typical of the small unit actions on Vella Lavella, PFC Ernest W. Allen, aged 27, from Center, Texas, of Alpha Company, 35th Infantry Regiment, posthumously earned the Silver Star. The award, conferred on 11 January 1944, recorded that

> while acting as a point for a patrol which had penetrated Japanese outposts Pfc Allen aggressively killed two of the enemy and assisted in killing a third with quick and accurate fire. One of the Japanese casualties was an officer carrying a map completely revealing the hostile positions. Through its use, our forces were enabled to expeditiously reduce enemy resistance.
>
> In subsequent actions, Pfc Allen was killed instantly by Japanese machine gun fire. By his courage, devotion to duty and at the sacrifice of his life, he contributed inestimably to the successful culmination of the operation.[48]

Jerome J. Hendrick found his opponents much tougher than the Japanese he had encountered on Guadalcanal:

> The worst part of Vella La Vella, is that these Japs, were in good shape. The Japs on Guadalcanal were starving to death. These guys had plenty of food. They had

Photograph taken on New Caledonia of men of the 35th Regiment. Left to right: Bill Daly, Jerome J. Hendrick, Larry Hayes, Jim Godfrey, "Zooter" Fjelsted, McManus (front) (photographer unknown; courtesy Terry Hendrick).

good equipment. Full uniforms. They probably came off a barge that couldn't get through the Slot. They were reinforcements for Guadalcanal that had gotten stranded on Vella Lavella. It didn't look like they had been on that island long. By the fourth or fifth day on that hell hole we were all sick again, shaking with Malaria. Later they said it was Dengue Fever. It was mostly a mop up operation so they sent us back a couple miles. We hadn't gotten very far and found the beach, what there was of it, and we didn't get any food. There wasn't any supplies. The whole operation was a total mess, something they had just thrown together without much planning. There were no maps of the island. The officers were new to the unit, some had gotten killed. It was just a mess. We're all sick and we're scrounging around for coconuts because there's no water fit to drink.[49]

When the Japanese tried to infiltrate American positions at night, close-quarter combat often resulted. Jerome Hendrick was part of a two-man BAR team. His partner was a big coal miner from Pennsylvania, Bill Matachevsky. Hendrick was impressed by Matachevsky's ability to dig a foxhole—"give him a shovel and twenty minutes and he would excavate a huge hole big enough to sleep in and four or five feet deep." The problem with the foxholes, however, was that huge rats and lizards would intrude on the foxhole's occupants. One night Hendrick's sound sleep was interrupted when he felt something drop

Bill Matachevsky (or Mazechevsky), a coal miner from Pennsylvania who could dig the deepest foxhole in the South Pacific (photographer unknown; courtesy Terry Hendrick).

on top of him. Thinking it was a rat, he threw it off him but, coming awake, to his horror realized it was a Japanese soldier.

> He's about 5 feet tall and probably a hundred pounds and I throw him off and jump up and he has a rifle and tries to bring the rifle around and it's too long. He can't bring it round. It hits the side of the foxhole and I grab him around the throat and his neck shrinks down to the size of a coke bottle and I look at him and he's about fifteen years old, just a kid, and I choked him to death and I feel guilty about that. I didn't need to kill him, he's a kid, he obviously doesn't know what he is doing. He isn't going to kill me, but I killed him.[50]

This experience haunted Hendrick in his post-war life and led to nightmares—"I see that kid's face a lot at night," he would tell his family.[51]

A request was made by the infantry for artillery support. Battery C, 64th Field Artillery, was ordered to proceed to Ruravai. This, however, was easier said than done. The simplest method would have been to move the battery by sea around the coast using a Landing Craft, Mechanized (LCM). However, there were no LCMs available; these craft were committed to supplying the infantry. Thus, the gunners had to use the road being built by the engineers along the shoreline.

> The "road" was a track roughly paralleling the beach trail made by a D-8 bulldozer, which snaked between the giant jungle trees and through occasional coconut groves. By the use of axes, shovels, and winches the 2½ ton 6 × 6 trucks towing the 105s [105mm artillery] made fairly good progress. The main obstacle was the numerous streams. These were passed by fording at low tide the sand bars that choked the stream mouths. One river, where the water was too deep for fording, the engineers bridged with a coconut-log trestle that would have made a state highway engineer cringe. Lacking spikes, the engineers had to wire the logs together. Though anyone in his right senses would have hesitated to cross in a jeep, the battery drove their 2½ tonners across loaded with ammunition. By nightfall 6 September, C Battery was in position at Ruravai.[52]

The captured Japanese map proved invaluable. With the aid of aerial photos, the Japanese positions were plotted and fire plans developed. Since Ruravai was about 9,000 yards from the front line, it was decided to concentrate on A, C and Headquarters batteries at Lambu Lambu to lessen the range and increase their lethality.

By 8 September the batteries were in place and supported 1st Battalion in its attack by providing a ten-minute barrage to soften up Japanese defenses. The CO of 1st Battalion reported, "The attack was executed as planned and was unopposed. The enemy had withdrawn just ahead of our assault companies, making possible the seizure of the day's objectives without firing a shot."[53]

Later the deadliness of the artillery fire was revealed: "Evidence of accurate artillery fire was found in every occupied area. 105mm shell hits were found in mortar and field gun emplacements. Dead Japs were found with shovels and picks in their hands as if they had been working in their foxholes and on the ridges."[54]

On 11 September, B and C Companies were struck by the Japanese and withdrew. Faced with this check, McClure ordered the 3rd Battalion to assist with an assault on the Japanese defenses. McClure's plan was that while the 1st Battalion struck toward Valapata to the southwest of Kokolope Bay, the 3rd Battalion would push northward, preventing the defenders from slipping away. What McClure had not taken into account was the effect that the dense jungle had on the movement of the 3rd Battalion. Although both the 1st and 3rd Battalions moved off on 14 September, the 3rd Battalion made slow progress, and when the 1st Battalion reached Valapata the Japanese were gone. The 3rd Battalion relieved the 1st Battalion at Valapata, allowing the 1st Battalion to search for Japanese.

Meanwhile, the 2nd Battalion extended its defensive perimeter northward to Nyanga Plantation on the west coast. Frank Marks recalled:

> We received our orders to leave Baracomba [*sic*] and go to the west shore of Vella Lavella and move north along the shore. We first had to move up a ridge in the center of the south end of the island before we could head west to the west shore. I was the point man when we started moving up the ridge. At six foot three, it wasn't long before word came from the troops in the rear asking that the long legged s.b. in the front, slow down as those in the rear were running and still couldn't keep up. Cy Drew, our C.O. then had Frank "Porky" Bystiga take over point. Porky was about 5′6″ and slightly rotund so he would be walking at a pace those in the rear could maintain. We would march 50 minutes and then get a ten-minute break. During one of the breaks I was resting between the roots of tree that was about 100 ft. tall. I heard a scratching noise on the other side of the tree roots, so I got up to take a look to see what it was. Here was a green lizard about 4 ft tall and from head to tail about 6 ft. long. It had claws about 4 inches long that it was using to try and scrape bugs out from around the roots. Needless to say he scared hell out of me and I scared hell out of him. I tore around the tree where my buddies were and he headed elsewhere.
>
> When we got to the west shore, we were supposed to mop up any Japs we encountered. We found none. Word came that there was a white woman seen on one of the little islets off our shore. They sent a Barge from Regiment with orders to send a patrol to the islet and rescue the white woman. Cy Drew picked Sgt. James B. "Jungle Jim" Dowdy to head the patrol. Jim picked the men he wanted to go on the patrol with him. They returned with the information that the "white woman" was an albino native woman. They did find a Japanese supply dump (no Japs), consisting of food rations, ammo and sake. Like any good F Company man, they destroyed the food and ammo, but brought the Sake back with them.

While moving along the west shore we were put on alert. We were told Japanese reinforcements were coming down the slot on our side of the island and would be coming under the cover of darkness. We set up a perimeter along the shore and dug in. At the north end of our perimeter some of the men strung a wire across a trail and hung empty ration cans on it as an alarm. First they gave us condition red, this meant that the Japs were on their way. Then came condition black, this meant they could be right in front of us, off shore. We waited in complete silence and you could only hear the lapping of the waves upon the shore and occasional clicking of the claws of sand crabs as they move[d] along the sand in front of us. All of a sudden the cans started rattling on the alarm wire the men had set and the men fired off a few rounds towards the trail. We were to learn that the alert had been a false alarm and the rattling of the cans on our wire alarm was caused by a three-legged dog. A short time later we were taken off of the coastwatch, as our section of the island was deemed secure. We were then sent to the top of the ridge on the center of the island and set up a bivouac, with kitchen, tents and all.[55]

Having taken virtually half the island, the Americans halted. This was the position when the New Zealanders arrived. So why didn't the 35th Infantry Regiment complete the job of eliminating the Japanese defenders? Possibly there was recognition that the Regiment had been in combat too long. The 35th Infantry Regiment rejoined its parent division on Guadalcanal on 20 October and from there was sent to New Zealand for rest, recovery, and absorption of replacements. The Regiment would later undergo further training and would distinguish itself in the bloody battles for Luzon in the Philippines in 1945. There may also have been a desire on the part of the American commanders to use New Zealand troops in a combat role. Given the New Zealanders' availability, their desire to be involved in combat rather than a garrison role, and the shortage of American troops in the immediate theater, it made sense to utilize New Zealand troops to eliminate the Japanese defenders.

The 58th NCB began surveying and clearing the swampy jungle for an airfield at Barakoma. Private James C. Cook of the 35th Infantry Regiment observed the Seabees at work and their stratagem to fool the Japanese. During the day the Seabees would work on the construction of the airfield. Knowing that the Japanese would attack at night, the Seabees piled up coral rocks some distance from the airfield and placed a light on the formation. Sure enough, it attracted Japanese bombs.[56] By 24 September 1943, a 4,000-foot fighter strip was operational and in daily use. Additional facilities, such as an aviation gas tank farm of six 1,000-barrel tanks, were established. A naval station was established at Biloa and a P.T. boat base was set up. The reef was deepened to facilitate access.

The Allies had one key intelligence advantage: Coastwatchers were able to provide information about the position and size of Japanese forces, and the Islanders provided guides. The importance of this was appreciated by Robert Kennington:

> I took two Navy officers on a patrol across the island. They were looking for a place to establish a PT-boat base. Their commander was Byron White, later a Supreme Court justice. We had three native guides, the best I'd ever worked with. There was a village near the mountaintop there. A French woman pretty much ran things. Before the war she and her husband operated a plantation. When the Japs came they killed the woman's husband, so she and her son fled to this village. They turned the villagers against the Japanese. The Navy guys weren't up to the trek, and we had to carry their rifles and packs. They slowed us up badly. We took five days' rations and were gone eight, so we were running very low on food. We saw a couple of groups of Japanese, but slipped by them, not looking for trouble. One morning the natives took off, promising to return in about an hour. They came back carrying some giant mussels they gathered on the ocean and had about three wild pineapples and a bunch of wild oranges. They dug a hole in the ground, filled it with a certain type of wood that gave off very little smoke, piled rocks all over the fire. When it got good and hot, the mussels opened up like poached oysters. It tasted as good as a T-bone steak. We had plenty of bananas, papayas, and taro roots that tasted like a sweet potato. When we made it to the shoreline, we borrowed a big native war-type canoe in the lagoon. We left the Navy folks there and P.T. boats picked them up.[57]

Naval Battle Off Horaniu—17/18 August 1943

The Japanese had intended to contest Kolombangara and had reinforced that island, but they left few men on Vella Lavella. The Japanese realized that if the Americans could establish themselves on Vella Lavella, then their garrison on Kolombangara would be cut off. They decided, as a countermeasure, to set up a barge station at Horaniu on the northeast coast of Vella Lavella to facilitate the evacuation of their soldiers on Kolombangara. Two IJA companies and a naval platoon amounting to 390 soldiers were earmarked for this operation.

Accordingly, a Japanese convoy of twenty small landing barges, accompanied by four destroyers (*Hamakaze, Isokaze, Sazanami* and *Shigure*), commanded by Rear Admiral Baron Ijuin Matsuji, was sent on 17 August to retrieve the soldiers from Kolombangara and ferry them to the barge staging point at Horaniu on Vella Lavella. American planes discovered Ijuin's force in the Slot, and Admiral Wilkinson gave orders for the Japanese to be intercepted. An American destroyer force of four ships (*Nicholas, O'Bannon, Taylor* and *Chevalier*), under the command of Captain Ryan, USN, sortied from Tulagi.

AIRSOLS sent two flights of TBF Avengers to launch a night attack on the Japanese. This was unsuccessful, but it slowed Ijuin's force and allowed Ryan's destroyers time to catch up to the Japanese.

In the early hours of 18 August, the two forces sighted each other in bright moonlight and the Japanese launched torpedoes at long range. As the two groups closed, they battered away at each other with gunfire. The Americans had the disadvantage of being silhouetted against a bright moon. That, however, was soon to be offset by the fog of war. At about 0100 hours Japanese radar erroneously indicated more Americans arriving and, based on this misinformation, the Japanese destroyers ran for Rabaul. The Japanese barges scattered, and the Americans were successful in sinking two. The battle was an American victory—two Japanese destroyers, *Izokaze* and *Hamakaze*, were slightly damaged. The Americans had shown their increased skills at night fighting and their enhanced capabilities in dealing with their foe. Nonetheless, the Japanese had succeeded in their primary purpose—by 19 August 1943 Japanese troops had landed at Horaniu.[58] Still, American naval confidence had been boosted and a destroyer sweep was repeated on the night of 19/20 August 1943.

For the Japanese, the repercussions reached to the very top. The historian John Prados comments, "When the emperor [Hirohito] learned of the battle he erupted at Admiral Nagano, accusing the Navy's destroyers of running away and leaving the Army troops to their fate."[59]

A Japanese soldier of the 41st Infantry Regiment, part of a unit commanded by Probational Officer Hiroji Hirose, recorded in his diary that he left for Vella Lavella on 17 August as part of a convoy escorted by destroyers and other warships. Although he arrived on Vella Lavella safely, the experience was a traumatic one: "This was the first time in my life I knew what fear was. Riding in a large landing barge over rough waters receiving enemy air attacks. In our dizzy condition we awaiting the hour wearing our life jackets, the only thing we could depend upon."[60]

For the next few days the soldier hid in the jungle on Vella Lavella and was involved in reloading material. On 19 August he linked up with his company commander and camped with his comrades in the open overnight "while listening to the roar of naval guns." On 28 August, he heard the news that out of some nine hundred soldiers of the 41st Infantry Regiment who had departed at the same time, only two hundred had been rescued and made it to Bougainville.[61] That was the last entry in his diary.

The South Pacific Scouts

The Americans decided to deploy the Scouts on Vella Lavella. On 25 August 1943 Major Charlie Tripp was ordered to move fifty of his men to Vella Lavella to carry out a scouting role. He chose his fittest and ablest men. The group comprised ten New Zealanders and fifty Fijians, as well as an officer and three sergeants from 3NZ Division who were attached for them to gain experience. The group left Guadalcanal on 29 August 1943 and arrived at Barakoma on 31 August, where they were attached to the U.S. 35th Regiment. The Scouts were split into three groups. One, comprising sixteen men led by Major Tripp, was to work in the east coast area up to the Lambu Lambu Cove sector. The second, led by Captain David Williams and consisting of twenty men, was instructed to provide protection for the Coastwatcher at Topolando and to reconnoiter the northern area. The third group of nine men under Lieutenant D.G. Graham, of 3NZ Division Intelligence, was ordered to go to the Oula River on the west coast and then to turn inland and watch the Japanese track across the center of the island.

The patrols worked alongside small groups of Americans. A patrol killed two Japanese at Baka Baka Mission on 3 September 1943.[62] The following day, twelve Japanese were killed by a company of Americans. A map was discovered on the body of a dead Japanese officer, revealing the Japanese defensive positions at the main Japanese base at Horaniu. Major Tripp sent this back to the Island Command Post, and the decision was made to send a battalion supported by artillery to attack the Japanese. The Scouts were sent out on daily patrols to locate Japanese positions and ensure they had not moved. Their efforts paid off when the American heavy artillery was deployed and pounded the Japanese positions. Direct hits were scored on the defenses and the Japanese fled, abandoning ten 20mm guns, two 90mm mortars, 75mm mountain guns, and ammunition and supplies. The supporting American infantry found the going easy. Sergeant H.B. Brereton, a New Zealander attached to 1 Fijian Commandos, noted:

> September 14. The arty put over a barrage about 0800hrs. The whole BN moved out for BAKA BAKA at 0830hrs. It was a hard day through heavy going but struck no opposition. When we reached BAKA BAKA we were very pleased to find that the Japs had withdrawn from good positions and had left all their heavy weapons behind, also rations and supplies. It was in this area that the arty had got several direct hits which must have been the cause of the Japs withdrawing.[63]

Tripp's men looted the Japanese stores, delighting in the "canned heat" (used for cooking rice) and tinned salmon. Tripp and his men continued their patrol along the eastern coast but did not encounter any further Japanese; they returned to Barakoma on 20 September.

The second patrol led by Captain David Williams, a pre-war New Zealand farmer, traversed fifty miles of steep, densely bush-covered terrain. They linked up with Coastwatcher Henry Josselyn. He provided Williams with detailed information on Japanese dispositions.

Patrols were sent out. One patrol, consisting of Williams and two Fijians, investigated Japanese activities on Umomo Island. On 7 September the patrol stealthily located ten Japanese on Umomo and twenty-two at the mouth of the Timbala River. Reinforced by other scouts, Williams was intent on using his twenty-five men to attack the Japanese around the Timbala River. However, he soon realized that the Japanese had also been reinforced and numbered about a hundred men—a suicidal proposition to attack. He wisely decided to return to the Island Command Post and get reinforcements. However, before doing so, he arranged for tracks to be cut into the bush close to the enemy positions as a launching-off point for the attackers. When he arrived at the post he discovered that 14 Brigade had been ordered to eliminate the enemy. Williams then decided to rejoin his men who were watching the Japanese.

Graham's group on the western coast reconnoitered Japanese tracks. On 16 September 213 Japanese were spotted heading toward Warambari Bay. Lt. Graham's patrol watched as 86 Japanese passed them, literally feet away. Japanese soldiers also came threateningly close to Josselyn's large radio near Topolando. Josselyn arranged for this to be moved to safety, but Captain Williams kept operating a smaller radio reporting on enemy movements. This information enabled the Americans to send aircraft to bomb and strafe Japanese troops when they tried to move by barge. The Scouts were positioned high up and could see quite some distance out to sea.[64]

The patrols were stealthy, but sometimes they could not avoid contact with the Japanese. On a patrol at Pakoi Bay with three Islanders, Captain Williams suddenly came across a dozen Japanese. Both sides were surprised by the encounter and, to Williams' amazement, the Japanese turned and fled.

The exhausted patrols were recalled to Barakoma on 18 September. Malaria had taken a heavy toll, and the Scouts of 1 Commando Fiji Guerrillas were withdrawn to Guadalcanal for recuperation on 26 September. The group was eventually returned to Fiji in 1944 and disbanded.[65] They were given medical treatment, and three-quarters of the unit were found to be medically unfit for further service.[66]

Air Battles Over Vella Lavella

One of the tasks allotted to No. 16 Fighter Squadron RNZAF was escorting two B-25 Mitchell twin-engine bombers in strikes against Japanese barges. Coastwatcher reports aided in this task. On 21 August there was contact. Eight P-40s escorting the American B-25s searching the northwest area of Vella Lavella found three Japanese boats at Marquana Bay and two at Paraso, which they proceeded to strafe. Later that afternoon, eight RNZAF P-40s escorted two Catalinas on a photographic mission over Vella Lavella. However, the more usual role for the RNZAF was escorting American bombers attacking enemy bases and airfields.[67] The New Zealanders acquired a reputation for providing effective low cover with their Kittyhawks while USAAF P-38 Lightnings provided high cover.

The Japanese continued to strike at Vella Lavella. On 17 September, James N. Cupp of VMF-213 was on patrol in his F4U Corsair over Vella Lavella and intercepted a large group of Vals and Zeros. The Americans seemingly shot down the fighter escort before attacking the Vals. Several Vals were destroyed, and then the Americans were unpleasantly surprised by four Zeros. Cupp's Corsair was hit by a 20mm shell but nonetheless responded to the controls when Cupp ran for home.

His luck, however, was destined to run out the following day. Undertaking a dawn patrol in the hope of catching "Washing Machine Charlie," Cupp saw a Japanese Betty bomber, which he proceeded to chase. The Betty had a reputation as an easy aircraft to destroy, but as Cupp approached the bomber, its bomb bay doors opened and a gunner opened fire. His aircraft was hit by cannon shells, causing the Corsair to catch fire. Cupp bailed out but was severely burned, which spelled the end of his flying career. He had accumulated thirteen kills and was one of the squadron's highest scoring aces. He received the Navy Cross for his efforts on 18 September.

Bob Alexander's Rough Landing

On 23 September the "Black Sheep Squadron" (VMF-214), a unit of USMC F4U Corsair fighters, was given the job of escorting a naval air strike.

The mission began to go wrong from the very start, with five of the fighters suffering mechanical problems, leaving only fifteen to carry out the mission. Unexpectedly, thirty to forty Japanese fighters were encountered near the Treasury Islands and swirling dogfights took place. Bob Alexander's

Corsair had mechanical problems, but he gallantly intervened when he saw several Zeros attacking a comrade's plane. Alexander dove away to escape but, to his consternation, found that his aircraft's engine had stopped. He restarted the engine, but his plane was experiencing power loss. Alexander radioed to Vella Lavella that he needed to make an emergency landing there. His aircraft barely cleared a small ridge on Vella Lavella's north coast, and he began looking for the airstrip. To his horror, he saw that the airstrip was still in the process of being built, with heavy construction equipment in the landing area. As aviation historian Bruce Gamble describes it,

> With no choice but to put down his crippled bird, Alexander side slipped to the safest looking portion of the strip and touched down on marshy earth. He bounced and swerved, missing some vehicles but hitting a ditch and careering out of control. He unstrapped his shoulder harness and seatbelt, then dived low into the roomy cockpit and hung on as the *Corsair* flipped. The unconventional decision literally saved his neck for the cockpit was crushed flat. Construction workers ran to the wreckage and dug him out. The first man to greet him as he emerged into the sunlight was a hometown friend from Davenport, now an ensign in the Seabees.[68]

Vella Lavella had received its first aircraft.

Six

The Kiwis Arrive

Preparations and Plans

One of the problems that was to bedevil the New Zealand commander of 3NZ Division, Major General Harold Barrowclough, was the role that would be assigned to his Division. Would it simply be a garrison follow-up force, would it provide labor for logistical purposes, or would it be involved in combat? There was no clarity regarding the Division's role at either a political or a military level. Barrowclough's men had undertaken extensive training, and most were keen to see combat. Barrowclough wanted his Division to fight the Japanese, but it was understrength and could not take the place of an American division in the front line. Any combat undertaken by Barrowclough's men would have to be at a small-scale level. Barrowclough lobbied Rear Admiral T.S. Wilkinson, USN. In his war diary on 4 September 1943, he recorded that he feared his Division would be broken into isolated groups and allotted a garrison role. He spoke with Wilkinson and lobbied for "an opportunity of undertaking real offensive action. I referred to the fact that General Harmon congratulated us on the records we had established in amphibious operations. I said that it would give us little satisfaction to know that we had broken a number of records in amphibious training operations if we were not regarded as fit to undertake amphibious operations against the enemy."[1] Wilkinson promised that he would discuss matters with COMSOPAC, Admiral Halsey.

Barrowclough did not have long to wait. On 9 September, he arrived at his H.Q. on Guadalcanal "to find a series of most conflicting arrangements being made by the various H.Q. of the American Forces situated here. They were all planning our move without reference to me and without my having yet receiv[ed] anything more than a copy of a cable addressed to General

Griswold instructing him to prepare a plan for the move forward of my Division."[2]

Colonel Linscott, the G3, U.S. Army, informed Barrowclough late in the afternoon of 9 September that as a result of Barrowclough's representations, "Admiral Wilkinson had been able to arrange a more active role for us, the precise nature of which Col. Linscott was not able to state." To add to the opaqueness, Barrowclough found himself unsure of who exactly was giving his Division orders:

> The U.S. set up in this theatre with its multiplicity of Headquarters and services is extremely complicated and one had difficulty in getting definite instructions on any particular point. At the moment the Division is attached to XIV Corps but the instructions seem to be coming from Gen. Harmon, Admiral Wilkinson and General Barrett and our actual move will probably be directed by the Commander of Task Force 31, and if past experience is to be repeated, he will probably prepare the plan without any reference to me. His HQ is in Noumea and he has little idea of the differences in our organisation from that of an American Division.[3]

Confusing though it may have been to Barrowclough, the American Navy had developed the use of task forces comprised of ships and men to accomplish a particular purpose, which would thereupon be disbanded and a new command structure set up. While having the advantage of flexibility, it did have the disadvantage of tangled lines of command. It is also noteworthy that for the American commanders the New Zealanders were simply another asset to be used, and consultation with Barrowclough was overlooked.

The following day Barrowclough met with Admirals Wilkinson and Fort, as well as General Barrett, the commander designate of IMAC. Barrowclough noted "that 14 Brigade would be employed rather defensively than offensively on VELLA LAVELLA. The possibilities of defensive action were, however, not inconsiderable considering the fact that there were some 5,000 Japs estimated to be in KOLUMBANGARA [sic] and that reinforcement from Bougainville and even RABAUL itself was possible unless the navy could intercept these reinforcements."[4]

Barrowclough held a meeting with his senior commanders on 11 September and explained what was required of the troops. Arrangements were made for 14 Brigade to move forward. Liaison officers were appointed between the New Zealand and American headquarters.

On 12 September Barrowclough had a long conference with Major General Oscar Griswold, the commander of XIV U.S. Corps, and it was agreed that Barrowclough would take a skeleton Divisional Headquarters to Vella Lavella, which would arrive at the same time as Brigadier Leslie Potter's two leading battalions. Arrangements were made to send an advanced party: "Twenty-one officers representing all units of 14 Brigade, who moved north via Munda on 13 September as an advanced party to select bivouac areas, had their first practice in evasive tactics when their open craft was attacked by enemy dive-bombers off Maravari Beach two days later."[5]

On 16 September the troops loaded up the three APDs and three LCIs, and in the afternoon they had a practice disembarkation from the LCIs. The sea was too rough for the APDs.[6]

Barrowclough left Guadalcanal on 17 September, traveling first by air to Munda and then by P.T. boat at night from Rendova bound for Biloa, Vella Lavella. It was an eventful trip, as the P.T. boat had to skirt several Japanese-held islands. The P.T. boat traveled at a steady 27 knots, leaving a broad, white phosphorescent wake that extended for at least a mile, betraying the position of the boat.[7] During the voyage Japanese bombers struck the Allied base at Munda, providing an impressive display of pyrotechnics in the darkness. Barrowclough and his party arrived at Biloa safely. The following morning he and his senior staff, including Brigadier Potter, were on the beach at Uzamba and Maravari to meet the incoming landing craft.[8]

14 Brigade En Route to Vella Lavella

The 14 Brigade moved 220 miles from its advance base at Guadalcanal to Vella Lavella. Some 3,700 soldiers were in the first echelon. The movement, taking two days, had to be made by sea using LSTs and ships provided by the USN. The convoy consisted of six LSTs, six APDs and six LCIs escorted by five destroyers. The troops traveled in varying degrees of comfort. Those on the LSTs found that there was air conditioning and the food was "good, with fresh eggs and liberal helpings of tinned fruit on the menu, coffee was on tap all day. It was a slightly different story on the LCIs where the fare consisted of dry K rations."[9] Far less comfortable would have been the crowded APDs, the special troop-carrying destroyers. One thing that perhaps diverted the minds of the soldiers was that on 18 September they were allowed to vote in the New Zealand Parliamentary elections. A soldier noted, "Never before, and we hoped never again, had we voted in such unusual circumstances—many were recording their first vote since reaching their majority."[10]

As the convoy traveled toward Vella Lavella,

> the moon came up in all its glory. It was a perfect night, perfect for only one thing in that part of the tropics—bombers. A general alarm was sounded during the evening but nothing eventuated. Across the water of Munda the flashing of guns

Private G.W. Wotherspoon of 30th Battalion placing his voting paper in a ballot box on board LST-167, bound for Vella Lavella (photographer unknown; courtesy Archives New Zealand/Te Rua Mahara o te Kāwanatanga, Wellington Office, WAII, 7 3, Official Photograph Album).

could be seen and fires showed where the enemy bombs had fallen. In the early hours of the morning a further alarm was relayed throughout the convoy and two protecting destroyers on the flanks opened fire on enemy aircraft. No damage to the convoy resulted from the enemy activity.[11]

A Kiwi soldier later recalled:

The journey was reasonably uneventful, except for the observation of heavy bombing raids on Kolombangara, Russell and Munda with spectacular ack-ack retorts. The accidental collision with an empty stray barge caused come concern, fire alarms during the night made sleeping rather fitful.[12]

The New Zealanders Land on Vella Lavella

Arriving at dawn on 18 September 1943, protected by fighter cover, the convoy began off-loading men and supplies at 0720 hours at Barakoma, Mar-

Second wave of New Zealand soldiers arrive at Barakoma from LCVPs on morning of 18 September 1943. Note mixture of tin helmets and lemon squeezers (U.S. Signal Corps; courtesy Archives New Zealand/Te Rua Mahara o te Kāwanatanga, Wellington Office, WAII, 7 3, Official Photograph Album).

avari and Uzamba beaches. Those on APDs were brought ashore by landing craft, and those on LCIs and LSTs were landed directly onto the beach. Speed in unloading was critical because Japanese observers on Kolombangara, a mere 13 miles away, had a clear view of the shipping.[13] "As the ramps of the massive LSTs clattered down, trucks, bulldozers and guns rolled out and bumped into the muddy jungle. Bulldozers tore down palms and trees to form causeways to the ramps of heavier craft which remained in water too deep for vehicles to negotiate. Waist deep in the water, men passed crated stores and equipment from ship to shore stacking them out of sight among the trees. Petrol, oil and ammunition also disappeared into the jungle, which grew almost to the water's edge."[14]

At Maravari the shoreline plunged deceptively downward into deep water, as a company sergeant major discovered to his consternation. Shouting "heartily 'follow me, my men' [he] stepped off the landing platform of an LCT into eight feet of water."[15]

The Japanese airpower threat was uppermost in Barrowclough's mind.

Barrowclough reported, "There were a number of LSTs in the convoy and they were particularly obvious targets from the air as they lay on the beaches."[16]

Officers who had gone ahead a few days previously acted as guides to bivouacs. Men, supplies and vehicles rapidly disembarked. Bulldozers were used to create beach exits and ramps to amphibious craft restricted to deeper water, so they could unload their vehicles. Men formed human chains, often in the water, and passed crated boxes and gear ashore. Unloading of the LSTs was completed by 1345 hours.

A soldier with the 37th Battalion recorded:

> We made the shore on the narrow beach at Maravari, where dense bush fringed with coconut palms came down to within a hundred yards of the water. Immediately on landing we dumped our packs a short distance in the bush and began unloading the barges. Spare moments were spent in digging temporary foxholes in which to seek protection should enemy bombers come over.... At the first alarm, everyone rushed to cover, but the only planes to be seen were our fighters and the all clear sounded after a few minutes.[17]

New Zealand soldiers disembarking at Barakoma (U.S. Signal Corps; courtesy Archives New Zealand/Te Rua Mahara o te Kāwanatanga, Wellington Office, WAII, 7 3, Official Photograph Album)

Jack Humphrey, an infantryman with the 35th Battalion, traveled to Vella Lavella by APD. As the ship sailed past Japanese-held Mundi Mundi, Japanese positions could be seen with binoculars. Fortunately, the Japanese held their fire and the ship sailed past unmolested. As Humphrey disembarked from the American ship, the crew jocularly called out, "Good luck, you bastards!"[18]

The men of 14 Brigade landed and began sorting out themselves and their equipment. Allied air cover was patchy, with regular "Condition Red" alerts being experienced by the troops.

The troops from the 35th Battalion arrived at Vella Lavella just after dawn and landed in an area held by the Americans.[19] Speed was essential because of the danger from Japanese aircraft, and the troops were rapidly unloaded and the ships left the area. As the troops trudged up the beach and into a muddy area, they caught sight of a Japanese prisoner held in a barbed-wire enclosure. A soldier noted, "He was a forlorn creature, absolutely lost and completely bewildered." Some of the Kiwis approached the prisoner and

Camouflaged New Zealand soldier leaps off landing craft at Barakoma (U.S. Signal Corps, 18 September 1943; courtesy Archives New Zealand/Te Rua Mahara o te Kāwanatanga, Wellington Office, WAII, 7 3, Official Photograph Album).

offered him cigarettes through the barbed wire. For them there was not yet the burning degree of fear and hate that made the war in the South Pacific a "war without mercy."

The Kiwis, weighed down with their packs and equipment, trudged along a track that "was a sea of stinking, clinging mud": "A mile and a half through the jungle, carrying our full range of equipment taxed many of us to the full, high temperature and humidity putting an additional weight on our backs."[20] The troops found the exertion hard and frequent rest stops necessary. As they trudged toward their new camp, they passed another battalion landing on the beach. There was a lot of grumbling about why they couldn't have been landed there, closer to their destination.[21]

Due to the muddy and congested roads, there was great difficulty moving northward. The Quad artillery vehicles from 35th Battery spent two hours on 18 September winching vehicles "through particularly bad pieces of road half a mile north of Maravari Village."[22]

No sooner had they reached their destination than the Japanese aircraft struck. The troops rushed to the shore, making sure they remained in shadow or cover. Although most of the ships had departed, the LSTs presented a prime target. A member of the 37th Battalion recorded that

> there had been two air raid alerts but Japanese planes were nowhere to be seen. Those who were inclined to be skeptical about these alarms had nothing to say after the next one. Barely had the ships' whistles finished their warning blasts when the unmistakable surging of the Jap planes could be heard in several parts of the sky. In unvarying style, they circled behind the clouds for some time before coming clear to drop their bombs. They released some in the distance, but our fighters were soon on them, while the AK/AK blazed away at others. Few of us remained completely in our foxholes, the majority gazing skywards to watch the thrills. "Give him everything," we cried out as one of our fighters pursued a *Zero*. A great cheer went up as we saw the Jap crash into the sea, leaving a trail of heavy black smoke. After some minutes, the sky was clear again and we continued unloading. As the air battle covered many miles of the sky, we had no idea of the score, but we heard unofficially that the Japs had lost 19 planes to one of ours.[23]

A Kiwi soldier observed:

> Out of nowhere came our airforce. RNZAF *Kittyhawks* flashed about the sky pressing home the attack. Down went a *Zero* in flames with a *Kittyhawk* still on its tail. A spontaneous and rousing cheer went up from those on the ground. Again a *Zero*—one moment it was there—the next just a puff of debris in the air. Some invisible hand plucked it out of the skies. Down at the landing beach, when the first bomb dropped, those who had been unloading started the fastest race of their lives. One second the beach was a hive of activity; the next second following a

loud explosion, all human activity centred on a violent race for deep cover in the bush. Soldiering in earnest had started.[24]

Barrowclough was particularly anxious about the threat from Japanese aircraft. He noted in his diary:

Fortunately, we were not observed until 1215 hrs when a flight of six Japanese planes came over and attempted to bomb the landing craft, particularly the LST's. They were engaged by our fighters who had been previously allotted to provide air cover and were operating from Munda airfield. The Hvy AA guns on the Island opened fire and at one stage the enemy planes came down so low that our Bofors guns, which had just landed on the beach, were able to engage them. From all sources five enemy aircraft were shot down.... No casualties and no damage to equipment or installations were caused and we were not further troubled throughout the day. There was great relief to get such a large convoy ashore with such little enemy interference.[25]

Ross Templeton was a driver with 4 MT, NZ Army Service Corps. He recalled that he landed with men of his unit on an LCI. He had been assured that the RNZAF would be there to provide air cover. To his dismay, his LCI never made it to shore because of a coral reef. He and his comrades thus had to wade through water up to their waists. They had partially unloaded the craft when they realized that they were on the wrong beach. The craft had to be reloaded and they had to travel further up the coast. Dogfights were swirling overhead, and Templeton saw one Japanese plane on fire, which seemed intent on crashing into a ship. Fortunately, it crashed into the sea instead. The Kiwis unloaded the ships and piled up the supplies under the cover of trees and undergrowth.

It was not a comfortable time for Templeton. He suffered from chronic dysentery and bled when he squatted down. This lasted for ten days and then eased off. Other men in his unit were similarly afflicted. An additional problem was that they lacked toilet paper in the first days after landing. Some men improvised and used leaves from local plants, only to suffer from very painful inflammation.

The Kiwis had been supplied with a malaria suppressant called Atabrine, which had the effect of turning the skin yellow. There was little fresh water available, and Templeton and his comrades succumbed to "Dhobies Itch," an inflammation around the crotch. Bathing in salt water only aggravated it.

Ross Templeton recalled that his unit went up an estuary on Vella Lavella and set up a camp there. They established a latrine that consisted of a deep hole with a log strung across it. One day five or six planes appeared overhead. Suddenly, the last one peeled off and began a strafing run. Having completed it, the plane then turned around and began another run. A burly soldier, "Ox"

Andrews, was desperate to escape the merciless Japanese fire and dived into the only cover he could find—the latrine. After the attack had ended Andrews emerged, unhurt but covered in feces.

Although Templeton's unit was a truck and supply unit, there were no roads to speak of and his unit spent most of its time unloading and storing supplies. The Japanese would fire shots into the camp and the Kiwis would fire back.[26] Fortunately, no casualties or damage were suffered.

Another Kiwi soldier recalled, "The usual routine of digging fox holes began, in use nine times against air raids the first night, shrapnel and bombs breaking the monotony."[27] Barrowclough likewise noted, "There was considerable enemy air activity during the night but without material results on either personnel or equipment."[28]

The men of No. 1 Company, New Zealand Corps of Signals, who were responsible for radios and communication, were warned by an Australian Coastwatcher

> that they could expect raids nightly, and the warning was fulfilled shortly after when falling bombs commenced to whistle overhead, landing with a dull crump between the airstrip and the camp. There were seven raids that night, all too close to be comfortable, and fox-holes were consequently improved the following day. The well-known trick of dropping beer bottles, bearing the label of the Kirin brewery, *Manchukuo*, was also resorted to by the Jap. The anti-morale effect was much the same as that of a falling bomb except that the long awaiting explosion never materialised.[29]

For the men of No. 2 platoon, MMG Company, "the nights were a time of dread for us all as Tojo was extremely active and would come over several times. After several nights of broken slumber most of the platoon decided to spend whole nights in fox-holes. This improved matters very little as one's imagination led one to think that every bomb was aimed especially at one's fox-hole."[30] "An ingenious idea was the transplanting of phosphorous plants along the mud tracks of the area as guidance for the speedy movement required to reach fox-holes during the air raids."[31]

Lawrence Baldwin recalled his first night on Vella Lavella: He and his fellow artillerymen had been told to head off into the bush and dig foxholes. This was hard because once the thin layer of soil had been removed, the soldiers' spades hit coral. Rudimentary foxholes having been scraped, the soldiers tried to get some sleep despite the cacophony of the jungle. The troops had been ordered to remain silent so that their positions would not be given away to the enemy. In the darkness a plaintive voice called out, "Doesn't it ever get light in this bloody jungle?"[32]

Frank Rennie, a young officer with the 37th Battalion, recalled that a tight defensive perimeter had been set up, and once the sun had gone down the jungle came alive with sounds ranging from the croaking of small frogs to the screeching of birds and clacking of cicadas. The troops' nerves were stretched taut as they strained to discern enemy movement. Gaps between the Kiwi positions were covered with vines, and ration tins were filled with pebbles in the hope that they would give early warning of intruders.

> On this particular night at about an hour after last light, I realized that someone was beside me, someone who whispered "Bula vinaka" from a flash of white teeth. A patrol of Fijian commandos had simply walked through our lines to report. They said they had watched us take up positions and considered it safer to approach us at night rather than appear in daylight. So much for our tight defensive perimeter.[33]

The defense of the perimeter extending from Barokomo to Joroveto was the responsibility of the 4th U.S. Marine Defense Battalion. Inside the perimeter were the American units, New Zealand Divisional Headquarters, 14th Brigade, the airstrip and a naval base at Biloa, just south of the strip.[34]

Barrowclough Takes Command

Barrowclough took command of the island at midnight on 18 September and became Commanding General Northern Landing Force (CGNLF). However, Barrowclough had little time to get accustomed to his new command. He visited Island Command HQ on 18 September and was briefed by Colonel Brown, who had been in temporary command since General McClure's departure. He came under the command of General Oscar Griswold of XIV Corps, U.S. Army, who was based on New Georgia. All of the various administrative tasks, such as supplies, medical, engineering, signals and transport, were taken over by 3NZ Division Headquarters. The New Zealand Headquarters staff worked alongside their counterparts from the 35th U.S. Infantry Regiment and rapidly learned, to their dismay, that many military terms and expressions used by the Americans differed from New Zealand usage. The New Zealanders found some "distinctly quaint and odd."[35] (Without doubt, their American equivalents were equally disconcerted by the New Zealanders' strange language and way of doing things.) Nor did the Divisional Headquarters staff find their surroundings convivial. Divisional Headquarters was established in the jungle behind Barakoma Beach with a poor access road. A shortage of road-making equipment was an immediate problem.[36]

The new site on Vella Lavella stank of decay and mud and fungus and was hidden far in the jungle under trees of such grandeur and thickness that a bonfire would have been invisible from the air. Jeeps and trucks churned the place into an evil-smelling bog and heavy downpours of rain kept everything in that glutinous state.... Exposed lights were not permitted at night despite the impenetrable canopy overhead, and two meals a day with a cup of tea and a biscuit of sorts at midday simplified the work of the cooks.[37]

The place was infested with land crabs, one of which had taken a liking to the general's boot polish and on a nightly basis dragged tins back to its hole.[38]

Brigadier Leslie Potter set up his own headquarters at Gill's Plantation near Joroveto, a deserted village on the eastern coast adjacent to the Joroveto River. Barrowclough inspected several sites for his Division HQ and decided that Gill's Plantation was the best. To his chagrin, on his way back his command car was put out of action by the butt of a tree striking the radiator.[39]

The POW compound at Gill's Plantation. Japanese prisoner of war being interrogated. At back left is New Zealand intelligence officer Capt. H. F. Foster, GSO 3 (I) 14 Brigade. (photographer unknown; courtesy Archives New Zealand/Te Rua Mahara o te Kāwana-tanga, Wellington Office, WAII, 7 3, Official Photograph Album).

Divisional Headquarters then moved into the more comfortable area of Gill's Plantation, Joroveto, on 2 October 1943. As soon as combat operations began, Potter set up an advanced headquarters at Matu Suroto.

Because of the danger of air attack shelters had to be dug. H.Q. Div Engineers and the 20th [Field Company], arriving first on Vella Lavella, dug in on the slopes of Gill's plantation, "but the coral a few feet below the surface everywhere made a compressor a most helpful item.... Coconut logs made good roofing, although in the early rush for head cover there was such indefensible action taken as making use of corrugated iron from the QM, tent bags of coconut matting or anything else that looked likely (even if quite unlikely) to stop a bit of shrapnel."[40]

Barrowclough hosted a large American group on 20 September made up of Admiral Halsey, Senator Huey Long and various others. Barrowclough laconically noted in his diary, "I saw them but nothing of any importance was discussed." However, the visit was of great consequence. General Griswold was part of the visiting group and asked Barrowclough to capture Gizo Island. This was not in Barrowclough's combat area, but he promised Griswold that he would attempt it once the 30th Battalion had arrived and it was clear that it would not be needed in the north of Vella Lavella.[41]

The 35th U.S. Infantry Regiment Departs

As the New Zealanders established themselves, the American troops of the 35th U.S. Infantry Regiment began to make preparations for withdrawal. However, there was some interaction between the different nationalities that highlighted their contrasting national characteristics. Much to their dismay, Frank Marks and his comrades endured the experience of coming under the New Zealand ration system:

New Zealand had the ration dump and our menu wasn't fit to eat. First off, we only had tea, no coffee, then we had canned lambs tongue which was promptly thrown away by the mess Sgt. We had flour for biscuits and the rest of the menu was salmon patties and beans for breakfast, corned beef patties and beans for lunch, salmon patties and beans for supper, corned beef patties and beans for breakfast, etc. etc. I heard that some of the men from weapons platoon took to shooting wild chickens, but they gave that up as the birds were too tough to eat. When you cooked them, it was like trying to eat shoe leather.

Our squad, the 1st squad 1st Pltn. decided to raid the ration dump and steal something that was fit to eat. We took care of the guard at the dump and a noncom that had been left in charge. We stole some canned bacon, powdered eggs, and coffee. When we returned to our area and started cooking our loot, we had to chase away other members of our platoon, as there wasn't enough to go around.

The New Zealanders had a cuisine based on mutton, butter and milk. New Zealand was, and still is, a major exporter of dairy products and sheep meat. For Americans used to beef, the New Zealand–supplied mutton was an abomination. Some of the Americans even suspected that they were being supplied with goat meat. For the New Zealanders, there was an equal detestation of the chili con carne, Vienna sausage and Spam that was provided by the Americans. One Kiwi veteran complained that the Yanks got the best food while the New Zealanders were deprived. The reality was that it was difficult in the tropical heat to provide nutritious, flavorsome meals capable of satisfying both nationalities.

Frank Marks noted, "We heard a rumor that the New Zealanders were going to come and take our place on the island. Then we had a New Zealand NCO come into our platoon with about a dozen Fijian 'Night Fighters.' I didn't pay too much attention as to what was going on at the time, but there were probably other New Zealanders and Fijians in our other platoons as well."

Marks and his comrades had one last experience highlighting interservice rivalries before they left Vella Lavella:

> Orders came that we were to leave the island and return to Guadalcanal. On our way to the beach we found that a Naval C.B. unit had dug out and installed a landing field on the east side of the island. When we finally got to the shore and were lining up to be picked up by landing barges, we were ordered to get back into the brush. Motion Picture cameras had been set up along the beach, the barges were coming in, when they hit the shore dropped the ramps on the front of the barges, Marines with bayonets on their rifles and faces blackened, came storming ashore yelling like banshees. When all this was over, they finally let us board the landing barges, which took us out to the ships lying off shore, then back to the Canal. (About 2–3 months later, when we were on R & R in New Zealand, a newsreel in a theater showed a caption, "Marines Take Yet Another Pacific Island—Vella Lavella"). When we left Vella, the Island had been pronounced "Secure." That so-called capture of Vella by the Marines, was just Marines landing to protect the new Air Strip that the C.B.'s had constructed.

Marks commented, "We were glad to be relieved and being sent back to the Canal, not because we were tired and worn down, but because we were bored from inactivity."[42]

The 35th Regiment returned to Guadalcanal and from there to New Zealand.

We landed at Auckland, New Zealand and were met by thousands of New Zealanders who gave us a "Hero's" welcome. We disembarked and loaded onto troop trucks, each regiment going to a different part of the island. Each of our Artillery units went to separate camps too. Our regiment the 35th went to an area just outside of a quaint little town called Papatoitoi [Papatoetoe]. Here we stayed for just over two and a half months. We hadn't been paid since the Division left Hawaii, so when we did receive our money we were pretty well heeled. The only rub was that we were paid in English Pounds instead of Dollars and many of the fellows really got taken, as they didn't know the value in the rate of the exchange.

The people were really wonderful opening their homes and taking some of our boys in. We would receive a one-day pass, which allowed us to go just to Papatoitoi [Papatoetoe]. It had one theater that showed the same show for a week, a couple of stores and a Pub that couldn't handle too many of our boys at a time, so not too many tried to frequent it. We did get some 3-day passes and then we could catch the train just outside of camp and get into either New Market or Auckland. The two towns were so close, you couldn't tell where one left off and the other began. There were six of us who hung out together pretty regularly. The first time we got a 3-day pass we all went on the train and got off at New Market. We asked the first person we saw where the local "Bar" was. He directed us down the street to a building and when we went in, it was a dairy store. This is what they called a Milk Bar. When it was determined that we wanted some beer, they told us we wanted to go to a Pub. It was about two in the afternoon and the Pubs there didn't open 'til four. So we walked around and found a roller skating rink that was open so we went in and skated until the pub opened. We ordered either a pint of ale or a pint of stout and were really disappointed as all their beer was room temperature. We found they did have a really good wine called "Manhattan Cocktail." We walked on to Auckland and went to a photographer's studio and had some group and individual pictures taken to send home.

Once again we were getting our rations from the New Zealanders. I was by our kitchen the first day one of their trucks came to that area. The driver asked our Mess Sgt. Marcus Roberts where he should put the 6 butchered lambs. Roberts had him walk through the kitchen to where we dumped our garbage. He said that was where the lambs belonged and if that was all they were going to deliver to never make that delivery again. They finally got the idea we Americans were beefeaters and that is what they delivered after that. They didn't have to deliver too much as most of us went to town and had our fill of steak, chips and tomatoes. Oh yes, and plenty of fresh milk and eggs.[43]

Jerome Hendrick's recollection of Vella Lavella was bitter:

We felt like we'd been forgotten and that the whole Vella Lavella operation was an afterthought and that no one was in charge. When we got to New Zealand they reorganized the whole regiment. New officers, new equipment, real organization. When we were sent to the Philippines it was a different story than Guadalcanal or Vella Lavella, but Vella Lavella was absolutely the worst.[44]

SEVEN

The Problem and the Plan

The Problem

The American forward positions consisted of one battalion supported by artillery anchored in the position at Horoniu with the remainder of a Regimental Combat Team covering the line of communication from Kokolope in the north to the airfield in the south.[1] However, that left the Japanese in control of the northern part of Vella Lavella.

Barrowclough's instructions were to "to eliminate all Japanese forces on the island so that we can proceed with the erection of radars on the North-East and North-West coasts." The establishment of these radar installations was viewed as being of primary importance due to their coverage of Japanese airfields on New Britain and Bougainville. The establishment of a P.T. boat base at Horaniu was a secondary objective. Looking forward to the next operations involving the capture of the Treasury Islands and the invasion of Bougainville, radar facilities and naval bases would be of considerable value.[2] "Sites at Kimbolia for a radar station and at Lambu Lambu for a more effective motor torpedo boat base were urgently required on the northern coast to assist in the next operations—the capture of the Treasury Group and a beachhead on Bougainville—and for this reason Vella Lavella was to be made secure."[3] The instructions were clear enough. The issue was how they could be carried out.

The Plan

On 19 September Barrowclough had a general conference on the tactical situation with American officers and his own staff. Also in attendance were the Rev. Archie Silvester, Lt. Graham and Major Tripp of the South Pacific Scouts, and Lt. Harwell, RAN. Later that day Barrowclough had a conference with Brigadier Potter, and a campaign plan was tentatively settled upon for eliminating Japanese forces in the northern part of Vella Lavella.[4]

In other operations, such as the later invasion of Bougainville, a small area would be seized and a defensive perimeter set up. This tactic was not

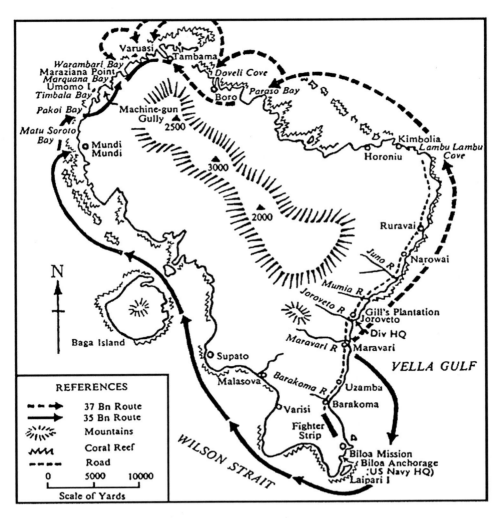

Map of Vella Lavella, Lands and Survey Department, New Zealand (*Medical Services in New Zealand and the Pacific*, Wellington, Historical Publications Branch, 1958, T. Duncan M. Stout, p. 39).

used on Vella Lavella. For the Allies, it was imperative that the island be fully cleared of Japanese troops. There were too many Japanese troops on neighboring islands, and the threat of reinforcement was a palpable one. The numbers of Japanese troops on Vella Lavella were thought to be reasonably significant and capable of organized action. The Japanese had to be mopped up, and based on prior experience on Guadalcanal and New Georgia, they could be counted on to be dogged and skillful defenders.

It was believed that there were about five hundred Japanese troops in the north of Vella Lavella—some one hundred at Timbala Bay, three hundred to four hundred at Warambari Bay and thirty at Tambama Bay. There was also an unknown number of Japanese at Varuasi.[5] It was thought that the Japanese around Varuasi were using it as a base for recce parties.[6] The intentions of the Japanese were unclear. They were believed to be the survivors of American artillery bombardments at Horaniu, having walked over the rugged mountains, a journey of several days.

According to the operations order, the intention was that "14 Brigade Group less 30 Bn Combat Team will eliminate all enemy remaining on VELLA LAVELLA and particularly within the areas PARASO BAY–MUNDI MUNDI."[7]

Potter's problem was that he had to neutralize the Japanese reasonably quickly, and he also had to avoid pushing them into the center of the island, where with supplies they could potentially hold out for some time and act as a base for Japanese reinforcements. It was thought that the Japanese were "anxious to avoid battle" and that they would "withdraw[,] resulting in a long and perhaps never-ending chase."[8] Potter had limited numbers of soldiers available to him, and they were, with few exceptions, experiencing combat for the first time. Although there were high expectations for the Kiwi soldiers, there was still the question of how they would fare in high-intensity jungle combat and whether they would master the complexities of amphibious warfare. Potter also knew that he could not be profligate with the lives of his men. They were precious assets, and the New Zealand government had indicated that 3NZ Division would not receive replacements. If Potter got his men into a meat grinder, as had occurred to American units at Munda, it would likely result in the disbandment of 3NZ Division. The effects of heavy casualties on the small New Zealand population would resonate through generations, as had the casualties from the World War I battles of Gallipoli, the Somme and Passchendaele.

Potter was limited in his planning by the threat of Japanese air attack. The Japanese effectively owned the skies over Vella Lavella, and Allied fighters could only linger over Vella Lavella for limited periods of time. The flight time for Japanese fighters based on nearby Japanese-held islands to reach Vella Lavella could be measured in minutes, and they had the ability to stay longer and attack targets of opportunity.

Information regarding the number of Japanese combatants, their health and motivation, and details of their weaponry was somewhat vague. In those circumstances, it was considered prudent to use a sufficiently large number of Allied troops to crush the defenders.

Potter realized that if he was to succeed, his men had to be moved quickly. Although some Japanese troops were reported "short of food and in a weakened condition it was feared that reinforcements were landing."[9] There were insufficient trails on Vella Lavella to move overland, and it would have taken weeks to create a jeep trail to supply combat troops with food, ammunition and other supplies.[10] To move speedily, his men had to go by water, and he was totally dependent upon the Americans to supply craft. (Potter had insufficient sea lift to move more than small numbers of men and supporting units.) There was also the consideration that the Imperial Japanese Navy, particularly its cruisers and destroyers, still packed a potent punch. Japanese night-fighting ability and their superb Long Lance torpedoes had been used to good effect during the naval battles around Guadalcanal. Potter did not have guaranteed U.S. Navy or air support. He could not risk moving in open water, so movement had to hug the coastal area.

Potter divided his resources into two Battalion Combat Teams built around the 35th and 37th Battalions and sought to carry out a pincer movement around the coast that would envelop and destroy the Japanese defenders. The 37th Battalion Combat Team was to operate north and west from its base at Paraso Bay, and the 35th Battalion Combat Team was to operate north and east of its base at Mundi Mundi. He was also under the pressure of time—he had to act quickly and decisively. Potter gave his men fourteen days to clear the island of Japanese.[11]

The planned move was only partially amphibious—while guns, heavy equipment and supplies were to be transported by barge, Potter intended for light infantry patrols to clear the areas between the amphibious bounds. "After establishing advanced bases, battalion commanders were instructed to move from bay to bay in bounds, first clearing selected areas by overland patrols before bringing their main forces forward by small landing craft after beachheads were secure." If the enemy could be located, fixed and destroyed, so much the better.

Two basic types of landing craft were to be used, both of American origin and crewed by USN personnel. The first was the Landing Craft, Vehicle

Personnel (or, to use the USN acronym, LCVP), more commonly known as the "Higgins Boat." These were wooden landing craft with a hinged ramp at the front that could be lowered to disgorge soldiers or light vehicles such as jeeps. Typically, the thirty-six-foot-long, ten-foot-wide landing craft could carry thirty-six men or 8,100 pounds of cargo. Capable of twelve knots, they were maneuverable and had the ability to land on a beach and then to retract. The crew consisted of a coxswain, an engineer and a crewman. The latter two manned two .30-caliber machine guns on the aft deck, but these positions lacked protection against small arms fire. Several coxswains were wounded by Japanese fire, and a later report recommended that anti-tank shields be adopted to provide protection. Packed into the LCVP, the soldiers felt highly vulnerable, and with good reason. Contemporary documents refer to the LCVPs as "barges," an unglamorous but accurate description.

The second landing craft was the Landing Craft, Mechanized (or LCM). These larger craft, some fifty feet in length and fourteen feet across, had a crew consisting of a coxswain, an engineer and two crewmen. They were armed with two .50-caliber machine guns. Although they could carry sixty soldiers, the LCMs' primary purpose was haulage of heavy vehicles (including tanks) and cargo. An LCM also had a hinged ramp and could beach and retract. The LCMs were more efficient for moving heavy bulk supplies, ammunition and the twenty-five-pounder field guns and their tractors. However, they would remain in chronically short supply.

The New Zealanders were newcomers to amphibious operations, but they did have the huge advantage of support from the USN, which had worked out procedures with its "Tentative Manual on Amphibious Operations" in the years preceding Pearl Harbor. Such manuals were provided to the Kiwis. In accordance with these manuals and the experience gathered in amphibious exercises, the Kiwis worked out how to establish beachheads. It was accepted that the invading soldiers would need to secure the "defensive perimeter unencumbered by supply problems," so it was arranged that they would carry 48 hours' worth of rations so they could be self-supporting until bulk supplies were landed.

Potter had sixteen landing craft, and he decided to utilize this capability by transporting infantry, artillery and heavy supplies in leaps "to feel forward with patrols and search the country and secure a base from which the next bound forward could be made." These bounds were governed by the openings in the reef so as to supply troops by boat. Potter planned to send out patrols from each beachhead to locate Japanese positions, pin them down, and prevent their freedom of movement. For the 37th BCT, the initial bounds planned for the infantry were to Paraso Bay, Doveli Cove and Tambama Bay. On reaching Tambama, it was planned to move the guns from Paraso Bay to Tambama Bay to cover the further advance of the infantry.[12] No forward plans were made from Tambama Bay onward.

Eight of the landing barges were allocated to each Combat Team, but in practice mechanical breakdowns meant that at one point the 35th BCT was reduced to only two and had to borrow from those allocated to the 37th.[13] In theory, 37th BCT had seven LCVPs and one LCM. However, this was never achieved, and visits from the LCM were spasmodic. Speed of operations was hampered by insufficient craft.[14]

Barrowclough had given orders that the troops were to go into combat as lightly equipped as possible—with the exception of the anti-aircraft personnel, they discarded their cumbersome steel helmets and dressed in drill jungle suits and peaked soft hats. Gear was restricted to waterproof capes and groundsheets, C and K rations, mosquito repellant and water bottles.[15] They were also issued with a supply of the malaria suppressant, Atabrine, but all too quickly a fatalistic attitude developed and they stopped taking the tablets.

Advanced Brigade Headquarters of 14 Brigade was established at Matu Suroto on the west coast of Vella Lavella, and this was effectively the operational command center. The rear Brigade Headquarters, which had the purpose of coordinating the flow of supplies and personnel, was set up at Joroveto on the east coast.[16]

Preparations were made by the troops for combat:

> Ammunition was checked over and distributed; grenades were primed and all weapons carefully oiled. Jungle medical kits, atebrine, insect repellant, C or K rations, and jungle suits were issued. There were, as usual only two sizes of jungle suits—too large and too small. They were made of a heavy green material which did not help to keep the body cool and the hat was similar to a jockey's cap fitting the skull closely, with a stiff peak for protection of the eyes from the sun. The web belt and small haversack containing waterproof cape, rations, spoon, tooth-brush, soap and spare socks completed the dress. The water bottle hung from the belt, to which two or three grenades were also fastened.[17]

Steel helmets were discarded in favor of the "jockey's caps" because it was felt the helmets were heavy, cumbersome and likely to snag on vegetation as the soldiers moved through the jungle. By contrast, the caps were lightweight, had a peak to protect the eyes and were comfortable to wear.

EIGHT

The Pincers and the Execution of Potter's Plan

The Japanese held the northern half of Vella Lavella and were believed to be concentrated in coastal pockets with a radio station on the western side of Vella Lavella at Umomo Island near Timbala Bay. The neutralization of this radio station (thus compromising Japanese command and control) was one of the prime objectives. The BCT from the 37th Battalion was ordered to carry out a series of amphibious bounds around the eastern side of the island, while the 35th Battalion would do likewise on the western side of the island. The tempo of operations was critical to keeping the Japanese off balance and preventing them from massing against one of the pincers. "Brown water" (or coastal) operations had not been attempted before by the New Zealand Army, and Potter's men were effectively learning on the job. Similarly, "mopping up" (clearance) operations against the Japanese were likely to be brutal, close-quarter affairs.

The two Battalion Combat Teams conducted operations separate from each other, and for the sake of coherence, it is necessary to describe them separately.

35th Battalion Combat Team—Barges, Barrages and an Elusive Enemy

Orders were given on 20 September to Lt. Col. Seaward to carry out "aggressive operations" against the Japanese troops located on the northwest coast of Vella Lavella. His 35th BCT was directed to assemble in the Mundi Mundi area. The soldiers were supplied with five days' worth of C rations, plus emergency rations and two units of fire (i.e., ammunition sufficient for two days of fighting). In theory, Seaward had at his disposal eight LCVPs and one LCM. However, to Seaward's frustration, throughout the operation, for various reasons (including mechanical breakdown), he would have less than this at his disposal.

The following day, 21 September, a platoon of picked men led by Lt. W.J. McNeight was sent as a reconnaissance party by LCVP southward from Maravari and around the western coast to Mundi Mundi. To their undoubted relief, they did not encounter any opposition. Instead, as Barrowclough noted in his war diary, they were "met by native scouts operating under Mr. Jocelyn [*sic*] and established themselves there for the night."[1]

Having secured a lodgment, Seaward moved his troops in large parties to Mundi Mundi by LCVP and established the Combat Team HQ there. Although the battalion history notes that the move on 23 September "was completed without incident," there were reminders of who owned the air space—"once or twice, as barges moved round the coast, Jap bombers flew overhead, but fortunately for us they were more interested in bombing the air-strip which was being developed than in annoying a few barges."[2]

Movement by sea was limited by the threat of Japanese airpower. Jack Humphrey recalled that as the 35th BCT moved around the coast of Vella Lavella, he twice encountered Japanese reconnaissance planes. These aircraft were able to spot the wake of landing craft. On both occasions, as soon as the crew knew they had been spotted, they steered the ship into an inlet, pulled in under the cover of jungle vegetation and waited for a quarter of an hour, by which time the Japanese had left.[3]

Lawrence Baldwin, a gunner with 35th Field Battery, also saw the effects of Japanese airpower. He traveled on a barge with twenty of his New Zealand comrades, as well as two American crew members. Japanese planes came over and bombed an LST. One of the American crew panicked and steered the barge to shore. The skipper pulled a pistol on him and yelled, "Lie down or I will shoot you!" The Kiwis were stunned. Fortunately, the air raid ended and calm was restored.[4]

Even though the Kiwis had trained in tropical conditions, their first experience of being at the front line stretched nerves tight. Jack Humphrey recalled that his first night in the jungle was hell. He knew that the Japs were out there and he "had the breeze up." But after two or three nights he began to get used to it. As a precaution, the Kiwis would set booby-traps consisting of a grenade in a fruit tin with the pin tied to a jungle vine. It was thought that this discouraged Japanese infiltrators.

The battalion history gives a flavor of Mundi Mundi:

> Mundi Mundi was a small area covered by a coconut plantation. The landing was
> a wet one, as a shallow shore prevented the barges from beaching. All stores had
> to be carried about 75 yards through water just over waist deep. Foxholes of the
> four-men type were dug immediately on landing and everybody settled down to
> keeping a perimeter such as they had practiced before, but this time it was not in
> fun. Few, if any, slept the first night they were in Mundi Mundi Bay. Thoughts of
> Japs creeping through the bush gave little peace to the nerves. Trees and shrubs
> seemed to move and every noise suggested undreamable things. Lying awake
> through the night the cacophony of sound seemed to be realized for the first time.
> Every living thing in the world seemed to be doing its best to make itself heard. It
> was a frightening and unnerving experience at first.[5]

However, no doubt due to the difficulties involved in unloading supplies,
Seaward concluded that Mundi Mundi was unsuitable as a base for operations.
Patrols were sent out to the next bay at Matu Suroto, and no Japanese were
encountered. Seaward therefore ordered his men to assemble at Matu Suroto;
this was accomplished on 24 September. Having some facilities made Matu
Suroto more attractive as a base, albeit with limitations:

> This area was really an inlet with a large storehouse and shed located just opposite
> a small jetty. A perimeter was set up and sentries posted. Fresh water was now in
> short supply and a great demand was made on coconuts. Agile chaps clambered
> up the palms and, with a cry "heads below," down would come a shower of coco-
> nuts. Bayonets made short work of the refreshing liquid within.[6]

Those soldiers still carrying steel helmets and gas masks were given the
order to leave these at Matu Suroto as preparations were made for the next
move forward. Seaward began deploying his men with the object of blocking
all tracks leading out of the Timbala–Marquana Bay area.[7] However, first
Seaward had to keep his own position hidden from the Japanese, and he also
had to locate where they were. The party of picked men led by Lt. McNeight
had

> established a forward listening and observation post to prevent a surprise attack.
> During their forward patrolling they had often seen the Japs. It was necessary, how-
> ever, in order to achieve success, not to disclose their presence. On one occasion,
> two members of the patrol, hidden behind a thick bush, calmly watched some Japs
> enjoying a swim. They had a few tense moments when the Japs retrieved their
> clothing in front of the bush in which our men were hiding.[8]

On 22 September 1943, parties of men from 17th Field Regiment left
for Mundi Mundi (12th Battery) and Paraso Bay (35th Battery) in support of
the infantry. Barges laden with guns, ammunition and the usual impedimenta
of artillery units were painstakingly moved forward. The artillerymen began

LCVP loaded with stores and troops of 35th BCT heading for Matu Suroto (photographer unknown; courtesy Archives New Zealand/Te Rua Mahara o te Kāwanatanga, Wellington Office, WAII, 7 3, Official Photograph Album).

the repetitive tasks of "backbreaking toil, clearing arcs of fire, digging and building gun-pits, digging interminable fox-holes, sweating and learning."[9]

On 25 September, five patrols were sent out in the direction of Pakoi Bay. Even the weather seemed to conspire to make the lot of the Kiwis as miserable as possible. Rain fell, drenching the men; it soaked their equipment and stores, turning the jungle into a bog, and made movement difficult. The primary task of the patrols was to ascertain whether the area was free of Japanese and, where minor resistance was encountered, to brush this aside so that the main body of men could advance by bounds, using landing craft where possible and avoiding a hard slog through the jungle. The patrols were never less than one officer and two sections, but they often consisted of just one platoon. The patrols were armed with rifles, sub-machine guns, light machine guns and grenades.

> Progress was slow, amounting to only 300 to 600 yards a day during contact with the enemy, and a company front was rarely more than 100 yards wide. The men moved along narrow tracks in single file, hindered by tree roots and clutching vines

Patrol from A Company 35th Battalion crossing a creek at Pakoi Bay with Islander guide, 28 September 1943 (photographer unknown; courtesy Archives New Zealand/Te Rua Mahara o te Kāwanatanga, Wellington Office, WAII, 7 3, Official Photograph Album).

and always on the alert against ambush or enemy traps. Every noise was suspect for the Japanese soldier, hidden among the roots of trees or up the tree themselves, held his fire until patrols came within five or ten yards.[10]

The problems of navigation through a dense, green landscape rapidly became evident:

Each patrol was accompanied by a native guide and two members of the signals platoon who were equipped with a No.48 wireless set which proved useless. Following a compass course which leads up hill and down is no fun when behind each tree and mound one expects a Jap to appear suddenly.

Native guides gave a lot of confidence to patrols as they slipped silently and easily through the tangled undergrowth. On occasions these natives would slip ahead and disappear from view, only to appear unexpectedly with a big toothsome grin adorning their faces, thus indicating that all was clear. Each guide faithfully carried a Jap rifle and ammunition and each told a varied and always bloody story of how these weapons were acquired.[11]

The New Zealand Army history *Guadalcanal to Nissan* records:

Loyal native guides, one of whom was named "Bamboo," warily moved with our patrols. Without them many more lives would have been lost and progress would have been slower. Those natives have an acute sense of smell and seemed to possess the ability to sniff out the Jap, who leaves a curious odour behind him. "No go there—Jap" they often said, tapping a squat nose with a finger.[12]

It is difficult to minimize the importance of the Islanders' assistance. For them, as untrained civilians, there was tremendous risk and the certainty of a slow, painful death if captured in possession of a Japanese rifle or ammunition. What is clear from the historical record is the determination of the Islanders to rid themselves of their Japanese invaders.

The patrols did not encounter any Japanese and set up a defensive perimeter. They were reinforced on 26 September when the remainder of the BCT moved to Pakoi Bay. It was believed that there was a large Japanese camp at the next bay, Timbala Bay, so precautions were taken to maintain secrecy— "smoking and loud talking were forbidden."[13] Lindsay Adams, an officer in 14 Brigade, commented on the tension among the troops:

> The leading section of the leading platoon whose turn it was to probe ahead close to the coast through steep jungle hills on barely discernable tracks in muddy conditions from persistent rain knew the terrors and the tensions of making first contact with the enemy. Would the first indication be the leading man falling to a sniper in the trees, or would it be an ambush of the whole section or of the whole platoon? Infantry soldiers are often the first to be sacrificed, while infantry nco's and infantry officers figure amongst the highest casualty statistics.[14]

Patrols were again sent out to locate the Japanese and, as advance elements, to occupy particular locations until reinforced by companies the following day. Most of D Company took up a position blocking the track in a southerly direction at Timbala Bay, while two ill-fated platoons under Lieutenants Beaumont and Albon were sent to cut the trails leading to the north of the island.

The plan was that the Japanese force around Timbala Bay would be encircled and annihilated:

> B Company on the right, C Company in the centre and a composite force of Captain Stronach's Bren gun personnel and others on the left would form a perimeter around Timbala Bay. D Company and the two platoons previously mentioned would block any attempted escapes or prevent further aid coming to the Japs. After an artillery barrage on Umomo Island B and C Companies plus the composite force would close in on the bay to destroy the enemy force. A Company was in reserve and was to be held in readiness just on the Pakoi side of Timbala Bay.[15]

Helmuth Von Moltke, the German strategist, famously quipped that "no battle plan survives contact with the enemy," and so it was to prove.

On 27 September, the 35th BCT soldiers

moved silently to their positions from which the assault would begin. It was a trying journey. Absolute silence was difficult to achieve, for a soldier must say something when, laden down with all his gear plus the weighty and much cursed anti-tank rifle,[16] he tripped. No smoking was permitted and this, although necessary, didn't help to sooth tempers which by now were on edge. The hard daily treks, weighty loads, shortness of water, tropical deluges, mud, mosquitoes, crabs, insects and the detested and tasteless C ration all contributed to building up the pitch of tempers.[17]

The BCT consisted of more than infantry, however. Lawrence Baldwin served with the 17th Field Regiment handling twenty-five-pounder guns as part of the 35th Battalion Combat Team. The guns were manhandled off the landing craft with the help of towing ropes and dug in for the night off the beach. The ammunition also had to be off-loaded from the barges. The twenty-five-pounder guns had tow ropes, which were used to maneuver the guns over sand and coral and into firing positions. The manhandling of guns had been practiced in training, but in combat conditions on difficult ground, it was strenuous work. The close jungle and smell of mangroves would remain a prevailing memory for veterans. Night fell quickly, and there was always the fear of what lay beyond the defensive perimeter. Calls for fire operations would come from a forward observer attached with the infantry. In all, Baldwin's unit moved about three or four times around the coast of Vella Lavella and fired supporting fire about half a dozen times. Vegetation had to be cleared away from gun positions to avoid shells detonating prematurely.[18]

The New Zealand gunners manning the twenty-five-pounder field guns, having hauled their guns and ammunition into position, relished the prospect of firing on the Japanese. It seemed that they would soon get their chance. Patrols from the 35th BCT had located likely Japanese positions at Timbala Bay and Umomo Island. The gunners set up positions at nearby Pakoi Bay and waited for orders.

On 26 September, 12th Battery began ranging its twenty-five-pounder guns on Umomo Island, "a thickly wooded island about seventy five by fifty yards," where there was a suspected Japanese radio located in a native hut and a watchtower. The gunners had been warned by Captain Hatch, their American artillery liaison officer, that the aerial photographs provided to the gunners had an eastward slew of about ten degrees. Despite this handicap, the "first ranging shots fell satisfactorily and the first two rounds of a battery salvo were reported as having set fire to a native hut. After a minor switch the watchtower was hit. After that intermittent artillery fire occurred till 0730hrs and 258 rounds were fired."[19]

Fire control was problematic because of the dense jungle and lack of landmarks. *The Gunners* noted that the battery's commander, Major L.J. Fahey, "stripped fairly extensively, blackened himself with some noisome concoction of dubbin, bootblack and grease and sallied further off Pakoi Bay and controlled his fire by radio from there. This sounds easy and quite fun in retrospect, but he and his wireless operator were under fire and quite glad to get back when the job was done."[20]

The artillery barrage began at 0630 hours and lasted an hour, after which the infantry began to advance. Scouts warned that the Japanese bivouac area was near, and the troops advanced cautiously, expecting at any moment to be hit by machine gun fire. However, the area was cleared with C Company and Captain Stronach's men meeting on the foreshore, neither group having had any contact with Japanese troops. They set up a perimeter and awaited word of B Company and the soldiers on the right bank of the river.

> Suddenly, a large tree overhanging the right bank of the river moved. Brens, tommies and rifles from the left bank positions drew a bead on the point of disturbance. The leaves shook, parted and a large dugout dinghy glided out manned by a green clad individual. Friend or foe? Features were indiscernible, so fire was held. The dinghy drew nearer and features of the paddler became clearer. It was the platoon commander of the right bank platoon. His report indicated that all ground his platoon had covered was clear, although three Japs, poorly clothed and apparently unarmed, had been chased without success. Areas had been found where Japs had been eating the roots of palms, a few crude shelters were also seen. The conditions contrasted strangely with the bivouac camp. Here was food by the barrel full, tinned fish, chopsticks and plenty of bush shelters which were fairly well made. Freshly opened tins with chopsticks sticking in the food and other goods strewn about indicated that the Japs had departed hurriedly during a meal.[21]

Timbala Bay was considered cleared—the elusive Japanese had disappeared. The platoon on the right bank was ordered to push forward and link up with B Company. The platoon moved warily along the track; as it reached the top of a slight rise, movement was detected up ahead. It turned out to be B Company. As soon as the link-up occurred, shots were fired by the Japanese, killing one New Zealander and wounding two. This occurred at 0918 hours, 28 September 1943, and the situation of the Kiwis began to progressively worsen as Japanese pressure became more intense:

> One platoon, under Lieutenant Crawford, had become isolated and ambushed. Runners brought only the vaguest information back, but sufficient to indicate that the officer had been wounded and others killed. Lieutenant Griffiths, the intelligence officer, located the platoon and took charge, Lieutenant Crawford being evacuated. The platoon of C Company remained with B Company to help strengthen its defence, while another platoon of B Company attempted to outflank the Japs.

It seemed apparent that this position was one which the Japs had prepared before-hand and to which they had automatically evacuated from their bivouac area. This strong pocket of resistance could not be liquidated. In the early afternoon A Company crossed the river and moved up to B Company. The river being wide, deep and infested with crocodiles made the crossing an extremely slow one. About ten men at a time made the crossing in the dugout dinghy. By the time A and C Companies had moved up, there was only enough time left to move out to new positions, establish a perimeter and settle down for the night.[22]

The New Zealanders were learning hard lessons about jungle warfare, but their discipline and cohesion had held. The comment was made, "It is doubtful if many of us saw a Jap that day, yet several lives had been lost and other men wounded."[23] A common feature of twentieth-century battlefields, especially in the tropics, was the invisibility of the enemy, with soldiers rarely, if ever, seeing their foe.

The Kiwis had to quickly learn the rudiments of jungle warfare. A veteran recalled:

> Grenades were frequently used in jungle warfare. Unlike the flash of a rifle when fired, throwing a grenade did not give away your position. You could throw a grenade as far as you could throw a cricket ball. The trouble was in the Solomon Islands in the jungle the trees often have large flanges at the base. A grenade could bounce back at you if you were unwary.
>
> The rule at night was not to move out of the perimeter, not even to go to crap. Anything moving around was liable to be either fired on or have a grenade thrown at it. Often you had no idea what was happening in the blackness. We knew that the Japanese would creep up on the perimeters edge.[24]

Perimeter defenses were set up and at dusk the sentries were brought in. After that, no further movement was allowed. This ceded the initiative to the Japanese but was a practical way of ensuring security and resting the troops.

> Of every fox-hole group of four, one man was awake. Thus all night a quarter of the company would be on the alert. The most nerve-racking part of the evening was the time when one's turn came around for keeping watch. From a fitful sleep you would be awakened by the pressure of a hand on your foot. Then it was your turn; your turn to peer through the inky blackness, and to listen to the disturbing noises of the night.[25]

The artillery again proved their usefulness—a twenty-minute intense artillery barrage commencing at 0800 hours the next day, 29 September, pulverized the area held by the Japanese the day before. The questions were whether there were any Japanese still under the barrage and, if so, whether any had survived. For the Kiwi soldiers, the barrage had its downside: "A few shells fell short and bits of shrapnel whistled and thudded overhead."[26]

Close support of the Kiwi soldiers was necessary, but it was found that the infantry had to keep well within 60–70 yards of the target area in order to take advantage of the shock-and-awe effect of the artillery. Understandably, there was some reluctance to go too far forward for fear of being hit by the barrage. Accurately deploying artillery was difficult due to the close nature of the terrain and the tendency for artillery to explode in tree bursts.

While the barrage was taking place, the soldiers received a delivery of mail from home. For one soldier it was a cause for glumness—his mail had wished him many happy returns for his birthday, but he was stuck on a tropical island facing Japanese intent on killing him. He exclaimed "Who'd want a return of this!"[27]

After the barrage had finished, the three companies advanced. C Company found out that some Japanese were still in the area and very much in a fighting mood. A sniper began firing at the Kiwis. It was suspected that he was located in a tree, and shells from a 2-inch mortar were fired. The second shell exploded and the sniping ceased.[28] Movement through the dense jungle was difficult, and keeping contact with the adjoining companies was problematic. B Company linked up with C Company but lost contact with A Company in the thick jungle. For A Company, all hell was about to break loose as it entered a Japanese kill zone.

It was later realized that Japanese tactics involved using rifle-armed soldiers on the flanks to funnel New Zealand soldiers into areas dominated by well-concealed Japanese machine guns. The Kiwis were about to experience the full effect of this strategy.

At 1115 hours a fusillade of shots rang out, and it was clear that A Company had run into opposition. They were in a valley and had advanced into a trap. Japanese machine gun bullets ripped through the foliage, and three Kiwis fell wounded.

Following their battle drills, the leading platoon attempted to move around and encircle the Japanese defenders. However, the Japanese countered this, and one section was pinned down by intense machine gun fire. Complicating matters, there were now wounded soldiers under Japanese fire, and attempts were made to rescue them. The Kiwis attempted to maneuver:

> The leading platoon remained in position while another platoon went on the right flank on slightly rising ground, the remaining platoon and company headquarters guarding the rear. The right flanking platoon was then caught in heavy fire along well concealed fire lanes. Corporal Clifford's section bore the brunt of this attack. The platoon, Lieutenant McNeight's, was skillfully extricated from the trap. The platoon commander, with Corporal Stewart and Private Cooper, volunteered to

get the wounded from the tight corner in which they were caught. In carrying out this most courageous act, both Corporal Stewart and Private Cooper were killed.[29]

Jack Humphrey recalled that he and his comrades in the 35th BCT had been pinned down at "Machine Gun Gully" and were not making progress. It was suggested that the infantry fix bayonets to their rifles and charge the Japanese positions. His response was to say, "You get Mr. Seaward [the commanding officer], and we will tell Mrs. Seaward he died a hero." The infantrymen were "chased back" by the Japanese defenders.[30] Ultimately, it was intense artillery fire that pried the Japanese loose from their stronghold and forced them back.

Sometimes the attackers and defenders were in close proximity. The Kiwis and Japanese traded insults, one group insulting Emperor Hirohito and the other King George. The aim was to try to get opponents to give their position away. Most times this tactic failed, but it contributed to the wearing down of nerves.

Meanwhile, B and C Companies had advanced without any opposition. As night began to fall, A Company joined them and a defensive perimeter was established.

Concerns began to be felt as to the fate of the men led by Lt. Albon and Lt. Beaumont. Arrangements had been made to resupply them with food and ammunition at a rendezvous point at Marquana Bay. A resupply party had arrived at the agreed location, but there was no sign of the soldiers. There were, however, quantities of New Zealand stores, ammunition and equipment strewn about.

The 30th of September was relatively quiet—C Company sent out patrols to the left flank and the coast. No Japanese were encountered. Later, a patrol recovered the body of Private D.R. Bird, who had been killed during the first contact. Another patrol provided cover, but it was clear that the Japanese had left. A haversack belonging to a dead Japanese soldier was found to contain maps, photos and letters. These were sent on for analysis by intelligence officers.

September had been hard for the battalion—three days of intense fighting had resulted in eight killed and twelve wounded (although one man's injuries were minor). The weather did not help the morale of the soldiers—rain began falling on the night of 29-30 September and fell unrelentingly:

> Fox-holes turned into mud baths. No words can give an accurate description of what it is like to lie down in a fox-hole with several inches of sloppy mud in the bottom of it, to have such unwelcome guests as land crabs crawling over the body, to have no hot drinks, no cigarettes, tasteless compressed rations and, despite the

presence of so much water only a sip per meal. Clothes stank and clung to the body, socks were wet and no one had shaved or washed for days. In addition it was depressingly cold whenever rain poured down.[31]

Given these circumstances, it is easy to understand how the tired, wet and ill-fed troops let their anti-malaria precautions lapse. They would pay for this later.

C Company and troops under the command of Captain Stronach advanced 300 yards. A force using canoes paddled across to Umomo Island only to find bits of dried blood and wrecked Japanese radio gear. The Japanese had gone.

C Company then probed along the coastline and encountered a Japanese post. The Kiwis used 2-inch mortars but seemingly to little effect. There was insufficient time to call down an artillery barrage, and, with light failing, the soldiers retreated to a defensive perimeter.

The area where the Japanese machine guns had been encountered earned the nickname "Machine Gun Gully." Rather than incur further casualties, it was decided to use artillery to blast the Japanese defenders out. However, the artillery forward observer experienced difficulty with radio communication.

On 2 October, C and D Companies moved to the coast and to the farthest point that had been previously reached. There a patrol made contact with Japanese defenders. Artillery fire was called down, producing an unusual response:

> Jap snipers moved under the barrage towards the company positions, firing indiscriminately but mainly towards the sound of the artillery officer's raised voice as he hurled a mixture of oaths and corrections down the line to the battery positions. Another patrol was sent out but found that the Jap position was still intact. A Jap machine gun was being fired over a large log straight down the track. Any encircling movement by our troops was frustrated by vicious sniper fire from Japs up in trees. Private Bevin was wounded during this encounter and was evacuated by company stretcher bearers under fire. Further artillery fire was brought down, but as time did not permit of further reconnaissance both C and D Companies returned to their previous night's bivouac area.[32]

The thick jungle limited both visibility and movement. In order to locate the defenders, the attackers had to expose themselves to the defenders' fire, which invariably meant wounded men. "After that, in true Jap style, any endeavor to evacuate the wounded men meant a fusillade of shots. It almost seemed as if the Jap policy was to wound one man so that others, in trying to evacuate him, would make a target of themselves, such was the Jap cunning."[33] In fact, it was common practice by the Japanese soldiers in World War II to exploit the Western tendency to recover wounded men or the bodies of those killed and, in the process, for the rescuers to set themselves up as easy targets.

The Kiwis responded to the Japanese resistance by having their artillery plaster the area with fire. Patrols were then sent in to probe the Japanese defenses. B Company's patrol encountered Japanese snipers; several soldiers were hit, and one killed. A Company's patrol tried to help by swinging around to the right. However, this patrol ran straight into Japanese machine gun fire. After recovering their wounded, both patrols prudently pulled back and let the artillery do its work. Once the barrage had ceased another patrol gingerly advanced and recovered the Thompson Sub-Machine Gun and ammunition that had belonged to a dead B Company soldier. Further probes encountered Japanese resistance.

On the afternoon of 2 October, a force of New Zealand soldiers under Lieutenant R.B. Lockett, commander of 2 Platoon, 14 Brigade, MMG Company, seized Umomo Island. The mortar platoon and Vickers Machine Gun platoon set up their weapons so as to barrage any Japanese positions. The Kiwis used their weaponry to good effect. The firepower of Vickers Machine Guns had been demonstrated in World War I, when concentrated fire had been used for suppression. In a similar way, the Kiwis sited guns on Umomo Island and used them to fire along the coastal strip where infantry forces were advancing. It was estimated that the Vickers had an effective penetration into the jungle of up to fifty yards. The guns were relatively heavy and based on tripods. Their use was dependent upon having stable ground, and they were most useful in covering flank positions.

Harassing fire continued at night, except when Japanese float planes were overhead. This force would play a key role in the rescue of some trapped New Zealand soldiers.

Allied air support was intermittent, and the movement of artillery and supporting units was limited by the threat of Japanese air attack. On 2 October Japanese aircraft located and attacked the 12th Battery guns and Regimental HQ at Matu Suroto. There were no casualties, but it reinforced the need for dispersal. Preparations were made to move a troop forward to Pakoi Bay.

About this time the Japanese were running short of food and so each night a float-plane arrived with food for the enemy and bombs for us. He was not quite sure where his friends were, so he distributed his red and white striped parachutes of food with reasonable impartiality. The Japanese jungle food in compressed form seemed more palatable to us than our own, though that may have been due to our being tired of our C and K rations on alternate days. His bombs[,] few in number and fairly small, were entirely reserved for us and were not so palatable as his rations. He was known to the locals as "Washing Machine Charlie" from the peculiar sound of his motor as he loafed up and down at what seemed in the velvety blackness of the night to be tree-top height.[34]

On Sunday, 3 October, C Company sent a reconnaissance patrol forward into the area held by the Japanese. There was no contact. A and B Companies broke contact with the Japanese to their front and linked up with C Company. A defensive perimeter was then established. It was decided to probe forward and, if the area was clear of Japanese, to set up a bivouac. Two platoons led by officers were given this task. Using the coast as its left flank, the patrol advanced three hundred yards with no contact. A suitable bivouac area was located, but it was decided to ensure the security of this site by advancing another 150 yards. No sooner had the troops begun to advance than a whistle was heard. It was known that the Japanese used birdlike whistles to signal the approach of Allied soldiers, so the Kiwis cautiously went to ground and established a defensive perimeter with the coast at their rear. At first nothing seemed to happen. Then a small group was sent forward:

> These men moved slowly forward and disappeared from sight. Suddenly the silence was shattered by two shots. A fusillade of shots followed. A runner came back and stated that two men had been hit. The party had withdrawn slightly, but were still covering the wounded men. A plan was quickly formulated for the rescue of these men and their weapons. Two fields of fire were laid down in the shape of a V, the point of the V culminating at the enemy positions. Inside this V a small party went in and collected one of the wounded men and his tommy gun. As they withdrew the V of fire was drawn tighter towards them. Stretcher bearers who had been hastily summoned took charge of the wounded man and evacuated him under guard to the rear.[35]

There are a number of things here worthy of comment. The first is that amid the cacophony of jungle noises the Kiwis had been able to pick up the sound of a Japanese wooden whistle and recognize it for what it was. Second, their battle craft had been followed—they had formed a defensive perimeter and avoided an ambush. Third, the Kiwis had used suppressive fire in a very effective way to recover the wounded soldier. Fourth, the New Zealanders had recovered the Thompson Sub-Machine Gun. These were in short supply and valued as jungle fighting weapons.

For the wounded man, the story, sadly, did not end there. He was being taken to the rear for treatment by stretcher bearers accompanied by an armed guard. They entered a clearing, where "they were fired on by a tree sniper. The guards replied to the fire while the stretcher bearers hurried into the cover of the jungle. Once more the fire plan was laid down and the other man was recovered, but unfortunately he was beyond human aid."[36]

During this firefight a Japanese soldier broke cover and ran. He was "fired at and bowled over several times before collapsing."[37] The curious thing is that when the Kiwis searched for the body the next morning, they could not find it. The Japanese also had a cultural norm that bodies, or at least parts of deceased soldiers (such as fingernail clippings), be recovered so that funeral rites could be carried out.

One other unusual feature of the firefight had been the role of the mortar crews: "The 2 inch mortars had done a splendid job of work. In order to obtain an unobstructed flight for the bombs the mortar men had waded into the sea. Only about three inches of the barrel could be seen above the water, yet all the bombs were successfully fired."[38]

Another platoon of C Company covered the withdrawal of the patrol to the safe haven of the perimeter. An officer from the patrol and a forward observer artillery officer then got into a canoe and, staying some two hundred yards offshore, proceeded to call down an artillery barrage on the Japanese positions.

The problem for artillery was that the area was unmapped, with numerous tree trunks and obscuring vegetation, making observed fire difficult. Air observation was extremely challenging because the smoke from the marker shells rarely rose above the jungle.[39] It was virtually impossible to fire with pinpoint accuracy. Frequently, the only option was for forward observers to creep close to Japanese positions and observe the fall of shot. Captains P.M. Blundell and R.E. Williams would lie a mere 25 to 50 yards away from shell bursts as they tried to direct the artillery onto Japanese positions. It was highly risky work, considering the possibility of a short round exploding in their vicinity or even shells being deflected off vegetation. Sergeant J.T. Walsh gained praise for his role in pinpointing Japanese machine gun nests.[40] And sometimes the gunners got lucky. On Sunday, 3 October, Captain McKewen again directed artillery fire on Machine Gun Gully. On this occasion the infantry moved forward, and the soldiers found that a round had hit the forked root of a tree where a Japanese machine gun had been sited. The round had not exploded, but it must have shattered the nerves of the Japanese.[41] Despite all its limitations, concentrated artillery fire still remained the attackers' best weapon for dealing with static Japanese fortifications.

After the heavy artillery fire on Machine Gun Gully, A and B Companies moved down the gully without opposition and reached the coast, where they linked up with C and D Companies. On 4 October, the combined companies advanced, passing through a Japanese bivouac that had been mortared: "For once the Japs had not buried their dead, thus giving us a stinking, horrid and unforgettable sight of what damage had been done by our men."[42]

Two patrols were sent out on 5 October to the long inlet of Marquana Bay. Encountering no Japanese, the companies moved forward and set up a defensive perimeter. They encountered a coconut plantation:

> Strewn everywhere were opened coconuts showing that the Japs had been there. Evidently they were short of food and water as hundreds of coconuts littered the ground. Parachutes of red and white bands of cloth were found nearby. Food had been dropped by plane every night, but apparently not sufficient for all the Japs. From the shallow water of the coast several white parachutes were retrieved. Attached to these was the well-known Jap Knee mortar, but no ammunition was found for these weapons.[43]

At 1700 hours on 5 October, soldiers from the 35th Battalion saw friendly landing craft entering Warambari Bay, the next bay up the coast. Firing was heard, but the soldiers were heartened to know that the end was in sight, "with the Japanese trapped between the two Combat Teams and the artillery, Vickers and 3 inch mortars of both combat teams were all set to give the Japs a night of unholy hell. They gave it to them."[44]

However, before describing the ending, it is necessary to backtrack and describe other events that were occurring, including the fate of the soldiers sent to block the Japanese retreat and the experience of the 37th BCT.

The Bloody 25th of September 1943—30th Battalion Arrives

The two New Zealand battalions on Vella Lavella were reinforced by their sister battalion, 30th Battalion. Even though the beachhead had been secured, it was believed that the Japanese had observation posts on Gizo and Kolombangara Islands. This meant that it was imperative to get the shipping unloaded and away as quickly as possible in order to minimize Japanese airstrikes. The battalion historian recorded:

> Soon after dawn on 25 September the destroyers passed Gizo Island and at 6.30am assault boats were lowered to the water. The troops landed at Mumia Beach, where members of the advanced party were waiting. Very soon an LST nosed its way into the beach. While men were stacking rations and ammunition, a Jap fighter plane made a cheeky mast-high run over the ship.[45]

The troops of the 30th Battalion took over the area and tents left by the 37th Battalion. The role given to the 30th Battalion was to take Gizo Island, but in the meantime it would act as a reserve unit. As the troops disembarked, they could hear the ominous sound of bombs exploding further down the coast.

The Marines Arrive

Admiral Halsey decided to set up a forward operating base on Vella Lavella, and on 17 September 1943 he issued orders to Major General C.D. Barrett to put this plan into effect. Barrett in turn placed Major Donald M. Schmuck in command of a task force consisting of units from the 77th Naval Construction Battalion, 3rd Special Weapons Battalion, the Motor Transport Corps, and 4th Base Depot, as well as communications personnel from III Amphibious Force and selected personnel from the 3rd Marine Division.[46]

On 25 September nine hundred Marines of 1 Marine Amphibious Corps landed on the east-central coast at the mouths of the Juno and Ruravai Rivers. This base force was designated Corps Forward Staging Area, Vella Lavella, and had deployed from Guadalcanal to clear out Japanese opposition and to establish a base from which to support future operations on Choiseul and later on Bougainville.

A small provisional force under Major Donald M. Schmuck, USMC, consisting of two hastily put-together rifle companies, an AA Platoon, and Motor Transport Section, together with various supporting elements, had been landed on Ruravai Beach—the wrong beach. Schmuck recalled the tension between himself and the captain of the troop transport as they gingerly sailed past Japanese-held islands. The captain wanted the troops unloaded as quickly as possible so he could get his ship away to safety. On reaching Vella Lavella, both Schmuck and the captain had peered intently at the coastline, seeking a beach suitable for landing. The decision to unload at Ruravai proved to be a fateful one.[47]

Nor was Schmuck clear on the chain of command. Was the operation being run from 3rd Marine Divisional Headquarters located at Guadalcanal, or was it IMAC based on New Caledonia? He later found out it was IMAC.

Air attacks on this base force resulted in almost as many casualties as suffered by the army.[48]

Japanese air attacks greeted the arrival of 77th NCB on 25 September. The Seabees lived up to their motto ("We build, we fight"), manning guns and helping with casualties. Despite the attacks, the Seabees set to work building roads and bridges, gun emplacements and LST facilities.[49] Urgency was given to the construction of hospital and medical facilities in anticipation of receiving casualties from the impending invasion of Bougainville.

A Japanese air raid on 25 September hit the New Zealanders' advanced Brigade HQ at Matu Suroto, resulting in five dead and fifteen wounded.

Carnage at Ruravai Beach

Worst of all were the Japanese airstrikes on Ruravai Beach at the eastern side of Vella Lavella. The 25th of September was a black day in the history of the U.S. Coast Guard. Japanese aircraft struck at shipping clustered around the beach at Ruravai. Since this beach had not previously been used, it lacked air defenses, and beaching and unloading facilities had not been developed. Consequently, when LST-167, crewed by U.S. Coast Guard personnel, beached at 0745 hours, it took time to unload its cargo of the 77th Marine Combat Battalion's equipment. This was unloaded by 1115 hours, but at 1116 hours a possible "bogie" was reported forty miles out. A patrol plane then reported "lots of bogies and about twenty angels." Three Japanese dive-bombers struck a few seconds later, coming out of the sun. The twenty guns on the LST opened fire, but it was too late. Two Japanese bombs scored hits, a third being a near miss. One bomb hit the main deck on the port side, and the second hit the main forward deck, exploding in the provision room. The explosions knocked nearly everyone off their feet. A fire started on the tank deck, and petrol and oil that had not been unloaded added to the conflagration. The cargo hatch was aflame, and fire spread through the aft ventilators. Electrical circuits were damaged and power failed. It was a scene of carnage with dead and wounded and flames. The order was given for the ship to be abandoned. Efforts were made to move casualties, and an emergency casualty station was set up in an Islander's hut.[50]

Denny Frangos, a Seabee with the 77th NCB, was on LST-167. He recalled that the ship was about six hundred yards from the shore when the Japanese bombs struck. The doors were open, but the ramp was still up. Frangos glimpsed a crew member through the flames operating the crank by hand to lower the ramp and let people off. Frangos jumped off into eight feet of water but immediately found that the surface of the water was on fire from burning fuel oil. He took a deep breath and dove underneath the burning oil. Every now and then, when he ran out of breath, he had to surface, gulp some air and dive down again. Despite the gravity of the situation, Frangos clutched at his Thompson Sub-Machine Gun. Although it was heavy, he believed it was his protection and he was determined not to jettison it. Frangos suffered burns to his ear and the tips of his fingers. Once he reached clear water, he yelled out to a friend, "Hey Boomer, I can't swim." His friend said, "Jump on board," so Frangos grabbed him and was towed into the shallows. Once he got into waist-deep water, Frangos walked to the beach unaided.

His clothes were badly burned. He saw a young, dead Marine on the beach. He was the same size as Frangos, so Frangos opened up the Marine's pack and took a shirt and pants, which he then put on. Frangos' finger tips and an ear were burned. The horror was not ended, however. He looked down the beach and saw that a tarp had been set up to keep the sun off the wounded, and medical staff were at work, including carrying out amputations. He wandered over and saw a young Marine covered with a blanket who had a facial injury. The young soldier waved to Frangos and asked for a cigarette. Frangos gave him one, and the injured man inhaled twice and died. Frangos then lifted the blanket and saw that the dead man had a large hole in his body.[51]

Attempts at firefighting on LST-167 were hampered by there being no pressure on the fire main. Ammunition for the 40mm gun began cooking off at 1140, and it became too dangerous to continue firefighting activities; the order was given to leave the ship. The fire continued raging, with ammunition exploding through the night, and it was not until 1530 hours on 26 September that the fire had subsided to the point that a portable fire pump could be used. The burned-out LST-167 was unbeached and towed to Rendova. She was irreparable and struck from the Naval Register on 6 December 1943.

The severity of the fire can be gauged by the casualties: Two officers and five enlisted men were killed in action, and three enlisted men died of wounds. Five enlisted men were missing in action. One officer and 19 enlisted men were listed as wounded.[52]

Colin Ramsay was a New Zealand Army Service Corps driver who found himself attached to 22 Field Ambulance as a driver. His unit received word of the airstrike:

> We drove up with the medical personnel and after dressings were applied on the beach we drove the wounded back to our hospital. After we had recovered them all, we went back to pick up the dead, who had to be buried within three to four hours as the heat very quickly bloated their bodies. Some would get so bad that if you poked them with a stick the foul gases would easily escape. Because of the internal explosion on the ship, those inside had their bodies terribly mutilated and we were often just recovering torsos, heads, limbs and chunks of flesh. It was the first time I had seen blood and guts on this scale, so it was a bit unsettling for me. A large communal grave was dug and all the human bits and pieces were thrown in and quickly buried.[53]

In war, timing can be everything. The Seabees of the 77th Naval Construction Battalion had more than their fair share of luck. As their cruisebook records, "Fortunately, most of our men were at the beach instead of on the ship when the bombs fell. An attack a few minutes earlier or later could have meant a heavy toll of lives. A few minutes difference could have meant that the 77th chow line would have stood on the very section of the deck that was pierced by a bomb."[54]

Denny Frangos later found himself assigned to an unusual duty: he became the personal bodyguard of an Australian plantation owner, Mr. Gill.

> He was a great big six-foot-four guy, but he wouldn't take a gun for self-preservation. But he insisted on going because he knew that island and we had no aerial maps except tree tops, and that didn't tell you what was underneath. So we knew nothing about the topal [topography] of the island. So he sat in on the plans and knew what was going on and nobody else did. And they were afraid if the Japanese captured him, they'd learn about our going up further and the dates. So they had me and another guy as his bodyguard, and if it looks like he's gonna get captured, shoot him. He was real nice guy, I wouldn't do that. But he knew of a nice cave in the coral. About six-five or six foot high and eight feet deep. Real nice, dry cave. So we headed for that, because at nighttime with that burning LST beached, that was a good landmark for the next wave of bombers to come over, which they did. They bombed all our equipment and everything that we happened to land. The only thing we saved as far as food goes were these five gallon tins of fruit cocktail—that's what we had to eat for a week.[55]

Pharmacist's Mate, Second Class, USNR, Rex H. Gregor

Valor is not the exclusive province of those who carry or operate weapons. That is proven by the extreme heroism of Rex Gregor, a 21-year-old U.S. Naval Reserve pharmacist's mate, on the beach at Ruravai.

Gregor had landed with others from his unit and was on the beach when Japanese planes struck. A bomb landed on the LST that Gregor had arrived in and set it ablaze. As people streamed off the stricken ship, Gregor hurried back onto it, determined to get his medical kit. Dodging flames and explosions as the ship's ammunition cooked off, Gregor succeeded in grabbing his kit and some plasma, and then, almost miraculously, he made it off the ship. Gregor later commented, "I put my head down and raced through this blazing inferno of hell and made it through without a scratch!" As he reached the beach, Japanese aircraft struck again. Unperturbed by the continuing air raid, Gregor sterilized his instruments and went to work on casualties. One man had his leg almost blown off, and Gregor realized that in order for the man to survive, he would have to receive emergency surgery. No doctors were available. Gregor had never attempted an amputation before, but he recalled the training that he had received. With assistance from other corpsmen, Gregor clamped off the arteries of the mutilated leg and went to work with his scalpel. Having stabilized the injured man, Gregor then arranged for him to be sent on to a field hospital. The patient survived due to Gregor's skill. Gregor continued to distinguish himself in later days by tending to air raid victims dashing from foxhole to foxhole. Gregor's commander, First Lieutenant Grant J. Limegrover, commented, "In a month of action on Vella Lavella I saw many heroic deeds, but none to compare with Gregor's actions."[56]

The sequel was that Gregor was recommended for America's highest award for valor—the Congressional Medal of Honor. However, he never received it, and the reason soon became evident to Gregor. He was summoned to report to the commander of the Special Troops Medical Detachment at Division Headquarters. Gregor observed that the commander appeared to be affected by alcohol. The commander then took Gregor to task for unauthorized surgery, commenting that if he were in the States, he would be prosecuted for performing surgery without a licence. The commander then stated that Gregor was lucky not to face a court martial and that Gregor was sadly mistaken if he thought approval was going to be forthcoming for unauthorized surgery. "If you get an award for amputating a leg then every knife happy corpsman in the Navy will be striking for a medal."[57] Happily, the commander was wrong. Although Gregor did not receive the Medal of Honor, Halsey awarded him the Silver Star.

The Japanese had mounted a maximum effort in their air raids on 25 September and had inflicted thirty-two killed and fifty-eight wounded casualties on the Allies. Once again the lethality of Japanese airpower had been demonstrated.

A special unit citation was awarded to 3rd Platoon, Battery A, 3rd Special Weapons Battalion, 3rd Marine Division, for its actions on 25 September 1943. Major General Turnage, commanding officer of 3rd Marine Division, praised their outstanding courage under enemy fire in continuing to fight despite having had two guns hit and suffering significant casualties.

The Seabees of the 77th Naval Construction Battalion had the relative good fortune to have suffered only three injured men:

> After the confusion arising from the vicious attack had been put under control, all hands set to making camp, which included setting up tents, getting adequate water supply, making foxholes, helped by bulldozers and draglines. During the night the camp was kept in a nervous state by several air raid warnings and one bombing during the early morning. The ship burned all night making a clear target. Our situation was further accentuated by continuous explosions of munitions on board LST-167.[58]

The following day the Seabees moved to a new campsite near the Juno River. They were kept busy unloading LSTs, building roads and milling timber for construction projects.

For the Kiwis, the arrival of the 8th Echelon was a mixed blessing. On the one hand, two bulldozers (a D-7 and D-4) and a power grader opened up the possibility of constructing an all-weather road to Gill's Plantation. The arrival of additional signal equipment held the prospect of improved radio communications. On the other hand, however, as Barrowclough observed, the additional traffic consequent on the handling of cargo from the 8th Echelon made the forest vehicle tracks almost impassable in spite of strenuous efforts on the part of all concerned.[59]

The Engineers

It may sound paradoxical in an environment where rain falls in great quantities, but clean drinking water was in short supply. The role of engineers in providing drinkable water was critical to the health of the troops. Lieutenant Syme, a New Zealand engineer, later wrote:

The recce party left on 30 September for Timbala Bay, arriving in heavy rain but unopposed. In ground of hard coral and mud we commenced to dig in, taking up positions on the infantry defensive scheme. We erected a lean-to shelter roofed with palm leaves and took cover. A small well which had been discovered by an infantry recce party was inspected. The walls were boxed and the water clear. It had obviously been used by the enemy but was found pure on testing. A minimum dose of purification was added as a precaution. We dug water holes for washing and drinking, these being about four feet square and requiring again a minimum dose of chlorination.

Lieutenant Syme, Sergeant Burnie, Sappers Philip and Findlay, the last named the diviner, went on a water recce to Susulatolo Bay. Two infantry officers and six guerrillas [South Pacific Scouts] accompanied us and left us shortly after arrival to recce for a stream which was thought to be not far away. We had four guerrillas to protect us while we worked, since freshly opened coconuts and some Jap clothing hung up to dry gave evidence of enemy troops in the vicinity. We dug a trial hole first about 50 yards from the shore and had to place a small charge to breach the coral. The water cleared rapidly but was slightly brackish and suitable only for washing. We then decided to move into the jungle, strong indications of water being found about 250 yards in. We had just begun to dig when the picket corporal warned us that Japs were coming. We immediately took up our weapons which were handy and made a dive towards where the corporal was. Before we reached him we heard him call, "Hands up" and then a shot. This was followed immediately by another shot from Sergeant Burnie who had moved up to assist the now spread out covering party. The corporal had seen two Japanese and thought that he had winged one. The other escaped in the denseness of the undergrowth. Sergeant Burnie said that the Jap fell to the corporal's shot just as he himself had fired. Upon going forward we found that the Jap was indeed killed. He had a rusty knife in one hand and a grenade firmly clasped in the other. He wore trousers and a green cap with an anchor worked on it and had a purse with several coins and two 10-yen notes. We continued with our water hole. Water was struck at two feet six inches below the first layer of coral and proved to be almost pure. The recce party returned having failed to find the stream as the going was very arduous and mostly through mangroves with very little visibility. After we had told our story the whole party moved into the jungle in search of the escapee and any others who might be about. We found only a few ill-defined tracks and as it was getting late, 1730 hours, we returned to the barge. There was continual air activity during the night with some bombing about a mile away. Ack-ack and heavy naval gunfire did not make a restful night, explosions being heard on this and other nights and the flashes of gunfire seen.[60]

37th Battalion Combat Team—A Hard Slog

The experience of the soldiers of the 37th Battalion was in many ways similar to that of its sister 35th Battalion. They also had to wrestle with the logistical problems of brown water warfare and eliminating determined Japanese defenders. An advance party of a platoon from the 37th BCT was sent on 21 September from Maravari to Paraso Bay. They were accompanied by a member of the Intelligence Section who had been given instructions to return with the landing craft and report on progress. Having arrived at Paraso Bay, they carried out a short reconnaissance and met up with a group of scouts. There were signs of recent Japanese presence, but the only Japanese soldier discovered was sick and in a pitiful state, and thus easily captured.

> He was a wizened little fellow and evidently had been lost or left behind when the enemy made across country. All he wore was a pair of ragged trousers and seemed half starved. His face lit up, however, when he knew that his captors were New Zealanders. He was given a packet of cigarettes and continued chain smoking until they were finished. Lieutenant R.A. Stokes brought the prisoner back by barge to Brigade where he was fitted out with clothes and fed. He seemed very grateful and bowed and scraped to everyone.[61]

The platoon commander reported back that Paraso Bay was unsuitable as a base because boats could not get any closer than fifty yards from the shore. This meant that guns could not be off-loaded.

The plan had been for a full company with reconnaissance parties to move to Paraso Bay. The company commander, Captain Edwards, was told to go ashore at Paraso, consult with the platoon commander about the situation, and then push on and look for a more suitable landing spot.

On the following day, Wednesday, 22 September, D Company left Maravari at 0800 hours and reached Paraso Bay. The platoon commander indicated that, on the basis of his own reconnaissance and the reports from Josselyn's scouts, there were no Japanese in sufficient strength to stop the New Zealanders from landing at Marisi or Dovelli Cove. Reacting to the changing situation, the company commander decided to push on to Dovelli. The force reached Dovelli Cove at 1240 hours without opposition and established a defensive perimeter.

Reinforcements in the form of Combat HQ, a detachment of 22 Field Ambulance, Battalion HQ, A Company and part of its HQ, and signaling detachments arrived at noon the following day. D Company sent out protective patrols while the remainder of the force dug themselves into a defensive perimeter.

On 23 September, 37th BCT moved out from its base at Maravari Bay, traveling along the east coast. A soldier recalled:

> Our first hop in the barges was to Dovelli Cove, where we made a beachhead and camped. It had been eerie enough, cruising along in the barges about 400 yards from the jungle-fringed shore, a sitting shot for aeroplanes, and fresh meat for any snipers on the island, but it was even worse when I took my platoon on a patrol to Paraso Bay with a native guide who lost the track. When we eventually arrived, the cupboard was bare, although we combed the inlet in open formation for two hours. The white, blinding beach was littered with debris from wrecked ships— ammunition, gasoline, equipment. We destroyed what we could and returned to the defensive perimeter at Dovelli. It was still a game.[62]

Another soldier from the 37th Battalion remembered:

> Vella Lavella was fringed by mangrove vegetation to the water's edge, any jungle movement was only possible by following Native or Japanese tracks, sitting shots of course for any snipers. Our main method of transport was by water and as Guerrillas we would precede the main body, establishing suitable battalion beachheads, ensuring suitable water supply and [attempting] to make some sort of contact with the enemy. Occasionally we were accompanied by a platoon from another company. We would also have the company of some natives as guides, they seemed pleased to be with us, but would melt away into the jungle at the proximity of the enemy. The Japanese had a distinctive odour, very early sensed by our native companions. At Paraso, an open bay fringed by coconut palms and a very shallow coast line, we waded ashore without the expected retaliation, and there caught our first Jap. What a disgrace for him, he begged to be shot, pointing to our rifles and then to his forehead, probably thinking of his beloved emperor. Instead, I understand that he was sent back to N.Z., probably a participant in the subsequent Featherston riots.
>
> Dovelli Cove was another venture, a pleasant spot with that rare article, good water, here the platoon camped in thatched native huts. Apparently hunted by the Japanese the natives had left their seaside habitations. The 23rd [of] September saw us on jungle patrol, rough going, sometimes waist-deep in mangrove mud.

There were signs that the enemy was close and we spent a wet miserable night in foxholes which we dared not leave after dark when friend and foe look alike. Further on, still by American L.C.P. [LCVP] we crept into a small inlet, jungle overhanging the water's edge which had been used to camouflage Japanese vessels while moored. "Go straight in," said the officer. Fortunately, no boat was there at the time. "Step ashore" he said, "see what you can find." All we found were sandals out to dry, a bucket of fresh water covered by a palm leaf, cases of medical gear including many gallons of plasma, later used in our military hospitals. There was no contact with Japanese, but our native guides were scared, a certain sign of their proximity. Back to headquarters we sailed, returning the next day with a complement of fifty men anchoring for the night. Then we followed Japanese tracks overland to Verusai, still no contact. The .303 rifle and pack, ammunition and grenades provided sufficient weight, but my sympathy went to the Bren gun carriers. Our nerves were on edge.[63]

On Friday, 24 September, the balance of the 37th BCT and some of the 25 pounders of 35th Battery arrived. The perimeter was enlarged. Patrols found signs of Japanese activity four or five days old. Josselyn reported that there were about forty Japanese at Tambama Point.

Portions of the 35th Battery and light anti-aircraft guns arrived on 25 September. The anti-aircraft guns would have been especially welcome, as Paraso Bay had been bombed on the previous two days.

Patrols were dispatched to Paraso Bay and Tambama Village, and one patrol was also sent by boat to the head of Sanusukuru Bay. The patrol sent to Tambama found traces of fifteen Japanese who were believed bound for Warambari Bay. The Sanusukuru patrol was delayed because of boat problems. Nonetheless, they found a Japanese food dump, which they destroyed. Medical supplies were also seized and brought back.

On Sunday, 26 September, more guns from the 35th Battery, light AA, anti-tank and an MMG platoon arrived at Dovelli Cove. Two platoons of infantry were dispatched to Sanusukuru Bay with orders to search Tambama Village and the northern part of Tambama Bay. They were instructed to eliminate any Japanese and to reconnoiter Tambama Point as a potential next landing point.

The following day, 27 September, the remainder of the Combat Team reached Dovelli Cove. Ammunition and rations were in hand. The patrol at Tambama Point sighted a camouflaged Japanese barge coming through the entrance to the bay; their experience will be described shortly.

The 37th BCT moved northward in a series of bounds using barges. The barges kept close to the shore even though several times they were grounded on coral. When Japanese planes were seen overhead, everyone sought cover.

As the soldiers of the 37th BCT moved forward by barge to Dovelli Cove, they had to be especially careful regarding Japanese planes, which could be seen overhead. "Everyone sought cover when enemy planes came near during unloading and prayers were that the pilots had not observed them. It was realized at night that they had not because few enemy planes were about and no bombs were dropped in the vicinity."[64]

Movement round the coast in barges in broad daylight made the troops sitting targets for Japanese planes. This reality was rammed home to the men of the MMG Company on 25 September: "During the trip around the coast considerable consternation was caused by the appearance of two Jap planes which came down very low over the barges to investigate. Strangely enough they did not strafe us, their failure to do so being attributed to lack of ammunition."[65] (An alternative explanation is that the Japanese pilots may not have been able to positively identify the barges as enemy craft and consequently did not open fire.)

Progress was made to Dovelli Cove, where the troops unloaded. There they also had to contend with the weather. "Rain fell towards morning and it was very unpleasant lying wet through in slit trenches."[66] They set about weatherproofing their foxholes:

Groundsheets were slung overhead, and waterproof capes used for lining the trenches. The only clothes we had with us were those we were wearing and the rest of our gear was at a minimum. The average soldier's pack contained his groundsheet, cape, jungle boots, spare pair of socks, a spoon, towel, toothbrush and paste, insect repellant, atabrine tablets and smokes. Our respirators were an incumbrance [sic] and we hoped for word to discard them.[67]

The role of the Islanders in assisting the 37th BCT proved invaluable. On 24 September, the 37th Battalion diarist noted:

More patrols went inland during the day, receiving valuable assistance from the natives, who were just as keen as we were to defeat the Japs. The natives were not well built physically, but were intelligent and good trackers. They spoke understandable English and the leaders spent many hours with Lieut. D.S. Dean and his I Section. From their statements, it appears that the Japs were making for the other side of the island, where the 35th Battalion had landed.[68]

For the soldiers, progress was difficult:

Patrols were out during the day and they found the going by no means easy. The dampness of the jungle made footholds difficult and even on the defined trails a good deal of cutting was necessary owing to the quick growth of vines and saplings. Much of the area was swampy and the patrols had to move knee deep in mud and slush.[69]

HMS Confident—*A Prize of War*

One of the major problems for the Kiwis was a lack of sealift capability. They had only a small number of American landing craft available, and what they did have was prone to mechanical breakdown. However, help was at hand from a most unexpected quarter, and the Kiwis would acquire one of the strangest and most dangerous craft ever to be used by the New Zealand armed forces.

On 27 September 1943, a patrol from the 37th Battalion reached Tambama Point. One of the patrol members recalled:

> That night we camped at the head of Tambama Bay when in the early dawn, what appeared to be a floating island of greenery approached our position from the sea, [which] proved to be a large Japanese barge. Had it landed at our spot, history could have been very different as it was manned with three large quick firing machine guns, but it sailed quietly past and anchored about a half mile further into the bay with us in pursuit through the jungle at the water's edge.[70]

What occurred next is described by one of the officers, Lieutenant S.J. Bartos:

HMS *Confident* **(photographer unknown; courtesy Archives New Zealand/Te Rua Mahara o te Kāwanatanga, Wellington Office, WAII, 7 3, Official Photograph Album).**

On the night of the 26th, Captain Adams, Lieutenant Stokes and myself lay in our bivouac and complained of our hard luck in being always a jump behind the Jap—little did we realize what was in store for us. In the early grey hours of the morning, we heard the sound of a motor out to sea. We looked out, and there, heavily camouflaged by green foliage, was a lugger making its way past the point into the bay on our left. We recognized it at once as being Jap. We could hear them talking. Plans were quickly made. My platoon was to stay at the point and pour all our firepower into the ship should she attempt to leave. The guerrilla platoon, with Captain Adams and Lieutenant Stokes[,] moved towards the head of the bay to attempt the capture of the ship. Years seemed to pass as we waited for something to happen. Then it came—the whole sky and ground seemed to shake with gunfire. I could tell that there were far heavier guns in action than we possessed. It seem[ed] as though we might be needed. I left eight of my men with two Brens at the mouth of the bay in case any of the Japs tried to escape by boat and the rest of us made our way as fast as possible in the direction of the firing.

Whether they realized it or not, the Kiwis were facing a formidable opponent. The *Daihatsu* was armed with a Lewis Gun on the bridge (probably captured from British forces in Malaya), a .50-caliber machine gun on the bow and a 20mm gun in the stern.[71] The boat was fifty foot long and heavily laden with fifty tons of ammunition, weapons and stores.

The sequence of events provides an interesting reflection on the Kiwis' lack of combat experience and their attitude toward the Japanese. The other platoon had found the barge anchored close to shore, with no sign of life. It seemed too good to be true, and the fear was that the wily Japanese had set a trap. Captain Adams conferred with Lieutenant R.A. Stokes and Lieutenant S.J. Bartos, and, despite the risks, it was decided that bold action should be taken. Bartos continued

> Whilst the rest of the platoon covered him Captain Adams waded out and climbed on board, only to find the ship deserted. Thanks to a lucky chance the Japs had gone ashore without leaving sentries. The whole platoon boarded her and prepared for battle. It was now 8am. The Japs were observed returning to the vessel by boat from the other side of the bay. They were called upon to surrender, but replied by opening fire. Everything then opened up on them, including their own 20mm gun on the ship. This was the gun I had heard from the point. It was the end for them. Those who did not fall victims to bullets were dealt with by our temporary allies, the crocodiles. Fourteen Japanese were accounted for.[72]

A defensive perimeter was formed around the barge. Lieutenant Bartos was then ordered to take a patrol and mop up any Japanese survivors. The Japanese fired their rifles but could not be located in the dense jungle. Bartos commented:

> In the afternoon I tried again with better luck. They opened up on us at 15 yards range with a machine gun, rifles and grenades. However, they were too ambitious.

They aimed at our heads and missed with their first shots and we were able to go to ground also. Hidden as they were among the roots of a large banyan tree, they presented a difficult target. One of my patrol and myself were blown off our feet by Jap grenades. I remember saying in a surprised tone, "the swines are using grenades." That brought me back to earth and to the realization that we also had grenades. I sent Sergeant Hillis round the flank to get himself into a position to use grenades to the best advantage and then it was all over. We found that one of the victims was the captain of the ship, complete with dispatch case—at least his dispatch case was complete.[73]

Some seventeen Japanese had been killed—there were no survivors. The Japanese had paid the ultimate price for their carelessness in a combat area. However, the victory was not bloodless. Private David Rees had volunteered to man an exposed Lewis Gun on the Japanese barge and fired on the enemy. He then called out, "I've got my one!" Misinterpreting his meaning, the men below congratulated him, but he added, "I've got it in the stomach." He was taken into the hold and made comfortable until Jock Hudson arrived to treat him.[74]

Dave Rees was dead when the barge arrived at Boro. He was buried the same evening on the top of the hill near the native mission. Padre Harford conducted the simple service, and there was a tightening of muscle and a hardening of eye among those who gazed for the last time on the white face of the first soldier of the 37th Battalion to be killed in action.

Rees had joined the Battalion in July and had celebrated his 21st birthday only ten days before he was killed.

The barges began to return to their comrades at Dovelli Cove:

Everyone gathered on the shore to welcome them, but again the occasion was one of sadness. "Yes, it's Snowy Riddell, all right," remarked someone that saw the body that was brought ashore. He had been killed by Jap machine gun fire when returning from a patrol that afternoon. In the gathering darkness, Cpl. A.W. Riddell was buried beside Pte. Rees.... "If only those people in N.Z. who called us Pacific playboys could be here now," someone uttered after the burial and there was silent concurrence.[75]

Riddell was a well-liked member of A Company. His death occurred during the process of mopping up Japanese survivors. In the dense jungle there had been glimpses of Japanese soldiers, and efforts were made to find them. At about 1230 hours on 27 September shots had been heard, and Lieutenant Bartos and five men left the defensive perimeter around the barge "to investigate the area with the intention of bringing in live prisoners—to return to barge by 1415 hours." Things, however, did not go according to plan. The writer of the Battalion war diary noted:

1405 [hours] Lt Bartos and party came across 2 Japs by base of tree—there later proved to be three in vicinity. One Jap opened fire with light automatic weapon of some type (this weapon was not found). The Jap who opened fire killed one of our patrol (Cpl. Riddell). Our patrol retaliated with T.S.M.G. [Thompson Sub-Machine Guns] and hand grenades and killed the 3 Japs (1 officer and 2 ratings). Jap hand grenades thrown by enemy had great blasting power but no explosive fragmentation. They were thrown at our patrol from approx. 15 feet. Two of our patrol were knocked over but suffered no injury. Dead Japs were searched and found to be carrying nothing of value except [for an] officer who had a map case.[76]

These losses suffered had a sobering effect on the Kiwis. They had won their encounter with the Japanese but had suffered their first fatalities.

They had also had a grim lesson about the warrior code of the Japanese. Very few, if any, Allied soldiers who had experienced combat with the Japanese and their extreme unwillingness to surrender would have contemplated inviting the Japanese crew to give themselves up. Humane though the offer may have been, it was also foolish. The Americans had told the New Zealanders of the fate of the Goettge Patrol, an American attempt to arrange for the surrender of Japanese troops on Guadalcanal in 1942: the patrol had been overrun and butchered. The New Zealanders, however, had no understanding of the no-quarter nature of war against the Japanese and did not have the depth of hatred for the Japanese that American troops had acquired.

Another indication of the greenness of the New Zealand troops was that soldiers were allowed to loot the intelligence treasure trove aboard the Japanese barge. As an official history records, "The booty included considerable quantities of rations and much valuable enemy equipment and charts. Unfortunately souvenir hunters made excessive inroads into this material before it reached headquarters for examination by American-born Japanese interpreters."[77] The Kiwis "secured for themselves enemy rifles, ammunition pouches and water bottles, and a small amount of clothing was distributed among the battalion."[78]

The Kiwis were understandably jubilant about their victory: "Meanwhile, our boys had broached cases of Saki found on board and were in increasingly bright spirits as we approached B.H.Q, so much so that although we were still in the danger zone much diplomatic restraint was necessary to prevent them exploding Japanese rockets."[79]

For the soldiers the main prize was the Japanese barge, which was dubbed HMS *Confident* with a wry sense of humor, for the soldiers who had care of it were anything but confident in its reliability.[80] An indication of the barge's challenges was that its engines could not be restarted, and it had to be towed by four landing craft back to Dovelli Cove, where a full inspection was made.

Despite its problems, *Confident* was a welcome addition to the Battalion's fleet. Mechanical difficulties plagued even the American barges; this, together with the need to refuel, meant that the 37th Combat Team had only four barges available to it during the period 28 September–3 October. The practical consequence was that the planned move from Boro to Tambama Bay was delayed. On 5 October only two barges were available for use.

Confident, with its carrying capacity of fifty tons of cargo, was crewed by five New Zealanders and became the flagship of the 37th Battalion Combat Team.[81] Two of the crew were engineers, and their skills were needed to get the engines going. The engines were diesel and had to be heated with blow lamps before the compressed air was turned on to start the engines up. The New Zealanders could not read Japanese and had to improvise.[82]

Flames swept up through the engine skylight while Taffy and Pop flitted about below, turning various cocks on and off. If the temperature was not right the compressed air would be wasted and a compressor would be requisitioned from the engineers to blow up the compressed air tanks again. When she did start, with a deep throated roar, everyone joined in the cheers of the crew.[83]

Confident made her first run on 17 October 1943, leaving Maravari with 50 tons of cargo and passengers; however, she had engine trouble and had to anchor offshore for the night. The crew spent a harrowing night as the craft swung on its anchor and drifted against a coral reef. It was only by continuous pulling on the rope that she was kept from foundering and being pounded to pieces. Another barge lent assistance in the morning, and the trouble was overcome. Making a steady seven or eight knots, Dovelli Cove was reached in the early afternoon. The trip had been too much for some of the crew, who handed in their "resignations."[84]

Confident required hard work. On 21 October the crew of eight began the laborious task of taking down the engine and cleaning it.[85] However, *Confident* was too valuable to ignore and a replacement crew was found, so *Confident* continued her journey "sailing out from Dovelli Cove in a cloud of smoke."

Confident ultimately proved her worth, sometimes in unexpected ways. On 13 November an urgent call was received from Karaka.

Private George Scharvi had received burns about the head from a petrol fire and it was necessary to get him to the A.D.S. at Boro immediately. "The *Confident* is here, we'll see what can be done," said Lieutenant R.A. Stokes, the shipping controller at Boro. He was on the move as he hung up the receiver, and within a minute was discussing the situation with Skipper Widden. Orders were shouted to the engine room and within a few minutes the *Confident* was chugging out of the bay. She made record time and delivered the patient safely to the Field Ambulance.[86]

New Zealanders had a well-deserved reputation for scrounging and repairing broken equipment. Three further Japanese barges that had been wrecked on reefs around Vella Lavella were later salvaged and restored to working order. The reconditioned barges were of "inestimable value" in bringing men to film shows "as well as the numerous other fetch and carry tasks that arise between outlying areas."[87] Lieutenant Stokes found himself appointed as harbormaster at Boro and was engaged full time in organizing sea transport. *Confident* was used on a regular run from Maravari to Boro transporting men, rations and, most importantly, beer.[88]

There was an unfortunate downside to recovering enemy barges. On 5 December 1943, a captured Japanese barge (not the *Confident*) was being used to transport a padre to Tambama to visit his parishioners and conduct the Sunday service. At Suanatalia, off Vella Lavella, the barge became grounded. A large American flag had been draped across the deck and a large white star painted on the roof of the wheelhouse. Five New Zealanders had gone over the side to push the barge off the coral reef when two American Corsair fighters appeared and commenced a strafing run. Two soldiers, Sapper F.L. Knipe and Corporal J.J. Todd, were killed, and another, Sapper A.T. Quirke, was wounded. The dead men were from 20th Field Company, and the deaths were felt very keenly. An inquiry was later held, and the explanation given was that the flight leader had simply been test-firing his guns and his wingman had followed suit.[89] Major General Harmon acknowledged that there had been a flagrant breach of safety regulations and gross negligence. He informed the New Zealanders that one of the pilots had been killed in combat, while the other had received forfeiture of half a month's pay and a formal reprimand. Harmon said of the dead New Zealanders that "we mourn them as brothers in arms."[90] The 37th Battalion war diary likewise noted, "These men who had been with us since the unit moved north had done a great job and their death in such a manner was deeply regretted by everyone."[91]

The story of the shot-up Japanese barge did not end there, however— the 37th Battalion chronicler recorded:

> December 6: The ill-fated Jap barge came to an unexpected end this evening, but not before it had caused two more casualties. All day the barge had remained at the pier, and towards evening it was decided to use it to take a pile of empty tins out in the bay for disposal. Sgt. Stan Butler and Cpl. Arthur Haselmore were in the engine room endeavouring to start up, when an explosion occurred and they were enveloped in sheets of flame. They were able to escape through a small door and Cpl. Haselmore dived overboard into the sea. Sgt. Butler staggered ashore with severe burns to his face and body. Both men were treated at the R.A.P. before being moved to the A.D.S. where their condition was reported later to be satisfactory.[92]

HMS *Confident* (photographer unknown; courtesy Archives New Zealand/Te Rua Mahara o te Kāwanatanga, Wellington Office, WAII, 7 3, Official Photograph Album).

The fire blazed fiercely in the engine room and deck, and a 44-gallon drum of petrol added to the fierceness of the fire. Men from the Quartermasters Store began shifting stacks of ammunition and petrol from the dock until the heat from the flames became too dangerous. Fortunately, the fire did not reach the stores of ammunition and petrol that were located in the bow of the barge, and the fire eventually burned itself out.

One outcome of the tragedy was that *Confident* was given a new coat of navy gray, and a large white star was painted on her hatch in the hope that this would deter aerial attacks.

Confident and the other *Daihatsu* were not the only craft used by the

Recommissioned Japanese barge used by New Zealand personnel for supplies (photographer unknown; courtesy Archives New Zealand/Te Rua Mahara o te Kāwanatanga, Wellington Office, WAII, 7 3, Official Photograph Album).

troops. Justifying their reputation for improvisation, the men of the Transport Platoon of the 35th Battalion used two Japanese collapsible boats, two outriggers, a heavy canoe and a light canoe around Umomo Island to carry water, rations and ammunition to companies deployed on the coast. The Transport Platoon jokingly referred to themselves as "The Umomo General Freight and Passenger (No Deadheads) Transport Corporation (unlicensed)." The outrigger was the fastest and could carry eight passengers and several pounds of cargo, in contrast to the slowest, the big dugout that was capable of taking three-quarters of a ton.[93]

It was not, however, only recycled Japanese barges that attracted air attacks. It is an army axiom that no pilot's brain works under five hundred feet from the ground. The sight of barges proved irresistible for some pilots. On Saturday, 16 October 1943, the USN barge K51-5, of the 35th Battalion Combat Team, left Matu Suroto for Wataro with the intention of delivering supplies and gear. At 0915 hours, when the barge was in open water just south of Mundi Mundi, four Corsairs were sighted. One peeled off, dove straight at the barge, and opened fire. It killed the coxswain, N. Blackmore, USNR, and wounded C.W. Sorrells, USNR; Private Lincoln, 16 MT Company, ASC; and Private N.D. Kingdon, also of 16 MT Company. Private Lincoln's arm had to be amputated, and he later died. "Lt. L.T. McMillan and the coxswain had a marvelous escape, the steering wheel being splintered and the barge well peppered."[94] McMillan and the coxswain were the only ones left uninjured, so he immediately headed back to Matu Suroto at full speed. The New Zealanders were perplexed by the attack, since no enemy barges had been seen in daylight for at least three weeks prior to the attack.

In order to prevent further casualties, orders were issued that "in view of the Air Force practice of testing guns on wrecked barges round the coast, wrecks will be given a wide berth and it is forbidden to visit them."[95]

Sadly, fratricidal attacks were a common feature of the war in the South Pacific. This is exemplified by the attacks on three P.T. boats by aircraft based at the Green Islands on 29 April 1944, which resulted in twenty-five dead and twenty-four wounded. Airpower was an immensely powerful weapon, but the consequences were dire when it was misused.

Fog of War

Lindsay Adams, an officer in 14 Brigade, experienced the frustrations of the fog of war on Vella Lavella:

> My job as a liaison officer from Div to Brigade was ill defined in the situation that the two HQ's were close to each other. I became a floating, fairly useless sort of cog in the machine. I linked with Seaward's combat team, travelling frequently in the assault boat which daily took supplies, clothing and sick or replacement soldiers back and forth. I found it very difficult to get any information about how the leading patrols were getting on, short of joining such patrols. This was not practicable for various reasons and in any case I would have been in the road and not wanted. On the one occasion that I reported something I had been told by a soldier returning from the forward areas, it turned out to be incorrect and the brigadier castigated me for listening to hearsay from someone who knew nothing. Signals communication, usually very good, was proving difficult so that the brigadier [Potter] was not getting a clear picture of progress or action. Not even Seaward could get a clear picture. His company commanders go to a meeting each morning to plan what they would do. They felt happier relying on their own initiative [rather] than waiting for orders from someone partly in the dark.[96]

Barrowclough also had his problems. For him, the communication difficulties meant that he was largely in the dark. Additional signal equipment and personnel arrived on Vella Lavella on 25 September 1943, much to Barrowclough's relief. He recorded in his diary, "At the present time communications are almost non-existent except by the slowest of means and I feel very much out of touch with my command."[97]

The reason for Barrowclough's concerns lay largely in the limitations imposed by Vella Lavella's geography and the relatively primitive state of communications equipment. Barrowclough's communications personnel had arrived early in the process and attempted to link in with the American communications set up and to lay communication cables connecting Gill's Plantation and the island command at Barakoma. Wireless nets were set up in an attempt to connect the disparate command structures—advanced brigade headquarters at Matsu Suroto, 37th Battalion combat headquarters at Boro, rear brigade headquarters at Gill's Plantation and advanced divisional headquarters at Barakoma. To the frustration of all concerned, "Conditions at Matsu Suroto proved extremely bad for wireless reception and transmission, while at other stations throughout the island they were only mediocre even during daylight hours. After dark, conditions became impossible with the types of sets in use."[98] The "heavy electrical interference and the screening of the wet jungle" all added to the problem.[99] On occasions, runners had to be used to deliver messages.

From a tactical perspective, one of the problems encountered by the troops in the jungle was that of communication. The No. 48 radio sets were found to be unsatisfactory due to the "weakness of transmitters, ineffectiveness of vertical aerial and maintenance of batteries supply." The heavier No. 21, however, sets worked reasonably well from the forward battalion "back to rear area of combat team. They proved satisfactory for boat patrols and were successfully used by arty for comms from observers in boats to gun posns."[100]

The No. 11 sets were found unsatisfactory. They were ineffective at night and suffered severe limitations due to the terrain and weather conditions. Valve radios tended to be fragile and unreliable. Batteries were heavy. One way that forward infantry could remain anchored to their supporting artillery and command centers was to spool out communications wire as they advanced. "Combat wire was used by patrols with good results."

Oliver Gillespie's *The Pacific* records:

> Communication difficulties were not easily overcome. Seeping moisture, continual rain and violent electrical storms played havoc with No.11 and No.12 wireless sets. Even the sets in use were not sufficiently strong to overcome the effect of the heavy

Divisional signals radio operator in the jungle using set number 11 (photographer unknown; courtesy Archives New Zealand/Te Rua Mahara o te Kāwanatanga, Wellington Office, WAII, 7 3, Official Photograph Album).

mat of jungle overhead. Forward units were frequently out of touch with rear formations, particularly at night, when conditions were at their worst. Field telephones were finally used in the forward areas and the more reliable runner when all else failed.[101]

Communications, part of the Third Division unofficial history, *Headquarters*, voiced the frustrations of the signalers:

Bogey of the unit on all the islands was the climate and the resultant condensation which day and night played havoc with wireless sets, switchboards, telephones, tents and personal effects. Mechanical equipment which possessed no apparent technical faults just suddenly ceased to operate due to the tricks of nature, thus keeping constantly employed section technicians and maintenance sections in full-time opposition; warming devices were required alongside many of the switchboards and many ingenious arrangements were devised to assist. A visual example of the severity of the climate was witnessed when a new canvas kitbag became completely covered in mildew within two hours of being put into use; the comparative effect on delicate mechanical instruments was not hard to imagine.[102]

The use of ciphers under the fast-moving pressures of combat proved problematic. "The delay involved in encoding and decoding messages was unsatisfactory" and it was considered that sending messages "in clear" should only be done where it would not prejudice the success of the operation.[103]

Eventually matters improved when some seventy miles of telephone wire was laid, linking up the various units, bases and depots.[104]

37th Battalion Struggles Onward to Tambama Bay

On 29 September, rain fell incessantly as the men of the 37th Battalion prepared to move toward Tambama, where the *Confident* had been seized. Because of problems with sealift, only B Company was able to move to Tambama Bay, while the rest of the troops had to spend another night at Dovelli Cove. Those troops had dismantled their bivouacs in anticipation of the move. "Before we had time to rebuild our shelters, rain came down in torrents and everyone was soon soaking wet. After the rain abated there was little drying in the damp atmosphere and the prospect was a night in wet clothes."

The men of B Company suffered a different form of discomfort. That night they were attacked by low-flying Japanese planes, and bombs landed within 50 yards of their foxholes. Fortunately, the foxholes were well dug and no damage was suffered.[105]

The following day, the Battalion HQ and A and D Companies moved to Tambama Bay to reinforce B Company. The troops had no reprieve from the weather—incessant rain fell and all of the soldiers received another soaking.

Once at Tambama Bay, the soldiers had to set up defensive positions:

Company areas were laid out and the difficult job of digging foxholes on the coral lined shore was commenced. It was night before we all settled in, but the prospect of sleep did not appear too bright. Our clothes were still damp and in addition sea water oozed through the bottom of the foxholes. Still, all except the guards had to be below ground level, so there was nothing to do but make the most of it. Those who slept for more than a few minutes at a time were lucky. The navy further down the coast kept up an hour after hour shelling of Kolombangara Island from Vella Gulf and the noise of this, together with numerous visits of Jap bombers made sleep well nigh impossible. In addition every man was on guard as usual for at least three hours of the night.[106]

Patrols were sent out to search the countryside to the north and south. On 2 October, contact was made with two Japanese by a recce party at Susu Bay. One Japanese soldier was killed, and the other escaped into the jungle. The 35th Battery was positioned so that it could fire in support of the infantry.

New Zealand soldiers on Vella Lavella, 1943, examine a captured Japanese model 99 (27mm) LMG (courtesy Alexander Turnbull Library, Wellington, New Zealand, reference number WH-0237).

Susu Bay was occupied by a company of infantry on 3 October, this time without incident.

Orders were issued by Sugden on 4 October that forward patrolling and searching of the countryside was to cease. He wanted the infantry to reach Warambari Bay on 5 October. To assist, three barges from the 35th Combat Team arrived at Susu Bay on the morning of 5 October. These were needed because only two barges were available from the 37th BCT's pool due to mechanical breakdowns and supply operations.

Plans were made for landing at Warambari Bay.

Toward Warambari Bay

As the Kiwis moved toward their destination, one of the soldiers recorded:

Matters were warming up, and as we heard by radio about this time that the 35th had made contact on the other coast and were driving the Japs toward us, we began to feel that tautness of expectation which is the prelude to battle. I was like a wound-up spring, when, on October 5, it became the turn of my company to make the first hop, form the beachhead, and reconnoiter.

No lovelier morning could be imagined as we chugged from the bay. The hour was about nine o'clock. The sea was glassy. Underneath were the fantastic shapes of the coral, overhead the vast blue belt of the sky, cloudless. It seemed as if we were making a pleasure cruise, only the rough ammunition in all my pockets, and the pile of equipment in the barge, made me remember facts. We would probably have to fight—for our lives, and no one knew, or could guess, from where the bullet, the bomb, was going to come.

In the first of the three barges was myself and platoon, company headquarters, and signals. The plan was for my platoon to land, push in fifty yards, and then if we met no trouble, I would fire a green flare. The barges outside could land. We took with us rations for four meals, (Rations K and C, with which we were just getting acquainted), and our armament was Brens, Tommys, rifles and grenades, plus an anti-tank rifle and a two-inch mortar. Our dress was green bush shirt and peaked hat like a jockey's. Faces were still light-hearted and smiling under those peaks as the ramp banged down and we scraped past the boxes of rations and gear, fanning out in three sections through the treacherous, evil-smelling swamp on the edge of the bay.

Soon my native guide was sniffing in the mud. Suddenly he stiffened. "Jap here, okay" he said. "Here show foot." I looked and yes, there in the mud were the prints, the unmistakable prints of the one-toed Jap climbing boot. The print seemed fairly old. "Long-time?" I asked. "Made—longtime," he replied after a further examination.

We scouted further till we were fifty yards from the water, and still there was nothing fresh. Having decided that all was clear, I jumped up on a rotting log, picked out a clear space in the canopy above, and through it fired my green flare, which finned up through the dark jungle air, then was gone in the brilliant sky. Immediately I heard the engines of the waiting barges boom into voice, heard them grounding with the rattling clank as their ramps hit the coral. Then came the knocking of equipment as one platoon went to our left and another to our right. I started to light a cigarette.

"Look! What's that over there?" I heard an excited whisper from the chap nearest me. I looked in the direction of his finger. Flitting through the undergrowth, like ghosts or moving shadows, I could see seven shapes in green, with peaked hats. Unconsciously we had both raised our rifles. "Hold on," I said, "They may be our own blokes coming round from the right." I passed the warning through my fan of men, and made my way in quick tree-to-tree rushes, back to the company commander. "Are any of our patrols out on the right flank?" There were none. "Then there are seven Japs at least working round to your left flank." He agreed to send out a patrol to investigate and I went back to our position.

Nearly back to my log, I went into the mud like an arrow as a frantic burst of firing opened on the left—running commentary from the Brens, the jab of the Lee-Enfield, and occasionally, the lighter bark of the Nip rifle. I twisted round to look at my watch in the jungle twilight. It was eleven thirty—and we had to wait there, staring out in front trying to pick out the real from the unnatural shadows, sometimes drawing a bead and firing.

After half an hour a runner came with word to withdraw. D Company had arrived in response to a radio message, and a platoon would replace us, man for man, while we reformed towards the beach. We managed this without injury. Still a game!

Our next task was to test the Jap position on the left. This was no cake-walk. For the first time I was uneasy and wondered how we would get on. The Japs were invisible, well-placed, numerous, with several machine guns. And we had had nothing to eat.

I arranged with the platoon to advance in a shuttling system, two sections, one on each flank, to cover the centre section as it advanced ten yards: then vice versa. Sometime after twelve we started, and I remember the comfort of seeing streams of tracer from the Brens, like a luminous wall on either side. We could never tell whether we were being shot at, owing to the din of our own ambuscade.

Sixty yards, and then I stopped. In front of me someone was shouting the words: "Tojo, Tojo!" Then the voice became a scream: "Moeji, Moeji! (The Japanese Emperor)." Finally it broke into song, and then started jabbering Japanese. A wounded Jap, ten yards ahead in the undergrowth, was making his peace with his Gods—and perhaps warning his mates of our position. Jim, one of my boys, said that he could see him. "Finish him off," I called. Jim, who had been kneeling behind a tree, now stood up to fire. I heard a crack and thought that he had fired. "They've got me—across the back!" He slumped down into the hollow. The bullet had entered his shoulder and emerged from the back, cutting the V piece of the web, so that I saw it drop. I yelled to the platoon to give concentrated fire on the Jap position, while another chap hauled Jim back to the dressing station in the rear. This was done, and I was just sinking back thankfully into the mud when I felt a smack on the chin—put my hands up, and pulled out two wood splinters. There was round hole in the tree-root six inches in front of my nose.

Now I knew the game was serious. Before this the platoon had been shouting gleefully about the wounded Jap: "Get the swine, let him have it." Now that one of us had been wounded, perhaps killed, it was different. Gone was the fun and games.

I decided to advance closer, and we managed another ten yards. But now the air was burnt with bullets. I learnt afterwards that a stream of chips was flying out from the log behind which I had flopped after the dash. Every time I spoke there was a grim whistle. Also, by the loud explosions, and clouds of mud, I knew that the Japs were using a knee-mortar from the ridge behind. It was obvious that we were stuck, with machine guns left and right, and a mortar in front. I had decided to attack on the left, when a runner came up and said that another platoon was on that job, and that we were to stay until the battalion had formed its perimeter for the night.

The next three hours—Ah, the next three hours! May I never go through them again! I was face down in the mud, and had covered my face with it, so that it would be harder to pick up. I was lying in the V formed by two flanges of a tree-root. Round these I peered and fired when I saw any part of a man—that was all I ever saw. Gradually, as the slow minutes crept into slow hours, as my feet became numb in spite of my wiggling my toes in their boots, and my fingers became stiff, and as the jungle twilight, darkened to the jungle night, I began to give up hope. Were we to be left there all night? If so the Japs would certainly get us, being isolated. Perhaps a sniper had a bead on me that moment, was waiting, finger on trigger. And still the minutes, the hours went by.

Perhaps at four, perhaps at five—I don't know, a runner came to say we were to withdraw to the main perimeter for the night. The best news I'd ever heard.

Back as we had gone up—in ten yard dashes, covered by flanking fire. I leap from tree to tree with new vigour as the blood comes back to feet and hands. Ten yards—wait and fire. Now they're all back—our turn again. I leap out from cover, run a couple of yards, slip on a root, stumble, fall into mud, waist high. The man on each side is the same. The bullets begin to churn up the mud around us—some of it goes up my nose. I shout to the sections to turn and fire while the others of my section haul two of us out. Dash for cover! I look around for the third man. He is still chest deep in mud, almost invisible, it is so dark. Two volunteers go to get him out. They drag him five yards when they stoop in their tracks and shout: "He's dead—back of his head's blown off." "All right, come in," I say tiredly.

A few more shots and we are back in the perimeter, our job done.

We had eaten nothing since eight o'clock that day, but now, sitting up to our ankles in mud, we could not eat. I managed a biscuit and a sip of water. Round us squelched the mangrove mud, soon complete blackout came down, and with it the unceasing cacophony of the jungle night. Our first clash was over.[107]

Despite the intense training the New Zealanders had received, they were still green and had to grapple with the realities of jungle warfare. The commander of A Company, 35th BCT, reported, "This type of warfare is a heavy strain on men's nerves, as the enemy is hidden anywhere and seldom seen. After two weeks of it, often in mud and rain fully 12½ percent of troops were suffering from skin trouble which could only be cleared up by withdrawal to clean surroundings and also from diarrhea."[108]

The shock of combat was quickly overcome. The role of good leadership on the part of junior NCOs was an integral part of this recovery.[109]

Landing at Warambari Bay

On Tuesday, 5 October, C Company of the 37th BCT landed at Warambari Bay at 1145 hours. Patrols were sent out to reconnoiter the area. Within a quarter of an hour they encountered Japanese in unknown numbers but supported by a light machine gun and a medium or heavy gun. Despite this, the landing went smoothly, with the perimeter gradually being extended as more barges carrying troops arrived.

At midday a platoon was sent out, led by Lieutenant Shirley, to push the Japanese back. Using fire and movement, Shirley's men were successful in forcing the Japanese back to 100 to 150 yards from the beachhead perimeter. However, the Japanese retreated to a more favorable defensive position concealed by logs and tree roots. The problem for Shirley was that the area between his men and the Japanese had opened out and was so exposed to Japanese fire that his men could no longer maneuver. Lieutenant Bartos was ordered to take his platoon, move to the right of Shirley's position and clear out the Japanese. But this was easier said than done—the Japanese were in well-placed, camouflaged defensive positions supported by guns. The Kiwis paid in blood, with five killed and six wounded.

In the face of determined enemy resistance, and in view of the fact that more troops and stores had arrived at the beachhead, the decision was made at 1730 hours, with darkness falling, to pull the two platoons back to the perimeter.

Things were not particularly safe in the perimeter, either. A determined Japanese sniper had set himself up in a tree within the perimeter and inflicted casualties. He was dealt with in the late afternoon by Bren gunfire.

Artillery had landed at the beachhead, and one troop of twenty-five-pounder guns was used to hit the area occupied by the Japanese. It was thought that the 37th BCT had come into contact with a party of thirty to forty Japanese soldiers who had been sent from Marquana to prevent an Allied landing at Warambari Bay. This group had been at an old Japanese bivouac at Warambari Bay when the first New Zealand troops landed. Fortunately for the New Zealanders, C Company had sufficient time to get ashore and organized before the Japanese could launch an attack. The most vulnerable time in any amphibious operation is when only part of the invading force has landed and is still relatively disorganized.

The fact that, on the other coast, the 35th BCT on 5 October had not met any resistance led to the thought that the Japanese had withdrawn from their South Marquana position and were making their way to Warambari Bay. It was decided that the 37th BCT would strengthen its perimeter and send a company to the head of the bay, patrolling the area of the old Japanese bivouac and the track to the southern area of the bay.

The following day, 6 October 1943, the artillery pounded the area around the old Japanese bivouac to soften up any defenders. Then B Company, under Lieutenant Hobbs, was sent to the southern side of the bay to clear the area of any Japanese defenders. Further patrols were sent out to search the old Japanese bivouac and the southern track.

An incoming Allied barge was fired at by a Japanese light machine gun sited at the southern end of the bay at 0730 hours. A patrol led by Lieutenant D. Law was making a recce of the southern area, and contact with the Japanese was established at 0900 hours. Law's patrol was on its way back to the perimeter, and Law was in the invidious position of having the Japanese force between his men and the safety of the perimeter. Law found himself under a heavy barrage—every move drew Japanese fire. Pinned down, Law and his men were unable to withdraw or try to move around the flank of the Japanese. Law prudently decided to stay where he was for the time being. Two Kiwi soldiers were killed, and one was wounded. It was thought that four Japanese were killed. At nightfall Law and his men were successful in breaking off contact with the Japanese and retreating to the perimeter. The wounded man was brought with them.

B Company had a comparatively easier time of it. They did not have any contact and returned to the perimeter with the information that there were no Japanese in the area between the perimeter and the head of Warambari Bay. In the meantime, Kiwi artillery fired at the area of the old Japanese bivouac between 1800 and 1830 hours.

The BCT commander's appreciation of the situation on 6 October was that the Japanese had not established any defensive positions, and that the contacts made by the New Zealand patrols further indicated that the Japanese were feeling out the New Zealand positions with the intention of attacking. He told Brigade HQ his view that the beachhead should be held in strength and further searches should be undertaken before the next leap forward was made to Marquana Bay. Brigadier Potter agreed to this plan. It is an indication that the New Zealanders were now viewing the Japanese not as a mere passive force to be hunted down and destroyed, but rather as a dangerous foe who had the ability to turn and strike back.

A plan was developed for offensive patrols to be sent out on 7 October on the left flank and toward Mende Bay. Preparatory shelling of Mende Bay occurred. No contact was made on the left flank. D Company, led by Captain Edwards, found that there were Japanese bivouacs around the coastal strip to Mende Point. There were, however, signs that the Japanese had been on the beach on 6 October—discarded Japanese equipment and heavy machine guns were found.

Lance Corporal Brewster and Private Walker behind their Vickers Machine Gun at Marquana Bay (photographer unknown; courtesy Archives New Zealand/Te Rua Mahara o te Kāwanatanga, Wellington Office, WAII, 7 3, Official Photograph Album).

A Situation Report from Advanced Brigade HQ stated that the U.S. Navy warned that the Japanese in the Marquana area were to be evacuated on the night of 5-6 October. A plan was devised to send patrols by the coastal route to Maraziana Point and the Warambari-Marquana track.[110]

Supply

Supplying troops with food, water and ammunition was essential if they were to maintain their combat effectiveness. Five days' worth of rations were sent with each flight of troops from the rear area to the forward zone. Bulk supply was maintained at the Combat Team rear area and sent onward. Subsidiary dumps were established further forward depending on the tactical circumstances. Rations were moved forward by landing craft and carrying parties.

If the Allied soldiers had problems with their supplies, those problems paled into insignificance when compared to those of their Japanese foe. Yoshio Ninoishi of the Regimental Gun Company, 229th Infantry Regiment, arrived on Vella Lavella on 18 August 1943; after fighting for 25 days, his unit was marched to Tambama, taking 11 days to arrive. "Since we lacked food we ate coconuts during the march." On 27 September his unit encountered enemy soldiers and engaged in combat. As he described in his diary, "Our rations are dropped, along with ammunition, from about one plane per day, which gives us soldiers (there are over 600 of us) a daily ration of about two small bowls of rice. It looks as though even the coconuts and taro will be eaten up within four or five days."[111] Poignantly, that was his last diary entry.

Intelligence Gathering

The contribution of Vella Lavella Islanders enlisted in the Allied cause to the gathering of intelligence was significant. The Islanders were under the control of Coastwatcher Henry Josselyn. Because Josselyn was familiar with the Islanders' language and culture, he was considered the best person to speak to them. On a cautionary note, it was "found best to send two or three natives out together and question them independently on their return as they often exaggerate."[112]

The South Pacific Scouts monitored the Japanese until they were withdrawn on 26 September 1943. Lt. Graham was recalled to Barakoma on 18 September, and he was able to brief his countrymen on the location of the Japanese. The Scouts did not take any part in the clearance operations, if only because there was considerable sickness among them.[113]

Japanese prisoners were another source of intelligence. Because the Japanese military eschewed the possibility of surrender, Japanese soldiers did not know how to deal with their captors and often became quite voluble, disclosing details of their units and background, as well as military secrets.

Japanese Tactics

Because the Japanese were on the defensive, there were few occasions when they attacked. Generally, Japanese offensive operations were at a low level and in the nature of patrol skirmishes. A report on Japanese tactics commented, "The attack was usually preceded by much shouting and noise after which he attempted to rush our position. When this failed he completely surrounded the position and adopted further rushing tactics." In addition, "effective use was made of snipers, sometimes in trees, who screened his movements on most occasions."

In defense the Japanese positions were well sited in places difficult to approach and usually consisted of LMGs and/or MMGs, effectively supported by riflemen who were disposed on either flank in checker-board formation. It was noted that "the enemy fire discipline was good and he usually waited until our troops were within five or ten yards before opening fire. He disposed his rifleman effectively to drive our troops into the lanes of fire for his automatic weapons."[114]

The Japanese were extremely skilled in field craft, and as regards the Japanese use of camouflage and concealment, the New Zealanders conceded that "he demonstrated his skill in both almost to the point of perfection and applied it not only to the individual but to whole defensive localities."[115] The Kiwis also acknowledged that "privation and hardship do not appear to restrict him in his desire to fight to the finish."

The Allies were uncomprehending of the Japanese willingness to fight to the last man and last bullet. It was suggested that "their peculiar attitude towards surrender may be partly the result of the belief that if taken prisoner they will be shot."[116] This revealed a cultural misunderstanding of the Japanese. There was a strict prohibition against surrender by Imperial Rescript, and the Japanese military could not envisage a situation in which its soldiers would bring everlasting shame to their service, their comrades and their families by surrendering. Generally, Japanese soldiers who were taken prisoner had either been rendered unconscious in combat or become emaciated, disease ridden and isolated from their comrades.

Even Japanese taken prisoner sought death at Allied hands. On 29 September, B Company of the 37th Battalion was en route by barge to Tambama Bay.

> Several miles out they saw two men paddling with their hands on an improvised raft. The men were picked up and they turned out to be Japs (a medical officer and an engineer). The officer spoke some English and it was learned from him that they were survivors from a ship which was sunk by our patrol boats on its way to Bougainville. They had been in the water for two nights and two days and were low in conditions when they were taken on the barge. The officer repeatedly asked to be shot. Had the Americans manning the barge had their way both of them would have been killed on the spot.[117]

The Japanese attitude to surrender was not confined to land forces. Doug Ross found himself on an LCI traveling around the coast of Vella Lavella. "We came across a downed Japanese pilot in the water. He pointed to his forehead inviting us to shoot him. The American crew were ready to oblige him but the company commander overrode them and insisted that the pilot be picked up."[118]

Lance Corporal Rob McLean of 5 Provost Company had the job of guarding 14 Brigade Headquarters at Pakoi Bay on the west coast of Vella Lavella. There were four Japanese prisoners held in a grass hut. They were each in a pair of shorts with their hands tied behind their backs. The concern was that "they'd make a go at you so that you'd have to shoot them. That's what they wanted. Being taken prisoner was one of the biggest disgraces and so they weren't happy." McLean found his prisoners "pretty sad." The prisoners were taken away individually by the Intelligence people, who were the only ones allowed to feed them. After three days the Japanese were taken south.[119]

Japanese prisoners taken in the South Pacific were usually sent to Australia or New Zealand. In Cowra, Australia, and Featherston, New Zealand, some Japanese prisoners intent on dying attacked their guards and were killed or wounded.

Treatment of Wounded and Medical Evacuation

Allied fatalities on Vella Lavella were mercifully low, in large measure due to the medical treatment available to wounded and sick soldiers. The medical personnel faced tremendous challenges, including the torrential rainfall, which did not allow blankets and clothing to dry properly; infestations of flies; and the sheer difficulty of moving casualties across rough country to medical facilities. It was easy to lose one's sense of direction in "a bewildering maze of tracks."[120]

Each of the BCTs had an Advanced Dressing Station provided by 22 Field Ambulance. A main dressing station was set up at Gill's Plantation, and sick or wounded troops were evacuated there by barge. I Field Surgical Unit was attached to the Medical Dressing Station (MDS). After initial battlefield treatment and stabilization, casualties were sent to a Casualty Clearing Station on Guadalcanal, usually being transported by plane.

The health of the troops was critical for their combat effectiveness. Tropical diseases had to be taken into account. The battalion medical services were organized, therefore, to treat not only battle casualties but also sickness.

All supplies were carried in portable haversacks, usually on the back, but in the trek up the coast, the main battalion medical supplies were able to be transported in native canoes. As soon as battalion headquarters moved forward, the battalion aid-post packed its equipment and reached its new site as soon as possible. There, a tarpaulin for protection against torrential rains was erected, and under it medical equipment such as blood plasma, splints, drugs, dressings and instruments was set out in preparation for casualties. It usually took eight men to get one wounded stretcher case back to the RAP, and the stretcher bearers found their work difficult in the extreme. However, the long months of training in New Zealand and New Caledonia enabled them to carry out their tasks creditably and well. When a man was wounded, first-aid was given on the spot by the company medical orderlies, and evacuation was carried out as rapidly as possible, first to the aid post where additional treatment was given, and thence by barge to the Advanced Dressing Station.

Even the transport of sick and wounded personnel has its lighter side:

On one occasion, a party of stretcher bearers conveyed a suspected case of acute appendicitis up hill and down dale, through swamp and jungle for a distance of

Wounded New Zealand soldier awaiting evacuation (photographer unknown; courtesy Archives New Zealand/Te Rua Mahara o te Kāwanatanga, Wellington Office, WAII, 7 3, Official Photograph Album).

nearly two miles back to the medical officer to find their patient was suffering merely from the common "belly ache," due to an unaccustomed diet of C and K rations. The perspiring stretcher bearers were not at all pleased when they later sighted their victim strolling about unconcernedly, and expressed this in no uncertain manner. Among other things it was suggested that the diet be persevered with![121]

For the New Zealanders, Vella Lavella was their first exposure to combat and casualties. To see their comrades wounded or killed was traumatic: "On 27 September contact was made with the enemy and wounded began to come in from the battalion. As we had known most of the chaps well from old 35th days, it was a shock to our boys, guarding the ADS and battalion headquarters to see them coming in badly smacked up."[122]

The Loss of LST-448—1 October 1943—Carnage and Heroism

It was one thing to invade Vella Lavell; it was another thing to hold it. To do so, adequate supplies of food ammunition, oil and all the other essential material of war had to be landed, sorted and stockpiled in an orderly fashion on Vella Lavella. The decision was made that a thirty-day stockpile of rations, gasoline and oil should be created. The vessels carrying this largesse knew that they had to run the gauntlet of Japanese airpower. The beaching of their ships would be the point of maximum danger for the large, cumbersome amphibious craft packed to the brim with often combustible supplies and ammunition. The swift unloading and safe removal of cargo was critical to the success of the enterprise.

The 6th Special Seabees were delegated to perform the loading at Guadalcanal and the unloading at Vella Lavella of LST-460. They knew that the island had not been secured, so they went into action kitted out with rifles and combat gear. To assist them, they had a USMC unit, Company B, First Corps Motor Transport Battalion. The men knew that it would be a race against time and that every minute heightened the risk of air attack. The Seabees' Cruisebook recorded the following:

In a driving rainstorm on September 29, the seven LST supply convoy left Guadalcanal for Vella Lavella with Echelon One and the Marine truck drivers aboard Large Slow Target 460. At one mile from the beach the LST crews completely undogged their doors and ramp and unclutched the ramp motor so that when the brake was released the ramp would fall of its own weight. The men on the deck watched for enemy planes. Navy gunners hung from the straps of their 20mm cannons, eyes skyward. To beef up their anti-aircraft defense, the Sixth men deck loaded the two New Zealand 40mm Bofors anti-aircraft cannons as well as all their own 50 caliber machine gun-equipped 6×6 trucks. A few hundred yards from shore the LSTs dropped their stern anchors and paid out the cables until seconds later they were crunching onto the beach. LST-460 grounded a little short of dry land, but Echelon One was prepared. As soon as their ramp splashed into the surf at 07.15 their bulldozer was disembarking[,] immediately followed by their five-ton tractor crane. As their bulldozer pushed a coral road up to the ramp, the Marine truck drivers on the tank deck waited with their engines idling. After the first trucks rushed out the Seabees installed the LST's elevator guides and lowered the 40mm cannons to the tank deck where they were attached to their prime movers and driven ashore. The Sixth men wasted no time in getting their own 20mm cannon and truck mounted 50 caliber anti-aircraft guns emplaced in positions ashore.

While their shipmates worked the ship the Seabee gunners stood by their weapons. Inside LST-460 tank deck 32 Stevedores worked at top speed to load the returning trucks. At 09.20 less than two hours after starting, Echelon One completed unloading their LST. The now empty LST 460 pumped out its ballast and prepared to haul in its stern anchor cable and retract from the beach. The Seabees began dispersing into the jungle, where they would dig their foxholes. LST 448 beached a half mile north of Echelon One, was still unloading. Marines had charge of the operation and it was not proceeding as quickly as it should have. Echelon One sent a work detail to assist discharging LST-448. At 09.30 a large force of Japanese fighters and dive-bombers raided the staging area. One veteran recalled how he was walking on the beach to retrieve his rifle and gear and saw a formation of about sixteen aircraft come out of the sun. He first thought they were Allied planes, but the sudden cry "air raid" and the formation's nosing over into a dive convinced him otherwise. The Seabees and Marines ran for the cover of the jungle as the anti-aircraft guns on ship and shore sputtered to life. Some men fired their rifles at the incoming planes. Two Japanese dive-bombers swept down and released their payloads on LST-448. The men watched helplessly as the bombs fell into the beached ship. There was a muffled explosion and the Sixth men could feel the ground tremble from the force of the blast though the exploding ship was half a mile away. Seconds after the impact of the bombs, the Sixth men took to their feet running down the beach toward LST-448. When Japanese fighters swept in and strafed the beach the 20 or so running Seabees dived into the jungle for cover, re-emerging to continue their dash as the enemy fighters passed. The Japanese planes bombed the dispersal areas too, wounding many among the work parties and gun crews. LST-448 was a twisted, burning wreck when the Seabees got to her. Ammunition was exploding in her hold and magazines. Marines were helping the wounded, assisted by the Sixth's medical officer who stayed on board throughout the afternoon despite the fires, exploding ordinance and a second attack. Many men were wounded. Of the work detail the Sixth had dispatched before the raid, eight men were wounded by shrapnel, two seriously, and another could not be found at all. Though he was listed as missing in action, it was clear two days later, when 21 unidentified bodies were pulled out of the wreckage[,] that Echelon One had lost one of its own.

The Sixth's first experience under fire was costly, but the men did not lose their sangfroid. They dug foxholes near their work area on the beach and waited for the next supply echelon to land. The Japanese attacked intermittently throughout the day and into the night, until about 22.30. The second Japanese air strike came at 10.00 at Ruravai about two miles up the beach from where the Sixth landed and LST-334 had still not finished discharging its cargo. It was on the shore as an inviting target. The Japanese hit it with a bomb but fortunately the damage was light. As the enemy planes swarmed over the beachhead, one *Val* dive bomber came hurtling across the cove at a very low altitude only to find cannon fire from the Sixth's 20mm anti-aircraft gun slamming into its nose. As the crippled plane reached the far end of the cove it suddenly exploded into pieces and fell into the sea. Later in the day the Airsols (Air Solomons Command), combat air patrol was on station above the staging base, and they helped deflect the worst of a 60-plane raid. Some enemy bombers still got through, and LST-448 was hit again. For the Japanese pilots there was no mistaking where the beachhead was as long as smoke belched out of the burning LST-448. In the last raid of the day the Japanese scored again, destroying 5 heavy trucks and two jeeps. The violence of the air attacks on Vella Lavella that continued, vividly illustrated for Echelon One the importance of anti-aircraft guns. While on the island the Sixth set about acquiring more 20mm cannon [and] .50 caliber machine guns and trained men in their operation when there was spare time. The corps staging area on Vella Lavella was considered secured by October 8. Air raids continued but the anti-aircraft defenses were by then beefed up. During Echelons One's [*sic*] seven and a half weeks on Vella, their gunners were part of the base's anti-aircraft defense.[123]

The Silver Star is the third highest award for the American military. It requires significant bravery in the face of the enemy. The loss of LST-448 resulted in a veritable cascade of Silver Stars.

The disaster that overwhelmed LST-448 turned ordinary men engaged in what were normally noncombat roles into heroes. This was the case with men from Company A, 4th Base Depot, USMC. First Lieutenant LeRoy Moore Cooke organized men to dump ammunition overboard from the flaming upper deck of the LST. Corporal Charles M. Adams was prominent in dumping the ammunition and leading others in evacuating injured men from the burning hold and upper deck. Assistant Cook Joseph J. Mayher repeatedly boarded the vessel despite the danger from fire and exploding gasoline and ammunition. He helped with salvage operations and then manned a hose deep in the hold until the pump failed. Mayher received multiple shrapnel wounds when Japanese planes again struck the LST. Private Howard C. Bennett helped in the evacuation of the injured. He was on the deck moving ammunition when he received shrapnel wounds from the second Japanese air attack. All were awarded the Silver Star for their bravery.

However, it was not just the 4th Base Depot men who earned the Silver

Star. First Lieutenant Burt H. Dreyer, USMCR, was Quartermaster of the 2nd Parachute Battalion, 1st Parachute Regiment, I MAC, and he was in charge of unloading. Dreyer rallied a group of Marines and led them into the burning vessel to rescue wounded men. First Lieutenant David I. Zeitlin, 3rd Marine Division, was involved with unloading operations for his unit when LST-448 was hit. Despite the strafing from Japanese aircraft and burning oil, Zeitlin swam to the rescue of wounded men in the water. He then assembled a group of volunteers who boarded the burning vessel. Zeitlin organized rescue operations even while the vessel was hit by further Japanese bombs.

A Marine Corps officer, Captain Fenwicke W. Holmes, was placed in command of Depot Company A, Branch 3, 4th Base Depot, Supply Service, I MAC. Between 19 September and 23 September, his men were given limited training, including rifle training. Most of his men were embarked on the APD USS *Crosby* on 23 September. He recalled that they landed on Vella Lavella on 25 September under air attack and experienced light casualties:

> We had no maps, but there was a photomontage of the area and by the time I had determined that we had landed 5 miles from the right beach, the USS *Crosby* was disappearing on the horizon. We skirmished up the dirt coastal road to the proper location and set up camp.
>
> Our mission was to set up a forward supply depot to support a possible future invasion of Bougainville. The Navy was supposed to send weekly convoys of LSTs with supplies and additional troops....
>
> October 1. This morning I had sent working teams to the various landing points to receive the LSTs due to arrive. I was in my jeep just south of the discharge point of LST-448 when we saw Japanese dive bombers attack that ship. The ship was on fire and ordinance was exploding as I arrived. Ships personnel rigged a fire hose to try to attack the flames. Several of my Marines were manning the hose. I set up an emergency treatment center for the wounded (This ship had brought in a large complement of Marines from the Parachute Regiment and several of them were killed or wounded). Some trucks had been off loaded before the bomb attack and they were being used to evacuate the wounded. In the melee a jeep arrived with a Marine Lt. Col who asked, who was in charge. "I guess it's me, Sir," I said. The Colonel said "Get these trucks out of here, get these men out of here. The Japs will be back, the Japs will be back." His driver gunned the jeep and that's the last I saw of Paratroop Lt. Colonel Victor H. Krulak. (When I retired in 1964 my commander was the same, but Lieutenant General Krulak).
>
> Krulak was right, the Japs came back and bombed the LST again. My small fire brigade was blown back from the ramps, and two of them were superficially wounded. That pretty much ended our attempt to salvage the burning ship.
>
> My corpsman reported that one of the wounded paratroopers was too badly wounded to make it by truck to the field hospital some miles away with the 8th [sic 14th Brigade] New Zealand Brigade. Could the captain find a small boat for the task? After trying futilely to use signal flags, I swam out to an LST that was

hanging some distance to the rear of the #448, and went up the gangway wearing only my shorts. When I announced to the duty officer that I was Captain Holmes and I needed a small boat to evacuate wounded, he acted immediately and the wounded marines were successfully evacuated. The title "Captain" impresses the hell out of Navy personnel!

Later that day I visited a site where another LST had been attacked but damaged only superficially and the equipment had been successfully unloaded. The Seabee Lieutenant in charge came to me and asked for advice on what to do because of the aerial attacks. I told him that if it were up to me I would use the heavy equipment that had been unloaded and start digging, get your men some shelter.

At no time during my stay on Vella Lavella did we have command of the skies. The Japanese had an airfield on Kolombangara, a volcanic island just to our north. We were attacked each time a convoy came up with supplies. Not to mention night attacks. It is my belief that the Vella Lavella operation was a failure and that we never successfully established a forward supply depot. The LST's we later off loaded on Bougainville had been dispatched from some rear echelon location such as New Caledonia.[124]

Fenwicke Holmes was later awarded the Silver Star for his part in directing salvage and casualty evacuation operations.

An American driver with the 6th Special NCB recalled, "I was a truck driver and the first one off and they were strafing down the road I was on. I got out of my truck and got behind a coconut log. I didn't get hit, but the one that did was very close by."[125]

In order to supply the Allied troops on Vella Lavella and to bring in equipment and New Zealand reinforcements, a series of convoys or "echelons" was organized. The Japanese contested the passage of these ships mainly through airpower. The Americans soon learned to respect the formidable combat power of the Aichi 99 Val dive-bombers.

When twelve 40mm Bofors AA guns from the 209th Light Anti-Aircraft Battery, a New Zealand unit, were scheduled to travel from Guadalcanal in late September to reinforce the AA defenses of Vella Lavella, the skipper of the LST they were to travel on arranged for the light anti-aircraft Bofors guns to be mounted on the deck. Barrowclough had concerns about this arrangement and gave orders that on arrival the guns were to be disembarked rapidly and emplaced as soon as possible. What Barrowclough had not counted on was the unpredictable Japanese and the reluctance of American skippers to disembark the guns. Without warning, at 0935 hours three Japanese planes attacked the LST-448 as it lay beached at Nargvai, Vella Lavella. Bombs struck the craft, causing fires to break out and gas drums to explode. With power gone, firefighting efforts were useless, and with ammunition beginning to explode, the order was given to abandon ship. Wounded were taken off and delivered to the New Zealand hospital. Another Japanese air attack later in the afternoon caused further damage. Efforts were made to fight the fires over the next few days, and water was pumped out. An attempt to tow LST-448 to Barakoma resulted in the craft sinking.

Seven New Zealand AA gunners on LST-448 died in the Japanese attack—John Hand, Neill Rae, Norman Young, William Feron, Jack McMahon, Ray Craw and Maurice Healy. Lt. Burt Dreyer, USMC, said that the pointer and trainer were found after the bomb burst slumped on their seats behind their sights, and the loader still had an unfired shell in his arms. Other members of the crew were lying in their regular positions. "I guess they must have kept on firing even when they saw the bombs dropping directly toward them. Brave men."[126]

Colin Ramsey of 22 Field Ambulance saw the aftermath of the attack:

> When we arrived the ship was on fire and down below were stores of fuel and munitions. The loading ramp was already down so we boarded and recovered the wounded and put them on the beach as soon as we could, all the while fearing the ship might blow up. We only had eight ambulances and each could only carry two casualties at a time. The hospital was five miles away so we had to make many return trips; meanwhile the wounded were lined up in order of priority, lying suffering on the beach in the sun and patiently awaiting their turn. The medical boys were doing what they could to make them comfortable. While all this was going on, dogfights were still happening overhead and one *Zero* was seen crashing into the sea. There was no one taking care of the wounded in the back, who depending on the road, could suffer terribly from the rough journey. If dressed wounds opened and bled, or if soldiers went into bad shock or were screaming with pain, nothing could be done for them until the ambulance arrived at its destination. Being mindful of this, we drove like hell, as fast and as safely as we could.[127]

Japanese air attacks were not limited to shipping. New Zealand ordnance personnel were caught up in an attack at 10 a.m. on 1 October. They were just about to disembark when the air raid began: "Fortunately, we had received the warning just in time to get off the ship and we rushed into the bush. Several of us found ourselves in the middle of a petrol dump as the strafing came through the trees. We made for a safer position and luckily stumbled along with some 20 others into a fox-hole intended for about eight."[128]

No. 17 Fighter Squadron, RNZAF, and U.S. pilots intercepted the third Japanese strike on shipping at Vella Lavella. There were twelve dive-bombers escorted by fifteen fighters. Opposing them were twelve F4-U Corsairs and eight RNZAF P-40 Kittyhawks. The New Zealand pilots shot down seven dive-bombers, and the Americans downed two fighters.[129] Squadron Leader M.J. Herrick, DFC, later reported:

1 October. No.15 F[ighter] Squadron on station over Vella Lavella—1430–1500 hours. Instructions to remain over shipping. I looked west and saw *Zeros* dog-fighting at considerable altitude up-sun, about 1430. We went in to attack about six *Vals* (plus).... We dived to meet them and they pulled out of their dive at about 2,000 feet. I then attacked one, firing a medium burst from above and astern at about 3,000 yards. Smoke started to come off his engine, another New Zealand P40 came in and finished it off. I then saw it hit the water. I also saw P40s everywhere, attacking *Vals* and several *Vals* crashing into the sea. I saw one *Val* heading up the "slot" at low level on the water and pursued him and saw smoke. He returned my fire. Ammunition short, so broke off attack and was followed by another *Zero* for about 10 or 15 miles at full bore 200 feet above the water making quarter attacks on me, but through violent skidding and jinking he did not hit me. I consider that the *Zero* that attacked me must be a new type with a new motor because it had plenty of speed.[130]

The aftermath of the Japanese air attack soured New Zealand–American relationships temporarily. Barrowclough confided to his diary that "among the casualties were the whole of the crew of one of our Bofor guns. The tragedy of this was that we had made arrangements for the early disembarkation of the Bofors guns and their move to preselected and prepared sites. The Captains of the LSTs would not facilitate the early landing of these guns with the result that they were less effective on board than they would have been on shore. I felt indignant about Navy's defiance of the instructions I had given."[131]

Barrowclough firmly believed that if his orders "had been carried out we would have suffered no casualties to that crew and it is just possible that with its better position ashore the gun might have saved the ship." He bitterly complained that his decisions had been "overruled by relatively Junior Naval Officers who are quite unfamiliar with our plans."[132] Wilkinson replied by expressing his condolences but pointed out that "the very fact that the gun was struck [meant] that it was in the best position to defend the ship against the planes coming directly at it."[133] The casualties would cause some sensitivity regarding the passage of New Zealand AA guns on LSTs in Operation Good-time (the invasion of the Treasury Islands, 27 October 1943). Barrowclough was determined that the experience would not be repeated.

The Marines' Frustrations

The Marine AA units on Vella Lavella found nights to be particularly frustrating. They were subjected to regular Japanese air raids but were under orders not to fire back in order to avoid giving away their gun positions.

Daytime also brought its frustrations. Some *Daihatsu* became so emboldened or desperate that they could be seen across the seven-mile strait separating Vella Lavella from Kolombangara. The Marines could not do anything about it, but some became so irritated that they fired their carbines at the barges.[134]

Vella Lavella and the Seabees

The Seabees of the 77th Naval Construction Battalion found more than their fair share of misery on Vella Lavella:

Each tent group dug a foxhole. Vella was a coral island and the rock was but thinly covered with top soil. The pick handles stung our hands as we chipped out small pieces of coral. The sweat poured into our eyes and coursed down our backs as we worked, for we were not yet fully acclimated to the heavy damp, tropic heat, but we got those holes down!

We needed those holes ... we spent most of each night in them, trying to avoid the dangers of from six to eight air raids a night was no picnic. An unbroken night's sleep was a blessing we were not to enjoy for many weeks. We sat in our holes with our heads stuck out like gophers through many dark hours watching the bright sprays of tracers, listening to the chatter of the 50s and the heavy bark of the 80mm, waiting for the earth-shaking "CRUMP" of the bombs. Ordinarily, we just got up a little before daylight and went to work, taking our sleepy eyes along with us.

Sometimes the vibrations of guns and bombs would cause a shower of ripe, ready-to-fall coconuts in our grove. There were always some falling, day or night and many men wore their steel helmets at all times. A coconut falling from a 50 foot palm deals a nasty blow! The ground was strewn with coconuts, some sprouting, some decaying.

Often, when a man left his tent in the unrelieved darkness of our complete blackouts, he would come upon a coconut in the wet grass so loaded with phosphorous that it glowed like a silver ball. Or he might find a wood or spray of grass that made a weirdly beautiful bouquet, another phenomena for our memories of the South Seas.[135]

Nor did the weather spare the Seabees:

Rain, hard driving, constant unending rain—and much rain meant much mud. This was a new sort of mud: stiff gooey mud that stuck to our feet and made them grow to the size of watermelons, so heavy we could hardly lift them. The dozers pushed the mud of the roads in camp and trucks churned up more mud. Finally, the roads went down three and four feet to solid rock and the truck wheels and dozer blades could cut no deeper, then the mud ran in from the sides and the roads were like canals holding a sluggish flow of mud. Always mud![136]

Japanese Aerial Supply

Despite the relatively small number of Japanese troops on Vella Lavella, they were not abandoned or forgotten by their commanders. Prior to the Pacific War the Japanese air forces had developed methods of aerial resupply, which they had used in their seizure of the Netherlands' East Indies and in the fighting along the coast of Papua New Guinea in 1942–1943. Similar attempts would be made to resupply the soldiers on Vella Lavella.

A New Zealand infantry patrol reported on 3 October having found "a parachute hanging from a tree 200 yards outside our perimeter. Upon investigation it was found to be attached to a large canvas bag containing medical

New Zealand troops display captured Japanese supply parachute container (photographer unknown; courtesy Archives New Zealand/Te Rua Mahara o te Kāwanatanga, Wellington Office, WAII, 7 3, Official Photograph Album).

supplies, food and cigarettes. It had probably been dropped by aircraft the previous night as it was thought the bombs dropped in the sea nearby were a signal to the Japs in the vicinity."[137]

The Japanese containers were dropped by multi-colored parachutes. Often these containers fell into the sea or into New Zealand hands. The New Zealanders were only too keen to use these "Tojo rations" to supplement their own.

The Japanese Response to the Seizure of Vella Lavella

The American capture of Munda on 5 August 1943 in large measure unhinged the Japanese defensive position in the Central Solomons. By 14 August, the Americans had the Munda airfield operational and were able to project airpower toward the heart of Japanese defenses. Between 6 August and 9 October 1943, the Japanese defense system in the Central Solomons began to collapse.[138] This was mainly due to Japanese inferiority in the air, leaving the Japanese unable to fend off Allied airstrikes and deliver blows of their own. As a result, they could not provide the necessary air support for their garrisons on Vella Lavella and Kolombangara.

The Allied seizure of Vella Lavella forced the Japanese to rethink their whole strategy regarding the Central Solomon Islands. The American invasion of Arundel, contemporaneous with the New Zealand clearing operations on Vella Lavella, demonstrated the Japanese soldiers' capacity for frustrating Allied plans. Japanese resistance on Arundel was intense and desperate as the Japanese commander, Major General Noboru Sasaki, fed reinforcements from the garrison on Kolombangara into the battle. Fighting petered out by 21 September largely because Sasaki had ordered the troops on Arundel to retreat to Kolombangara. The reason for this shift was that Imperial General Headquarters, disheartened by the declining Japanese fortunes in the Central Solomons, had resolved to abandon the New Georgia islands. It was decided to maintain the supply lines to the Japanese troops on Kolombangara with the intention that those troops would hold out for as long as they could and buy time for the Japanese to build up their defenses for the next battle on Bougainville.

The problem that the Japanese faced was that they did not know where the Allies would aim their main thrust—the Solomons or New Guinea. Imperial General Headquarters hedged its bets by decreeing that both areas were to be given equal priority. Rabaul received orders from Tokyo on 13 August

1943 that the forces in the Central Solomons were to resist while the defenses on Bougainville were built up, and that between late September and early October the Japanese would withdraw. Sasaki was not immediately told of the decision to abandon the Central Solomons, and he and his twelve thousand troops continued to work on establishing defenses. It was only after Sasaki had fed troops into the battle for Arundel that he learned of the change in strategy. His headquarters and planners from the Southeastern Fleet and 8th Fleet immediately began preparing for the withdrawal. Their plans involved pulling 12,435 soldiers out of harm's way. The resources available were limited and included between seventy to eighty *Daihatsus*, which could double as troop transports instead of supply barges.

Sasaki began collapsing his defenses, first ordering the withdrawal of troops from Gizo and Arundel to Kolombangara. Then the soldiers on Kolombangara began withdrawing in a series of evacuations on 28–29 September, 1–2 October, and 2–3 October. The withdrawals were implemented under cover of darkness. The U.S. Navy was not passive while Sasaki withdrew 9,400 soldiers. The Americans sank twenty-nine of the *Daihatsus* and torpedo boats and damaged a destroyer. Altogether, this was a small price to pay for the skillful withdrawal of so many soldiers.[139]

NINE

"Man Proposes, God Disposes"—
The Isolated Platoons

The Platoons Depart

War is full of tragedy. On Vella Lavella two inexperienced New Zealand platoons found themselves cut off from Allied lines and surrounded by Japanese soldiers intent on their annihilation. The story of these men reveals much about the fighting qualities of the New Zealanders and the vicious no-quarter nature of the war in the Solomons.

To the Allied commanders the situation appeared to be that the Japanese were falling back on Timbala Bay and that they were in disarray. They had been pounded and seemed to be a beaten force. The decision was made by Colonel Seaward to place a blocking force in their path of retreat as an anvil, so that the Japanese would be crushed by the hammer of the main force as it advanced to relieve the blocking force. At first sight, these assumptions appeared reasonable and the plan viable. However, events would show that jungle warfare, particularly against a determined Japanese foe, is complex and unforgiving.

The blocking force consisted of two platoons from the 35th Battalion, totaling some fifty men. The group led by Lt. John S. Albon, a thirty-nine-year-old pre-war salesman, was 14 Platoon. The second platoon was the Carrier Platoon, led by Lt. Joseph William Beaumont, a twenty-five-year-old regular soldier. The Carrier Platoon was a unit not normally used as infantry, and its deployment was indicative of the need to hurriedly cobble together the blocking force. Both platoons were trained but had yet to experience combat. The two lieutenants also were inexperienced.

On 26 September the two platoons were sent from Battalion Headquar-

Colonel Seaward and Islander guides at Timbala Bay (photographer unknown; courtesy Archives New Zealand/Te Rua Mahara o te Kāwanatanga, Wellington Office, WAII, 7 3, Official Photograph Album).

ters with orders from Colonel Seaward to occupy the top of a long ridge near Marquana, thereby creating a blocking position. It was intended that on 27 September, A, B and C Companies of the 35th Battalion, which were positioned at the mouth of the Tambala River, would, with the assistance of artillery, move forward and eventually relieve the blocking force. The plan seemed sound—what could possibly go wrong?

The two platoons left New Zealand lines and, guided by an Islander guide, Ati, marched all of Sunday but were still an hour away from the trail at dusk and had to call a halt. The march was resumed the following morning, and the track was reached. The platoons then proceeded to dig in and wait.

Although the track was relatively well worn by the Japanese since the American invasion, thick trees with flange-like roots predominated in the cleared areas. Some twenty to thirty yards from the trail the vegetation closed in; visibility was severely limited, and no landmarks could be seen.

Ambush

The first warning of trouble came from the Islander guide, who had been scouting forward. He saw forty Japanese soldiers close to the New Zealanders. "He was very excited and counted their numbers on his fingers."[1] The decision was made by Beaumont to split the force and send two sections up the trail, led by him, to ambush the Japanese. At midday the New Zealand troops were divided into two groups astride the trail, but "the approach of between ninety and 100 Japs froze them to the ground."[2] Successful ambushes in close jungle require considerable training, skill, fire discipline, good use of the ground and a measure of luck. In this case, the nature of the terrain made the use of infantry support weapons such as the Bren LMG difficult.

The ambush was botched. The Japanese were carrying rations and oblivious to the presence of Kiwi soldiers only some six feet away from them. The Kiwis did not know if further Japanese soldiers were in the area and realized that they faced envelopment and annihilation if an ambush failed. Beaumont in his report stated "with only two [sections] with me I did not think it wise to attempt an ambush."[3]

Beaumont's men held their fire and let the Japanese pass. That, however, left them in a highly vulnerable isolated position, and it left Albon's unsuspecting men in an even worse position. After the Japanese had passed, Beaumont and his men began to move back to rejoin the main group. However, as they did so, at about 1600 hours the Japanese attacked the main group in the gully. According to Beaumont, "The Japs had made a mass attack, jumping from tree to tree and letting go with all they had, light machine guns, grenades, and rifles. The platoon held them off with steady rifle fire and as soon as opportunity presented, the other platoon got a few bursts into the enemy's flank which allowed the platoon to rush over to the other side of the track and form a united defense. They poured a few magazines into the Japs who faded into the trees, losing several dead."[4]

Gillespie's official history, *The Pacific*, presents a slightly different version, with Beaumont and his men moving back to rejoin the main force only to hear Japanese machine gun fire in the distance. Albon's group had been surprised while having a meal (what about their sentries?) and had "rushed along the track and passed through Beaumont's men."[5] This suggests that Albon's group had left their food and gear behind and, having been routed, were running along the track, to be saved by Beaumont's men fortuitously arriving and providing covering fire.

Beaumont later described what occurred next:

They surrounded us as we lay on the side of a hill in a perimeter about twenty by thirty yards and roared round us shouting at the top of their voices and belting grenades and machine gun fire at us. They charged again, and we fired only when we saw a target. We tossed grenades behind trees and into hollows, and the Jap retired for half an hour. Then he came again, and one man, probably an officer, stood upright to take a look at us. Possibly he thought we were all dead, and he called out something. But we changed his shouting to a scream and no other Jap stood up to get the same fate.

Fortunately, we were left alone all night, though we could hear the Jap moving round us, and talking now and again. But he did not come in. We were short of rations now. We had had to abandon them in the first moments of the Jap attack. Our haversacks were lost too, and all that was left was what each man could carry in ammunition. Some did not even have their water bottles. The next day the Jap tried again, and every day until Friday, until the troops were so weak that they knew that remaining in their present position indefinitely would be fatal. On the Thursday, Lt. Albon and two men made a dash through the Jap lines to get word to headquarters, but the party on the ridge could wait no longer. They had taken sufficiently heavy toll of the enemy to make him extremely cautious. A score of Japs lay dead outside the Kiwi perimeter.[6]

As regards Albon, Beaumont later reported that on the Wednesday two men from Albon's platoon were reported missing. "Lt Albon also spoke to me on this day about getting a small party of two or three men out to bring back information to our HQ re our posn [position] etc." He then went on to write 'On Thur, Lt. Albon and two of his men made a break at approx. 1100 hrs. I did not speak to Lt. Albon during Thur morning.'[7]

Encircled

The men of 14 Platoon had been ambushed, and the hunters had become the hunted. Beaumont took command and formed an oblong defensive perimeter. The Japanese attempted to unnerve the defenders by screaming abuse in English and Japanese. They also attacked with machine guns, rifles and grenades during the day. By nightfall the defenders had suffered three killed and four wounded, including their signaler. To make matters worse, the wireless had been wrecked by machine gun fire, destroying any chance of communicating with Colonel Seaward. All firing ceased when night fell.

Back at headquarters there was concern at the lack of contact with the blocking platoons. Two platoons commanded by Major K. Haslett were sent on 27 September to locate the missing soldiers and rapidly ran into stiff opposition as they neared Marquana Bay. Haslett avoided a Japanese ambush and retreated back to safety. Torrential rain fell continuously, and wireless sets proved useless.[8]

News of what had happened to the blocking platoons was provided by Private D.W.T. Evans on the night of 29 September. He arrived at the New Zealand lines, gave an account of the ambush of Albon's platoon and had an incredible story to tell. He said that he had been captured by the Japanese but had managed to escape when his comrade, Private W.F.A. Bickley, had diverted their Japanese captors. Evans had followed the coast until he reached New Zealand lines. Sadly, his account was too vague to be of practical use.

His story was corroborated early the next morning when Private Bickley was picked up by a barge. He indicated that he, too, had escaped from the Japanese and had followed the coast to safety. "His story was that the Japs had stripped him naked. One 'Nip' was so intent on twisting Bickley's identity disc card round his neck that Bickley was able to kick him between the legs with his knee, pick up the rifle, swing it at the others and then go for his life through the bush to escape."[9] Both Evans and Bickley had escaped certain death at the hands of the Japanese. (One of their comrades was not so lucky.) But Bickley, like Evans, was very vague.[10] According to *The Pacific*, "Albon spoke to Beaumont on 29 September of attempting to reach headquarters to bring help. He slipped away the following morning taking two men with him, but when he reached headquarters his information was too vague to be of use."[11]

Seaward knew for certain that his two platoons were isolated and in deadly danger. The problem was fog of war—Seaward had no clear picture of what was happening.

Lindsay Adams was a liaison officer from Division HQ to Brigade HQ and found himself linked with Seaward's Combat Team. He recalled

> I found it difficult to get any information about how the leading patrols were getting on short of joining such patrols. This was not practicable for various reasons.... Signals communication, usually very good, was proving difficult so that the brigadier was not getting a clear picture of progress or action. His company commanders got to meeting each morning to plan what they would do. They felt happier relying on their own initiative than waiting for orders from someone partly in the dark.[12]

Seaward's worst fear was that the two platoons had been wiped out.

Although the trapped men had not been wiped out, their situation was desperate. Beaumont was not equipped to withstand a siege—most of the food, water and equipment had been lost in the Japanese ambush, and Beaumont's force faced dehydration, hunger, fatigue and the prospect of annihilation. Nonetheless, they held their perimeter for the next three days against determined Japanese attacks. Time was against Beaumont, as his men became progressively weaker. It was clear that they would be overwhelmed if they remained where they were. Beaumont made the decision to break through to the coast and, hopefully, help. The breakout began on the morning of 1 October. Beaumont recalled:

> So we cut poles for stretchers and prepared to fight our way to the coast, carrying the wounded with us. We had buried some of our dead; our losses in killed were very few. The morale of the wounded and unscathed was wonderful. Not a moan came from any of the wounded men. Those who could walk or help themselves did so. They needed water badly, but we had none to give them. We hoped to find some nearer the coast, and they had had nothing to eat for days.
>
> So on the Friday we fought our way out, through 1,000 yards of jungle track between us and the coast. We had plenty of fighting on the way, but it was better than sitting waiting to be picked off, and growing faint from hunger and thirst. It was wonderful how the men responded to the decision to get on the move. They brightened up, laughing as they fought down the hill, giving the Jap everything they had and taking good care of themselves. We had a few casualties, but nothing compared with what the enemy took.
>
> At the bottom, still inside the Japanese positions, we hauled the stretcher wounded through mangrove swamps of black mud oozing deep to our knees. There wasn't a groan from them. We managed to collect a little water after we had formed our new perimeter on the fringe of the bush—enough from a hole scraped in the mud and from the hollow of a tree stump to fill three water bottles. Two were reserved for the wounded. One I handed around amongst the rest. We had fifty-one in our party then, six of them wounded. When the one bottle had been passed around its allotted 45 men and came back to me there was still water in it. That will show the spirit of the men.[13]

Beaumont's position was established on the edge of the shore, and it was very precarious indeed. Then he and his men had an incredible stroke of good luck: an artillery officer in a barge, who had been cruising offshore looking for targets, noticed a group of men onshore waving wildly. The barge attempted to come closer but was prevented from landing by coral. Hopes of rescue rose. However, the Japanese were close at hand, as illustrated by the fact that Japanese aircraft dropped ration supplies by parachute to their soldiers on Friday evening, one of which landed in the center of Beaumont's perimeter. The men had their first meal in five days and relished fish cakes, plums, oatmeal and emergency food rations. The issue was whether their rescue would come in time or whether they would be annihilated.

The 35th Battalion history recounts:

> On Saturday, the sixth day, a barge returned with a rescue party on board. As it grated on the coral ledge off shore an artillery barrage was laid down just outside

the perimeter of the beleaguered troops while the main body of troops endeavored to force their way overland in support of the rescue.

One of the beach party crawled and swam towards the barge. Flashes of fire came from the screening bushes as two more of the beach party slowly crossed those 300 yards. One man reached the barge and an officer climbed over the side to help him in. He was shot from the shore as he leaned down to help the swimmer. A transport driver, who had volunteered to go with the original patrol and been the life and soul of the besieged party, clambered on board and manned a machine gun. A Jap bullet grazed his head and he fell to the bottom of the boat unconscious. On recovering he manned the gun again but was killed while his first bursts were peppering the bush on shore. The barge could not wait any longer and returned to its base.

The "transport driver" was Private R.J. ("Fitz") Fitzgerald, a popular member of the 35th Battalion. He was in the Motor Transport Section but had volunteered to be a rifleman. Before making his fateful swim to the barge, Fitz handed to one of his companions a Roman Catholic prayer book. This had been a source of great strength for him. He then swam out to what seemed to be the comparative safety of the evacuation barge. He clambered aboard and manned a Bren gun, providing suppressive fire. As noted above, he was knocked unconscious by Japanese fire but then recovered and recommenced firing. This time a Japanese sniper's bullet killed him.

Another rescue party was organized. Five men, including two officers, planned to swim ashore behind the protection of life jackets and haul in a rope by which at least the wounded could be evacuated. The barge moved in again, and the five men, vividly recollecting the fate of the first attempt, set out on that perilous crossing of the coral ledge. One stopped for a moment on the way in order to free the rope from a shelf of rock. He was the sole survivor. None ahead of him, who came directly into the Japanese fire, reached the shore, though Lieutenant Griffiths, who only two days before had gallantly led a platoon from a dangerous pocket under heavy fire, scrambled within a few yards of his goal before he fell.

The survivor of this group was 2nd Lt Gordon Graham. He commanded C Platoon, 35th Battalion. He later recalled:

> I became aware after the Brigade had begun combat operations that a couple of platoons had got into trouble. I understood that they were commanded by Lt Beaumont but I had not previously met him. I was at Battalion HQ when the Battalion commander came in and said "you've got to get on my boat and take it up. Do anything to help, help help!" He seemed desperate. I got into a landing craft with other people. It was a smallish American vessel. We had hardly arrived offshore when we encountered another similar vessel with three Yanks and a forward observer from the New Zealand army. We were offshore from Beaumont's patrol

and everything seemed quiet. Men were moving from the beach towards the vessels. We were aware that the patrol had wounded with them and they needed support to get to the rescue craft. A guy said to me to join their group which was going to take a telephone cable to the shore. It was daylight and there was no sound of gunfire. Beaumont's patrol seemed relatively close to where we were and they had wounded on shore. We took the cable and began dragging it to shore. At times we could walk on the coral and at other times the water was deep. There were seven of us in the rescue group. The cable became snagged on the coral. We could not go any further until it was cleared. I went back to the artillery FO's boat and pulled the cable free from the coral. I then went down the line towards the chaps of the rescue party who were almost ashore. I got close to them when I realized they were all dead. They had been shot by the Japanese. I was being shot at and decided to return to the boat. Thanks to my swimming experience I was able to save my life. I went deep underwater, would pop up and breathe and then go under water again. I reached the landing craft and got around to the opposite side to the shore. I got aboard. I told them what had happened. There were two casualties on the boat, one wounded and one killed by Japanese fire. It was decided to retreat out to sea. It was decided to send one craft back to return with the company commander and reinforcements. There was a call for volunteers to go ashore and bring out the survivors. Rubber dinghies were obtained. The volunteers got back about 7 pm and it was very dark. They got the wounded into the dinghies and the others had to walk or swim out. They got everybody back before midnight. Artillery was fired along the shore line. It was a bad morning but a good evening.[14]

Taking up their account once again, the 35th Battalion history recorded:

The night of the rescue, the shore party heard the barge engines about eight o'clock. Remembering the fate of the members of the rescue party who had died trying to reach the shore during the afternoon, they waited in suspense. The barge engines had stopped. There was no sound. They could see nothing in the blackness of the night. And then, six feet from the shore a head appeared, and another, and the dim outline of a canoe and rubber dinghy. A rope from the barges was secured, and first out were those who had been wounded. They were laid carefully in the two small craft. Their escort took knives to fight off the sharks. Then a dozen at a time the rest of the party slid into the water, crawled and swam to the boats. The perimeter on shore grew smaller, until at last six men, armed with grenades, remained. They slipped away unmolested. Clothing, watches, personal gear, were left on shore. Only the soldier's greatest friend, his rifle, Tommy gun or Bren gun went with him to safety.[15]

For the survivors, their deliverance seemed almost miraculous. The evening after their rescue they approached the padre and requested that a short service of thanksgiving be held. This spontaneous request made a powerful impression on the padre. He recorded:

Nor shall I ever forget the thanksgiving service which that little group of men spontaneously took part in behind the Iringila village Methodist Church on the

Sunday evening after the rescue. It was with deep sincerity and with a sense of great gratitude for a wonderful deliverance that they raised voices in unison in the words of the Doxology. I do not remember clearly what we talked about in that service, but I do recall that it was the most powerful and sincere time of worship that I have ever been privileged to conduct."[16]

The assumption that the Japanese were beaten had proven mistaken and their numbers grossly underestimated. However, the beleaguered force had maintained cohesion, and the fact that it carried off its wounded indicates good discipline. Potter later commented that "the action of this patrol in holding on to its position for that period (five days) was largely responsible for the success of the operation." Yet it had been too weak to be a blocking force, had been isolated for six days and had only been rescued by sheer luck and courage. The casualties involved constituted some of the heaviest in a 3NZ Division operation; on top of that, the Japanese were not blocked and were able to evacuate their forward positions and head toward Warambari Bay.

Seaward blamed the situation on bad information. In his post-action report he wrote:

"Man proposes and God disposes."
Our information proved to be far from correct. Instead of encountering 280 to 300 Japs half of which were believed to be unarmed and in poor condition while the remainder were believed to be armed with rifles and LMGs and in good condition, we ran into a hornet's nest consisting of 500 to 600 well-armed, hard fighting, first class Jap Marines.[17]

In assessing the conduct of Beaumont and Albon, Seaward reported:

Command of this party [referring to the two platoons] was assumed by Lieut. J.W. Beaumont when Lieut. Albon left them to, as he put it, get help. Lieut Beaumont's conduct throughout this operation has already been the subject of a special report to you. I consider his summary to be a true and elegant description of the trials his command suffered. The troops conduct throughout was most commendable.[18]

Beaumont was mentioned in dispatches. Yet, even so, Seaward did not recommend Beaumont for any award, nor, for that matter, any other members of the trapped platoons or those involved in their rescue. Gordon Graham discovered that he "had been recommended for a medal. However we were told that there were not going to be more than 22 medals awarded to the chaps in the Pacific. The chap from HQ who read me the letter suggesting I get a medal, later himself was awarded a medal. I did not get one."[19]

The rescue had been successful. John Rose, an officer with 35 Battalion recalled, "Seaward was in his mid 50s and had started to go to pieces under the strain. I went back and battalion operations were being run by Major Sid Moses from HQ. The rescue attempt was effectively run by the Adjutant and Company Commander."[20]

Seaward was making his operational decisions in a fog of war and in an ever-changing, dynamic, fluid environment. On some occasions New Zealand troops had encountered little or no opposition; on other occasions they encountered dug-in Japanese defenders who were only too willing to fight. Seaward's overconfidence is understandable, given his belief that he had superior resources to the Japanese, and he was under pressure to get his men moving forward to cut off what he believed were beaten, demoralized, ill-equipped Japanese defenders. Unfortunately, his men had to pay for his mistaken assumptions.

Major Burden of MIS tried to interest the Kiwis in dropping leaflets on Japanese positions inviting them to surrender. He was disappointed in the Kiwis' lack of interest in this idea.

Albon suffered a hernia as a result of fighting the Japanese. He reported that he had struck a tree root when throwing a grenade. He was exhausted by his experience and sent to a convalescent center, where he made a full recovery. He returned to New Zealand in 1944, where, on 10 June 1944, he was placed on the Reserve of Officers.[21]

Beaumont, by contrast, continued his career in the New Zealand Army. He rose to the rank of colonel and was involved in United Nations peace-keeping operations before his retirement.

Ten

The Final Push

As the Kiwis advanced to Warambari Bay, they encountered the problem of snipers. Doug Ross, an infantry officer with the 37th Battalion, had been sent to Vella Lavella to replace the platoon commander of B Company, who had been killed by a Japanese sniper. Ross noted that the snipers

> would tie themselves into the tops of trees and wait for us. When they were shot they would not fall because they had tied themselves in. We encountered isolated groups of Japanese who were covering the retreat of the main body. We would deal with them and then move on only to encounter another group. The Japanese were successful in evacuating their men from Vella Lavella. It should not have occurred but we were young officers and inexperienced. We did not always know what the hell was going on.[1]

Three companies of the 35th Combat Team had concentrated around Timbala Bay. The 35th Battalion War Diary notes, "1015, 28 September, Combat HQ reached Timbala Bay and met Coy. in vacated Jap bivouac area. Evidence of hasty evacuation during breakfast. Many cases of good rations including tinned salmon, herrings, and casks of fruit found besides rice. Also some 30 caliber ammunition. Number of Japs estimated thirty to forty." On 28 September, 12 Field Battery began firing at Japanese positions, with fire control undertaken by forward observers with the infantry and on a boat.[2] Once the artillery barrage ceased, the infantry advanced, though rain made progress extremely difficult.[3] B Company, to the north of Timbala Bay, encountered heavy resistance, called for reinforcements and dug in.[4] Potter ordered 35th Combat Team to cease large-scale attacks until the 37th Combat Team located the Japanese flank. On 1 October, 37th Combat Team established its artillery battery at Varuasi and both 35 Field Battery and 12 Field Battery were able to be mutually supporting. The Japanese had only Type 89 50mm "knee mortars" and could not counter the battery assaults, while their air attacks were largely ineffective because of the enveloping jungle, but efforts to push northwest were stymied by cunningly sited Japanese machine guns.

The Signalers

Communications were vital to the conduct of operations. However, the signalers faced considerable difficulties:

On 3 October Lance-Corporal D.E. Smith, Signalman C.A. Muir and M.G. Dwyer of E section, with a No. 21 set, participated in a landing by an advanced party of the 37th Battalion at Su Su Bay and were joined the next day by a further draft from the section. On the discovery by the infantry of the enemy's evacuation of this point a return was made to Tambama and preparation set afoot for a movement on 5 October when the section travelled in assault barges with the battalion to land under heavy automatic weapon fire at Warambari Bay. Signals were actually in the second barge to land, with the enemy less than 80 yards away, and their equipment was unloaded as bullets thudded into the trunks of the coconut palms fringing the water's edge. Local lines were laid within a confined perimeter, and wireless communication with advanced brigade headquarters was achieved "first call" by the ZC1 operator. Rear combat headquarters was also worked by wireless. Here, the wireless operators made the uncomfortable discovery that their set was only 50 yards away from an enemy sniper engaged in leisurely picking off troops from his tree top hideout, but a burst of Bren gun fire put an end to his activities. Lively skirmishes continued during that afternoon and night with members of the section remaining under fire as the beach-head was gradually enlarged. During the night the artillery commenced to shell the enemy positions, the shells falling barely 200 yards away from the perimeter. To members of E section inside the perimeter the thought of a "short one" was uppermost in their minds as they hugged the ground. During the first five days of October, No.1 company at advanced divisional headquarters had handled 1,000 dispatches for transmission by dispatch rider and safe handbag (air) while messages containing 14,887 groups, most of which were transmitted by wireless, had passed through their signal office.

On the completion of the composite cable party's task on the 35th Battalion side of the battle, its members were conveyed by barge to the 37th Battalion's field of activity, landing at Tambama to amalgamate with E section's cable party and commence the construction of a line through unpatrolled enemy territory to the 37th Battalion, newly dug in at Warambari. Allowing an extra mile and a half of cable for the unpredictable route of the jungle, the party carried 882 lbs of W110 cable in addition to their own personal effects and weapons as they commenced their expedition through the jungle—a map distance of three miles. With native guides (who were not always sure of their position in the jungle, but possessed an uncanny sense for "smelling out" the enemy) line was laid across knee-deep mangrove swamps and crocodile infested rivers. Visibility at its best was limited to 25 yards—it was usually not more than five yards but protection was still being accorded the party by the field security section. K rations and coconuts provided the only nourishment and at nightfall the party slept in a circle with every fourth man awake for a two-hour picket. To complete the nervous tension, no movement, no talking, and no smoking was permissible. Work commenced again at daybreak. On the second day the cable ran out, necessitating a request (over the line) for further supplies to be brought around the coast by barge. The cable soon arrived, together with a much appreciated replenishment of fresh water, and the barge returned to Tambama with a member of the party suffering from dysentery.[5]

The Pincers Clang Shut

As the Japanese were pushed further northward, their position became increasingly fraught with danger. Nonetheless, they still maintained dogged resistance.

On 3 October, 12 Battery assisted infantry with the neutralization of enemy positions in a gully at Joroveto at 0900 hours. There were pauses to allow the infantry to observe the results. Artillery fire continued to 1130 hours, and as night fell, harassing fire was maintained.

The Japanese continued to resist fiercely. On 5 October, during landing operations around Warambari Bay, Private A. McCullough was hit in both hands and one leg by Japanese machine gun fire. In the course of close-quarter fighting he picked up and flung back a Japanese grenade, which killed one of the enemy. For this he was given the Military Medal.[6]

On 6 October, 35 Battery found its role limited because infantry patrols were probing the area around Matu Suroto Bay. As night fell, the battery fired 172 shells on an area 200 yards south of the head of Marquana Bay. At Varuasi a Japanese machine gun position that had been causing casualties among the soldiers of the 37th Battalion was vigorously shelled by D troop, 35 Battery. Then A troop, 12 Battery, moved forward to Pakoi Bay. In the late afternoon, 12 Battery pounded Bolondu Island in the middle of Marquana Bay, where it was believed there was a concentration of Japanese. At night 35 Battery fired harassing fire, which had to cease due to low-flying Japanese planes. The noises of Japanese barges was heard offshore of Marquana Bay, but the temptation to open fire was resisted.[7]

One of the probing infantry patrols ran into trouble. An officer, Lt. Nicholls, was hit by Japanese fire close to their positions. He was seen by his men to fall. One of them, Corporal L.N. Dunlea, volunteered to go and bring Nicholls to safety. Despite heavy Japanese fire, he rushed forward, picked up Nicholls' body and returned to safety. Sadly, his efforts were in vain, for

Nicholls was found to be dead. Dunlea was later awarded the Distinguished Conduct Medal.[8]

> By nightfall on 6 October both battalions were in range of each other, with the Japanese trapped in a neck of land dividing Warambari Bay from Marquana Bay, towards which 35th Battalion had inched forward at 300 to 600 yards a day, finally losing contact with the enemy. A prisoner taken that day stated that about 500 well organised troops were trapped. They were short of food, evidence of which were the broken coconuts found in deserted bivouacs, and wished to surrender, but were prevented from doing so by their officers. Potter who had conducted the operation from advanced headquarters at Matu Soroto decided to close the gap. Both of the covering batteries were tied in on a common grid and came under regimental control.[9]

On 7 October, artillery pounded the area around the southern shore of Marquana Bay. This was repeated on 8 October. However, the presence of low-flying Japanese aircraft limited the firing, which ceased in order to avoid giving away the position of the guns.[10] As *The Pacific* laconically observes, "This lack of aggression undoubtedly enabled the enemy to escape!"[11] Maybe, but that judgment is made with the benefit of hindsight. At the time it made good tactical sense not to give away battery positions and render them vulnerable to air attack.

Lindsay Adams experienced the Japanese aircraft:

> That night [7 October] there had been a bit of light bombing of Vella Lavella by the Japs as an added nuisance. I was asleep at Div HQ that night when "condition red" was sounded on the siren to tell us to get into our compulsory "foxholes." Ron Wakefield and I had constructed a slit trench quite elaborately with a log roof of sorts. Suddenly the siren went and we heard the unmistakable sound of the light Jap plane which often at night flew over our campsites to drop small anti-personnel bombs here and there. A plane straight overhead with albeit a small bomb is disconcerting enough to make one value a slit trench. Some he-men pretended, but when "washing-machine Charlie" flew close enough for one to distinguish the unsynchronized sound of his engine, likened to that of an early vintage washing machine, the hardiest of men were quite pleased that the use of the slit trench was compulsory.
>
> The siren went and Ron beat me to our foxhole.[12]

For Barrowclough, the tactical situation was unclear. He noted in his diary on 7 October that he had received a report of a destroyer action north of Vella Lavella. He also noted that the expected LSTs had not arrived.

> In the battle area 35Bn was still out of touch with the enemy. There were some signs of a portion of the Jap garrison having been evacuated but this was not clearly demonstrated. At all events the enemy seem to have left the Marquana Bay area. Enemy points of resistance were being encountered by the 37 Bn in the WARAMBARI BAY area.[13]

At 10:30 a.m. patrols from A Company 35th Battalion linked up with patrols from B Company 37th Battalion in the vicinity of the Kazo River. All that could be found were abandoned Japanese bivouacs, equipment and bodies.

On 7 October, infantry patrols advanced toward Warambari and Marquana. By nightfall units had taken the southern end of Marquana Bay, and troops were moving in from the northern side. A smokescreen was laid by artillery fire to help a patrol land on Bolondu Island, where a Japanese prisoner was taken. He provided details regarding the location of the Japanese headquarters. Preparations were made to shell the Japanese positions the following morning preceding an infantry assault.

Attempts were made to persuade the Japanese to surrender. A leaflet in Japanese was distributed by Islanders in the Marquana-Warambari areas, urging the Japanese to give themselves up and promising that "we will gladly accept anyone that surrenders." The Japanese were instructed to go to the beach at 0900 hours, take their shirts off, put their hands over their head and with a white flag at the head of the group come out to the shore where the American troops are. "We promise that you will be given plenty of food, medical treatment and kind treatment." There is however, no evidence that any Japanese soldier acted on this leaflet.[14] An obvious reason is that by the time the leaflets were distributed, most of the Japanese would have left the island.

One Japanese sailor in a pitiable state was captured on 8 October in the area of Warambari Bay. Superior Seaman Toshio Yamashita, a 22-year-old former coal miner from Uwajima-Shi, had joined the Japanese Navy in 1942 and eventually was assigned to barge duty. Two *Daihatsu* barges left Buin around the middle of September to deliver rations and ammunition to Japanese troops. They stayed one night at Vella Lavella, and then both barges were sunk. Yamashita swam ashore and wandered around for three days, searching for coconuts and food. He was shot by .256-caliber bullets by an unseen rifleman in the darkness. He then crawled around the bush for five days. On 8 October a New Zealand patrol saw movement in the bush and heard what appeared to be crying. They captured Yamashita. His wounds were treated, and he was evacuated on 9 October 1943.[15]

On 8 October a friendly fire tragedy was narrowly averted. Patrols planned for the Marquana area were almost shelled by 12 Battery due to a breakdown in wireless communication. Fortunately, the barrage began before the infantry set out.

That same day the infantry moved into the Japanese positions, only to find them abandoned. As the U.S. Army historian John Miller observes, "The last organized bodies of Japanese had left the New Georgia area."[16] Barrow-clough noted in his diary, "Early morning situation reports still showed no contact with the enemy. At about 1100 hours we received advice from Brigadier Potter that the whole of the peninsula area had been searched with negative results and that all Japanese resistance had ceased. There were indications that some of the garrison had been evacuated."[17]

Potter declared at 10 a.m. on 9 October that the Brigade had completed its mission.[18] For the Kiwis, it seemed an anti-climax. As *The Gunners* observed:

> It seemed a disappointing finish. Although we had done our job and slain many of the enemy and cleared the island of the remainder it would have seemed more complete if the land forces had forced the surrender or death of them all. But our objective had been achieved. Brigadier Potter had undertaken to complete the operation in a fortnight and we had done it in 10 days.[19]

The Naval Battle of Vella Lavella, 6–7 October 1943

By October 1943 the Imperial Japanese Navy was being worn down in the South Pacific as the USN was reinforced, having absorbed the bitter lessons meted out by the IJN in the night fighting off Guadalcanal. Nonetheless, the IJN remained a formidable force, especially its cruisers and destroyers. One skill that the IJN had acquired was the evacuation of Japanese soldiers from South Pacific islands. The evacuation of the Japanese from Guadalcanal in January 1943, under the noses of the Americans, had been masterly. As the Japanese retreated up the Solomons chain, the skill of the IJN at pulling off a Japanese Dunkirk would be needed again.

From the Japanese perspective, there was no point in remaining on Vella Lavella. Forces on Kolombangara had been evacuated and an outpost on Vella Lavella was no longer necessary. The decision was made to evacuate the approximately six hundred Japanese troops from Vella Lavella. It was an article of faith that, despite intense interservice rivalry, the IJN would rescue its countrymen. Rear Admiral Baron Matsuji Ijuin was given the task by the Eighth Fleet. The resources he was given were three transport destroyers, four sub-chasers, twenty barges and six destroyers. The risk to these ships would have justified the abandonment and sacrifice of the Japanese troops on Vella Lavella. However, naval honor was involved, as well as an inherent sense of superiority over their American opponents.

Captain Tameichi Hara, the captain of *Shigure*, later characterized the operation as "ludicrous" and pointed out that the six hundred soldiers at

Horaniu were to be transported a mere fifty miles to Buin in southern Bougainville. To add particular pathos to the whole project, some four hundred of the evacuees from Vella Lavella had been delivered to Horaniu by Admiral Ijuin only six weeks earlier.[20] The result was, according to Hara, "one of the most confused encounters of the Pacific War."[21]

The Americans became aware on 6 October 1943 that the Japanese force had left Rabaul on its way southward. The problem that the USN commanders had was that there were only six destroyers available, and these were divided into two groups of three apiece separated by twenty miles.

The main Japanese transport group of barges was headed southeast to Vella Lavella escorted by six destroyers. Despite the risks of being outnumbered three to one and defeated, the American commander of the most northerly American destroyer group, Captain Frank R. Walker, decided to commit his force to battle rather than wait to be reinforced by the southern destroyer group commanded by Captain Harold Larson. The two opponents groped around each other amid rain squalls and utter darkness. American radar located the Japanese transport group at 2231 hours, and Japanese lookouts glimpsed the American force but overestimated its size. Both sides opened fire on each other at 2256 hours with guns and torpedoes. The superior Japanese Long Lance torpedoes scored their first hit on the American force when USS *Chevalier* was struck on the port bow, blowing it apart up to the ship's bridge. This disaster was compounded when the next destroyer in line, USS *O'Bannon*, rammed into the stricken *Chevalier*. The Japanese did not have it all their own way, though. HIJNS *Yugumo* was hit by American gunfire and torpedoes; having been torn apart, it sank quickly. The sole remaining USN destroyer, USS *Selfridge*, determinedly closed with the Japanese transports but found herself engaged by the destroyers *Shigure* and *Samidare*. The Japanese ships launched torpedoes, and at 2306 hours one struck the *Selfridge* on the forward port side, which brought her to a sudden stop.

Japanese aircraft then saw three American destroyers racing up the coast. Mistakenly, they reported their sighting as three cruisers. Thinking that he was likely to be facing a superior enemy force with the benefit of deadly radar-controlled guns, Ijuin ordered his eight ships to retire to their base at Rabaul. The Japanese destroyers retreated northward. When the southern destroyer group commanded by Commander Larson arrived on the scene, they found wreckage and men in the water. *Chevalier* was beyond salvage, and Larson ordered her sunk by torpedoes. The damaged *O'Bannon* and *Selfridge* limped back to Tulagi for repairs. Captain Henry Doscher recalled:

It was quite a sight when these destroyers limped into Tulagi Harbor, their bows completely blown off forward of their bridge area. Stub-nosed bulkheads just below the bridge were the most forward portion of each ship that remained visible. How they stayed afloat was a tribute to the resourcefulness of their officers and men. With help from the repair ship *Argonne*, each ship was shored-up as best as possible under the circumstances. This enabled each of them to make their way slowly across the Pacific in order to obtain major repairs and rebuilding so both could fight again.[22]

Strategically, the Japanese got the better of their American adversaries. While the battle was being fought, the barges crept stealthily into Marquana Bay, loaded up the soldiers and headed north to safety.

The following day American P.T. boats searching along the coast of Vella Lavella plucked seventy-eight survivors from the sunken *Yugumo*.[23] Despite this Japanese loss, the Americans had suffered the worst, losing *Chevalier* and sustaining significant damage to *O'Bannon* and *Selfridge*. However, Halsey was better able to absorb his losses than his Japanese counterpart. This would be one of the last Japanese surface victories of World War II.

More significantly, the Japanese had achieved the aim of their mission— they had pulled off another Japanese Dunkirk, and 589 of their soldiers survived to fight another day for their Emperor.[24] For the Japanese there were disturbing elements to this victory, however. The Americans had displayed incredible, almost suicidal aggression, attacking a larger Japanese force. As the historian Paul Dull observes, "Captain Walker should certainly have waited for Larson's destroyers—but he seemed to have a little bit of banzai in him, too."[25] As Hara later commented, "Naval battles are, always filled with blunders, illusions and surprises."[26]

For the USMC troops on Vella Lavella, the naval battle was cause for considerable anxiety. They thought that the Japanese might be counter-invading. Major Donald Schmuck recalled that they spent the night deployed on the beach, crouched in their foxholes with loaded guns ready to repel a Japanese invasion. The next morning he took an LCVP to sea in front of his unit's area, only to find the sea littered with wreckage, including unexploded torpedoes and bodies, some in parachutes.[27]

Frank Rennie recalled that three days after the evacuation of the Japanese troops, an Islander armed with a cane knife brought into the Kiwi camp a very nervous prisoner. The Islander explained that two Japanese had washed up on Vella Lavella, having been in the water for three days. One had been severely wounded, and the Islander had finished him off. The other he delivered to the Kiwis. The prisoner, having identified Rennie as an officer, requested that Rennie shoot him. When this was denied and the prisoner was given tea, a cigarette and dry clothing, he began to open up. He was a doctor in the Imperial Japanese Army and held the rank of staff sergeant. His English was understandable, and he questioned Rennie on how the New Zealanders felt about being in the Solomon Islands when the Japanese occupied New Zealand. Try as he might, Rennie could not shake him from this propaganda-based belief.[28]

Aftermath

General McClure was dissatisfied with the Kiwis' performance. He commented that he "believed that the Vella Lavella operation could have been shortened and the defenders wiped out." He maintained that "had sufficient landing craft been available I could have cut off Jap forces on Vella with small local amphibious operations." That was what Potter had attempted to do, but the lack of sealift assets had prevented his success. The jaws of the pincers clanged shut on an empty space. Potter did not stop the Japanese from withdrawing by sea, but neither did the U.S. Navy. Nonetheless, the complete annihilation of the Japanese force had come tantalizingly close for the New Zealanders. Full credit should be given to the Japanese Navy for carrying out an extremely difficult amphibious operation under Allied noses. To state the obvious, the New Zealanders had completed their primary mission—the elimination of Japanese forces from Vella Lavella—and they had done so in an expeditious fashion with limited casualties.

The butcher's bill for the New Zealanders was relatively small—four officers and 28 other ranks killed, and one officer and 31 other ranks wounded.[29] The Americans had 58 dead and 166 wounded.[30] Japanese casualties are unknown but were likely in excess of 250 soldiers killed.

Combat fatigue had set in for some. A New Zealand soldier, Jack Humphrey, recalled the recovery of a New Zealand casualty and being furious at what he thought was a waste of a life. He sat in a foxhole and was approached by Admiral "Bull" Halsey. Halsey consolingly said, "You have had a rough time of it," clearly recognizing that the Kiwi was upset.[31]

Warfare is full of vagaries and chance. A soldier from the 37th Battalion "recovered a machete from a dead Jap, the scabbard bearing the initials of a 35th friend of mine. Much later I learned that he had been on the sick list and it had been borrowed by a less fortunate soldier."[32]

ELEVEN

Consolidation and Development

Vella Lavella Is Secured

Even though Vella Lavella was declared to be secured, it was recognized that groups of desperate, hungry Japanese were still likely to be on the island, and precautions needed to be taken to prevent them from stealing supplies. An order laconically noted, "Parties proceeding inland must allow for the possibility of being fired upon."[1]

In the aftermath of the fighting, the various infantry companies were dispersed in campsites around the island. The 35th Battalion history records:

We continued to sleep on the ground with only a leaf shelter above us; the same C and K ration was still eaten and clothes could not be changed. Tropical deluges kept the ground in a continual state of slushy mud; thus we existed till such time as tents, personal gear and cookhouse gear arrived.... In most instances the complete gear for the companies did not arrive till the end of the month.[2]

On 11 October, the 35th Battalion War diary stated, "Personal gear started to arrive from MARAVARI. The receipt of this gear was much appreciated as it enabled all ranks to change from jungle suits which had been their clothing since the 21st Sept. Equally welcome was that cooking equipment began to arrive and this provided relief from the 'K' and 'C' rations the men had been eating."[3] The ability to wear clean clothes and shave did wonders for morale.

Japanese Air Raids—"Washing Machine Charlie"

The evacuation of their forces from the island merely meant that for Japanese aircraft the island became a free-fire zone. Japanese planes, on the night of 9-10 October, made this point by bombing the Kiwis' forward and gun positions. Thereafter nocturnal bombing raids occurred regularly:

Divisional Engineers' mascot "Sapper." HQ 3NZ Divisional Engineers, 1943 (photographer unknown; courtesy Archives New Zealand/Te Rua Mahara o te Kāwanatanga, Wellington Office, WAII, 7 3, Official Photograph Album).

In ones and twos, Japanese light-bombers and reconnaissance planes came over almost nightly and for the bombers their objective was the airstrip at Barakoma. Their aim was usually wide of the mark. Reactions to bombing were varied. There were those (a) who sat on the cot, tin hat in hand, waiting for the siren (b) those who made for the slit trench when the siren moaned (c) those who got in their shelters when the planes were overhead (d) those who jumped into anybody's shelter, nearly killing the occupants, when the bombs fell and (e) those who slept on. One very nervous soldier was dubbed "the man with the radar ears." He could hear Jap planes, or said he could, when no one else could. The story is told of Dave, an infanteer, who during an air raid was racing for his fox-hole. Unfortunately, he had left his braces trailing and his mate Tom, following hard on his heels, stepped on them. Dave was thrown on the flat of his back with a resounding smack. "Go for your life, Tom," he cried, "they've got me."[4]

The attitude of the men of the MMG Company to Japanese nocturnal bombing underwent a profound change after a nocturnal raider straddled their bivouac area with bombs. "A poor view was taken of this, especially by those who had dug fox-holes, as they found themselves more or less substituting as groundsheets for those who had not."[5]

As many as six air raids took place at night, which had a wearing effect on the troops. They became sleep deprived and exhausted. It was recognized that this could only be resolved by providing splinter-proof bomb shelters for sleeping. Ultimately it would be the suppression of Japanese airpower that solved matters.

There was a belief among the New Zealand wireless operators that the Japanese planes were homing in on the "send" signal emitted by their radio stations. "Some operators therefore took no chances on being on the receiving end of stick of bombs and they promptly switched off their sets on the approach of enemy planes."[6]

There was also the belief that the Japanese were dropping 250-kilo bombs with a delay fuse of two or three hours. This meant that unexploded bombs had to be marked and an area of 100 yards kept clear on all sides. Unexploded bombs had to be dealt with by specialist personnel.[7]

The nightly incursions of "Washing Machine Charlie" caused severe irritation to the New Zealand soldiers. The Japanese float plane, with its navigation lights on and cheekily flying only a few hundred feet from the ground, made regular trips over Vella Lavella to drop supplies for Japanese soldiers and bombs for the New Zealanders. In early October 1943 the machine gunners of No. 2 MMG Platoon, attached to the 35th Battalion, decided that they had had enough. They gathered together four Vickers and one Bren gun and decided to set up an ambush for their nocturnal visitor. They held a trial shoot just before dusk, which "produced a gratifying volume of fire." The soldiers then settled down and waited for their prey.

> About 8pm a droning could be heard in the distance and excitement ran high till, out of the darkness loomed four big bombers roaring towards us. Needless to say our murderous thoughts vanished like lightning as we dived for cover. As an anticlimax the bombers absolutely ignored us and droned serenely onwards. Evidently our friend "Charlie" had read our thoughts as we did not see him again after that.[8]

Sometimes Japanese aerial activity was of a more benign nature. The 37th Battalion war diary noted on 18 October 1943, "A food parachute showing little sign of the weather was found by C Coy Patrol in TAMBAMA BAY area. We wonder if the Japs really think we need food as badly as the dropping of a parachute would suggest!"[9]

New Zealand troops were used for the vital role of unloading supply vessels. The Japanese air raids had a wearing effect on the nerves of these men:

> In view of the determined attacks by Jap dive bombers on the LSTs battalion[,] working parties were a little "jittery" when unloading in the holds of the ships. At Barakoma beach one morning when the men were working inside the LST, an offi-

cer who had received word of an air raid alarm over the phone went to the entrance
of the ship and cried—"Condition red—air raid—condition red." He was nearly
killed in the rush as men spewed out of the hold and broke even time for the hundred yards as they sprinted for the jungle, tripping over coconut logs, their mates,
laughing and shouting and clutching their tin hats. But the Japs didn't come near,
for overhead was our fighter cover from the Munda, New Georgia airfields, with
pilots eager to get a Jap plane to their credit.[10]

An ambulance driver, Colin Ramsey, recalled:

> We were also subject to nuisance raids at night and we could always tell by the
> engine noise whether it was a Jap bomber overhead or one of ours. Not far from
> us was a fighter airstrip, so the bombers had a few targets to choose from. We called
> the Jap bombers "Washing Machine Charlie" because instead of the usual steady
> drone, the engines were unsynchronized and made a very distinctive sound. We
> had anti-aircraft guns around the hospital but didn't fire them at night, as every
> third shot was a tracer and that would give our position away. When the Japs
> dropped their bombs, you could hear them spinning through the air, and hoped
> they weren't going to land close to you. We got away with it most of the time.[11]

The Japanese ability to carry out daylight airstrikes was now severely
inhibited by their withdrawal from Kolombangara. They no longer had
observers on the island who could spot shipping movements and call in airstrikes. On 20 October 1943, Barrowclough noted that "12th Echelon arrived
without incident. There was not even a condition 'Red' throughout the day.
The Japs ability to interfere with our convoys seems to be at an end."[12]

Nocturnal air raids nonetheless continued. A New Zealand soldier
recalled:

> One night in December 1943 anti-personnel bombs were dropped by Jap bombers
> in the lines of A Company and the mortar platoon. Almost simultaneously with
> the sounding of the alarm bombs fell among the tents. A bridge evening was being
> held in the tents at A Company at the time, and as the explosions came closer nine
> frantic men endeavoured to get into the one fox-hole. One lad, who was at the end
> of the queue, saw that his prospects of getting in were nil and cried out what he
> thought would be his famous last words—"Good luck you fellows—good luck."
> On the same occasion another lad in his excitement tried to blow out his electric
> torch! It all sounds funny now but how little humour there was in those bombings
> at the time we all know.[13]

An Unpleasant Discovery

As life settled down, the body of a New Zealand private from the 35th
Battalion, Private H. G. Corcoran, part of Beaumont's platoon, was discov-

ered.[14] Corcoran had been posted as "missing" by Beaumont, but he had in fact been captured by the Japanese. He had been strung up to a tree and bayoneted by his captors.[15] Word of the atrocity spread among the Kiwi troops. The likelihood is that the unidentified perpetrators were killed either on Vella Lavella or elsewhere. No one was brought to account. Sadly, such atrocities were commonplace in the Pacific War.

The New Zealanders had not been exposed to the brutalizing effects of sustained combat. There was therefore a range of attitudes toward the Japanese. Some did not feel any hatred for them—they were simply an enemy to be vanquished, and once the job was done the soldier could return home. For others, influenced by Japanese atrocities and Allied propaganda, the Japanese were a subhuman species to be sent to the nether regions of hell.

Ralph Williams, a New Zealand signaler, described how he and his comrades had been sent on a reconnaissance patrol to find Japanese survivors:

> We had to go through the jungle and we had stuff on us to make ourselves inconspicuous—burnt chalk to camouflage ourselves. A man felt a bit of a goat, in a way, but we went. We came through the jungle to a sort of bivouac where the Japanese had been, and it had one survivor. This poor, emaciated little fellow, a Japanese soldier, the only one in the camp. And someone just shot him. I felt awful. To see a bloke shoot the Japanese. He had no weapon, nothing. And that really hit me hard. I said, "Look no need to do that. He was defenceless, he had nothing."
>
> Some were highly delighted that he'd knocked him off, but I felt it was awful because he was so pathetic, half starved, and he had no weapon. I didn't like that one little bit. I wasn't the only one who felt that way.[16]

Threats from Nature

Sometimes nature presented more of a threat than the Japanese. On 21 December 1943, a storm hit the island in the early hours of the morning.

> During the height of a storm, a huge tree, 70 feet long and over three feet through snapped off like a twig about four feet from the ground. The noise of the splintering trunk awoke the men sleeping nearby but they had not time to move before the heavy weight of timber crashed to earth. The tree fell right between two tents less than eight feet apart. Solid branches flattened both tents, and Len Cooper was struck heavily across the back. He suffered from shock and internal injuries and was removed to the ADS. Jack Pawsey was pinned to his bed and with tent folds enveloping him, he was nearly suffocated by the time his mates dragged him clear.[17]

Then, on the morning of Christmas Eve, the troops were awakened "by an earthquake which shook the ground for what seemed to be several minutes."[18]

Command Changes and Departures

The end of the fighting brought command changes. On 15 October, Barrowclough met with Colonel Seaward. He told Seaward that he was recommending him for the DSO, but that after it was received Barrowclough intended to send him back to New Zealand. Barrowclough explained that, at fifty-eight, he was too old for a battalion command, particularly now that there were younger officers with battle experience. Seaward indicated that he would be sorry to go, but he realized the fairness of the decision.[19] Seaward was not alone. Cornwall also relinquished command of the 30th Battalion. Barrowclough made the decision to purge all his officers over the age of forty-one unless there were special reasons for retaining them. He considered "the conditions of service here are so strenuous that they cannot be relied on from the physical point of view in a real emergency."[20] Barrowclough's aim was "to revitalize the whole force" with the infusion of new blood.

Another person leaving Vella Lavella was the "Bish." The Reverend Silvester left in November 1943 and returned to New Zealand. Two years later he and his wife came back to Vella Lavella and remained there until 1952. Silvester was awarded the American Medal of Merit by President Harry S Truman on 13 January 1946, "for extraordinary fidelity and exceptional meritorious conduct." Silvester continued as a Methodist minister and retired in 1966. As the Methodist history by G.G. Carter comments, "The resourcefulness, the cheerfulness of deep faith and commitment to Christ and his people were marks of 'Wattie' Silvester's service in peace and war."[21]

Josselyn also left Vella Lavella and was relieved by Flying Officer Spencer, RAAF, as Coastwatcher. Spencer visited the 35th Brigade on 17 October 1943, accompanied by Bamboo; arrangements were made for the building of bures for the soldiers, and the delicate issue of troops passing through villages and gardens was addressed.[22]

The Islanders

The Islanders had previously hidden in the hills. Now they began to return and survey the damage to their villages and their island. A New Zealander observed sadly that "it was educational to come across a little native boy gazing reflectively at one of our shell-holes, and perhaps marveling at the 'wonders' of civilization."[23] The end of the jungle fighting also meant that the troops now came into contact with the Islanders. The Islanders had fled into the hills when the Japanese arrived, and they had experienced a really hard time. The Kiwis were warned not to intrude but to let the local people make contact with them.

In the early hours of Christmas morning 1943, Frank Rennie and his comrades were awakened by a procession of Islanders moving through their tent lines singing "Hark the Herald Angels Sing!" The Islanders then climbed the track up to the hills. Rennie noted, "It was an experience as moving as it was unexpected."[24]

A common element shared by the New Zealanders and the Islanders was the Christian religion. The unofficial history *Headquarters* recorded:

> The natives were extremely friendly; most of them spoke exceptionally good English and Christian name greetings were always exchanged as friendships grew. Many men took the opportunity of attending the open air church services held by the natives in the jungle on Sundays. Deprived of their churches through enemy action the natives used logs to form the rostrum and seating accommodation for the congregation. The services were in native tongue interspersed with hymns by the Kiwis but the spontaneity of the strange native voices singing familiar hymns in four-part harmony was indeed a musical treat. On one occasion at Maravari the New Zealand band added to this scene of native sincerity which was exemplified by daily conduct and in the assistance given to New Zealand forces.[25]

The Islanders came to Kiwi lines to obtain medical treatment. There was puzzlement on the part of the Kiwis when the Islanders complained of "mission bell ears" and "head bit aches." The cause of this mysterious malady was that they had obtained a box of American Army hand grenades. The Islanders had tried to use these for fishing by throwing them into a pool to stun the fish. Unfortunately, in their eagerness they had leaped into the water once the grenades had been thrown in, with potentially deadly effects. The Kiwis then persuaded the Islanders to exchange the box of grenades for some bottles of aspirin.[26] Medical treatment by New Zealand medical personnel was also made available to locals on the outlying islands such as Simbo.[27]

The Islanders had provided informal Coastwatchers, guides, labor and succor, and they proved solidly pro–Allies. The 17th Field Regiment raised £300 in appreciation so that a hospital ward could be erected at Bilboa. The villagers of Mundau, near Boro, likewise provided men to build bures (native huts) for the soldiers of the 37th Battalion.

It was recognized that the relationship between the Islanders and the Allied troops needed to be handled with care and respect. Seaward issued an order that presents were not to be given directly to Islanders but sent through the Reverend Silvester in order to prevent jealousy. It was also suggested that gifts be in the form of goods rather than money because the Islanders did not appreciate the difference between one kind of money and another. An official trading post was set up where the soldiers could purchase souvenirs such as baskets, mats, canes, walking sticks and combs. Seaward commented, "The natives on the whole are friendly and entirely cooperative with our Forces. Do not abuse their friendship and do not make fun of their customs. On the other hand, do not allow them any too great liberties. Remember, in all dealings with natives be friendly yet firm." In the same order, Seaward pointed out that the prevalence of animal tuberculosis on Vella Lavella and the neighboring islands rendered the cattle unfit for human consumption. The troops were thus prohibited from shooting the cattle.[28] By contrast, Lieutenant Colonel Sugden took a much simpler approach and ordered that "donations to, and trading or other traffic with local natives is prohibited."[29]

Sometimes circumstances and cultural ignorance led to problems with the New Zealand–Islander relationship. One situation was the pilfering of fruit from local food supplies by the Kiwi soldiers. Complaints were received by Divisional HQ that New Zealanders were trespassing into local villages and taking food. In mid–November 1943, a New Zealand officer and fifty men were seen to march back into camp carrying bunches of unripe bananas, which the Islanders said had been planted by them for food. There was, however, no malevolent intent on the part of the Kiwis: "It has been found that the natives in several villages take to the bush immediately soldiers are observed approaching and the troops finding the villages empty think they have been abandoned and hutments are systematically rifled. Native villages are to be avoided."[30] The New Zealanders simply did not understand how important the Islanders' gardens were for their food supply. Orders were given that troops were not to enter inhabited native villages, including patrols.[31] In addition, troops were told to "respect native customs, avoid native women and children and generally behave themselves as befitting soldiers of the Allied Nations."[32]

The New Zealand commanders were also keen to ensure that the Islanders' canoes were left untouched. On 16 October 1943, Lt. Col. Sugden issued a routine order, noting, "A valuable native canoe has been broken by troops in this area. In view of the value of the canoes to the natives and the length of time it takes to season the wood and fashion them the use of native canoes is forbidden and the Chief, Bamboo, has been instructed to gather in all canoes."[33] For the troops, the canoes represented a recreational opportunity or items of curiosity. For the Islanders, however, the canoes were a vital means of transport and food gathering.

The Islanders continued to perform Coastwatching duties, a vital role in the security of the island. The 37th Battalion war diary recorded, "Bamboo's Coastwatchers from MUNDAU advised us that a ship, thought to be a destroyer was seen in the afternoon some miles off the N Coast of the island going in the direction of CHOISEUL."[34]

Gizo Island

There was concern that Japanese troops might still be on Gizo Island. As early as 20 September, General Griswold had asked Barrowclough to capture Gizo, and Barrowclough intended to make good on his promise to assist.[35] So it was that on 13 October a reconnaissance party was sent there with the intention that the brigade reserve, 30th Battalion and 37 Battery would be used to eliminate any Japanese entrenched there. The 30th Battalion history recorded:

> From information received by the colonel from friendly natives who made the five mile trip to Gizo by canoe, it was thought that in all probability the Japs had left Gizo. The natives reported that the usual enemy bivouac areas were not now occupied and it was therefore decided to send a strong reconnaissance party to the island. A couple of days were spent in preparation for the trip—studying maps and intelligence summaries, the issue of rations and checking up on equipment. The task of the party was to be purely reconnaissance, and it was to avoid any resistance in strength by the enemy. The detachment which assembled on Mumia beach on 10 October comprised Captain F.R. Watson (in charge), Lieutenant E. Roughton and some members of his intelligence section, Lieutenant J. (Spud) Murphy and his platoon (number seven) from A company, Lieutenant H.L. Bioletti and his platoon (number thirteen) from C company, medical orderlies and finally a section of divisional signals.
> Two assault boats were used and they were steered through the coral shoals near Gizo by aid of aerial photographic maps. Plans had been made for natives on Gizo to rendezvous in their canoe with the assault boats when they neared the island, and give the latest information about the Japs. A canoe was seen to put off from the shore and it came alongside the barge. In it were six natives and a white man— an American Coastwatcher. It was confirmed from this party that the Japs had left their usual areas. The assault boats landed at the picturesque Gizo anchorage. All round the foreshore were the now abandoned defensive positions which the Japs had constructed to ward off an attack. At the anchorage were the homes of officials, planters and traders, for Gizo had been an administrative centre for the British Solomon Islands Protectorate. The Japs had occupied these houses which showed signs of the strafing and bombing they had received from Allied planes over the past few months. Official correspondence of the administration littered the areas. Concrete floors had been burrowed under to serve as air raid shelters—even a billiards table had rubble heaped upon it to give protection. Crayon drawings by Jap

soldiers had been left on the walls, one with the title, "A soldier's dream of home." Left untouched by the Nips near one of the ransacked offices was a stone plinth erected to the memory of:

> "'The Old Commodore,' pioneer trader of the Solomon Islands.
> Whose life was work,
> Whose language ripe with rugged
> Maxims hewn from life."
> "He never sold the truth to save the hour."

The sunlight filtered through the trees to form a pattern on the path. Here a kiddie's tricycle; there a sea grass chair and flower beds a tangled mass of weeds which reminded one that once the anchorage had known happy days. Because of the encircling reefs there was not a great number of places on the coast where boats could be beached. A landing was made at Repo, a promontory, where it was found the Japs had fortified positions. The natives went in their canoe to get water from a neighbouring river and came back all smiles with a Jap prisoner. He had swum ashore some days before, he later told an interpreter, after having had his barge, in which he was evacuating soldiers from Kolambangara [sic], sunk in a naval action at night. Said the incorrigible Charlie, stropping his jungle knife on the palm of his hand, "Sir I promised my girl I'd send her a couple of pickled ears—could I er-er...." The Jap could not speak English (except for "watta") but he entertained the boys by drawing maps of New Zealand and putting in the main ports. He wasn't quite sure what was going to happen to him and was full of obsequious bows when given cigarettes or food and made frequent display of his excellent gold-edged teeth. It was a wonder the natives didn't kill him, for that was their usual treatment of lone Japs they caught. The men dug their fox-holes in the sand and that night had crabs by the score for company. A plane circled overhead for hours during the night and no one ever learned whether it was friend or foe.

Next day A Company platoon went on an all-day reconnaissance from Gizo anchorage of the middle portion of the island. C Company boys went to Zipo-zipolo and came upon the main Jap bivouac area. The whole hillside was a series of reinforced stronghold positions and air raid shelters, while interspersed with primitive sleeping quarters made from betel nut palm trunks. Cooking was done in huts with a small escape hole for the smoke which would have to be avoided as much as possible because of being spotted by American planes. Very little gear was left behind, but there still pervaded a sickly sweet smell of "fu-fu" powder in the living quarters. That was the name the men gave to the peculiar talc powder that the Japs apparently used on themselves. Corporal Albert Cockle was the envy of souvenir hunters when he found an American carbine under a Japanese officer's bed. All that the Japs had left were a few bags of salt, unpolished rice, medical comforts, two handed saws and empty sake bottles. On 12 October the party, except for C Company platoon, went by barge to Saegaragi. Thirteen platoon moved from the Nonsama River overland to Saegaragi, led by two native guides, old "Captain Betty" and youthful Daniel. In the mouth of the Nonsama River was a Jap barge from which one of the lads souvenired the compass. The section came upon another Jap bivouac area and, poking round, found pillaged goods, taken probably from the private homes on the island. There were snapshots too, that the

Nipponese had left, of a wife in her kimono, of the kiddies at the seaside, of family groups, and scenes at the fair with bunting, ferris wheels and all the fun of the roundabout. Which reminded one that apparently in their complex personalities some form of love does leaven their bestial traits. The platoon came upon cunningly concealed linked weapon posts and one had to admire their industry and the thoroughness of their work. Old "Captain Betty" was like a hen with chickens, darting now to the right, now to the left at any movement or noise in the jungle. But always with that innate sense of direction he came back onto the correct bearing.

From Saegaragi A company men moved further down the coast looking for any signs that might indicate that the Japs had left a Coastwatcher behind, but nothing was found to indicate that this was so. Fresh fish, obtained by the use of hand grenades, was on the menu for the evening meal. This may sound a very much simpler method than angling but actually when fish are stunned by underwater concussion they sink to the bottom. Retrieving fish at depths of 14 to 15 feet is painful to the ear drums. The natives disdained fish boiled in kerosene tins, preferring their own methods of wrapping them in banana leaves and cooking them on hot stones. It rained after the meal and in the shelter of the huts the natives, encouraged by the men, sang hymns and songs they had learned at the mission schools. If there were any Japs around even they must have been surely charmed to hear the Solomon Islanders harmonizing "In my Royal Hawaiian Hotel." Next morning, 13 October, the party returned to Vella Lavella.[36]

On 19 October a patrol from 4 Field Security traveled to Ganongga Island to ensure that it was free of Japanese. The soldiers found evidence of recent Japanese occupation but no Japanese. The Islanders did, however, say that sixty-seven Japanese bodies had been washed ashore.[37]

Defensive Positions

With the evacuation of the Japanese troops, the danger eased. However, there were still substantial Japanese forces on nearby islands, and there was always danger from Japanese stragglers and raiding parties. To both guard against attack and protect radar installations, two of the Battalion Combat Teams were deployed on the northern coast. The 37th Battalion Combat Team took over the area from Warambari Bay on the northwest coast through to Karaka on the northeast coast. The 35th Battalion Combat Team took over the area from Oulala River to Marquana Bay. The 30th Battalion Combat Team was also deployed around the area of the Mumia River, Gill's Plantation, to Subato Bay. There was a concern "that attempts may be made to land Coastwatchers or to locate our dispositions."[38] Patrols were ordered to be maintained and Native Scouts were instructed to keep in touch with patrols and inform them of any Japanese activity.[39]

As the teams were moving into defensive positions, efforts were made to make life more tolerable for the soldiers—cooking gear, tents and clothing were sent forward. As the 37th Battalion war diary notes, the troops began to settle in:

> The building of the camp area has proceeded apace and with the NZedders customary philosophical attitude, versatility and ingenuity; tents, cookhouses and mess huts are once again taking on the familiar appearance of the "home away from home." With the arrival of further gear and equipment most of the Units have set themselves up.[40]

Nonetheless, the troops had to maintain vigilance, and a stand-to was observed from 0530 to 0630 hours and 1800 to 1900 hours.[41] No noise or movement was allowed after 1800 hours; during the hours of darkness, a constant listening watch was maintained and no lights were permitted.[42]

For the Kiwis, the clearing of the island did not represent the end of hostilities. They knew that further operations were planned. "We did a lot of jungle training, particularly after the Japanese had evacuated the island. We did a lot of patrolling to pick up Japanese stragglers. This entailed moving through mangrove swamps, cutting through vines and thick undergrowth and dealing with triple canopy jungle."[43] For the 30th Battalion, this meant jungle training on the nearly Baga Island.

> In early November, D Company and later C Company spent three days on Baga Island doing jungle training. C Company sent a platoon to the island to precede the main body. When the rest of the company in its barges passed through the heads of the bay, this platoon opened fire with mortars and machine guns well in front of them. The American Coxswain of one of the barges had not been informed of the plan and he had to be forcibly restrained from opening fire on what he thought were Japs resisting the landing.[44]

For others, it meant incessant patrolling. The captured Japanese barges were employed to carry infantrymen on patrols. *Confident* was used to take patrols to Ganongga.[45] Constant heavy rain added to the misery of those undertaking the patrols.[46]

For Frank Rennie, the evacuation of the Japanese meant patrolling around the island to pick up any Japanese stragglers, pilots, or naval personnel washed ashore. The patrols, although routine, were not without incident. On one of his patrols Rennie came across what he thought must have been the largest crocodile in the world. It was about 50 yards away in the water. Rennie instructed his scout, George Mundell, to take no chances and to load his Lee

Enfield .303 rifle with the special armor-piercing ammunition. Mundell hit the croc in the head, and it proceeded to shake its head and make for the sea. Rennie and Mundell went over to check where the animal had been lying and were surprised to see marks in the sand showing that the crocodile had been shifted about a foot by the impact. Rennie concluded that the bullet must have ricocheted off the beast's head.[47] The seagoing crocodiles had a fearsome reputation, and Rennie noted that they took a tremendous toll on the natives, several of whom were missing arms or legs after surviving attacks.[48]

For the truly unfortunate among the troops, there was the unpleasant task of laying barbed wire along points that needed to be fortified. Barbed wire was laid in the area from Warambari Bay to Marquana Bay.

Seaborne Supply

One of the problems the New Zealand Army wrestled with was the need to continually supply its dispersed troops, which necessitated the construction of wharves and jetties for seaborne supply. For example, *Confident* was used to supply troops between Dovelli and Maravari, but she drew about seven feet of water and the beach at Maravari dropped away precipitously. Contending with a tidal variation of only two and a quarter feet between high and low tide, the New Zealand engineers set about building a wharf.

Hardwood jungle timber served as a base for this jetty, the logs being set into a coral shelf. Ten-inch-diameter coconut logs formed a simple crib superstructure that was packed up with coral spalls. Old truck tires made good fenders, and when access road and mooring bollards were finished, the 14 Brigade had a first-class jetty of its own.[49]

The engineers were also called upon to create mooring bollards for the LSTs and LCTs that regularly brought supplies to Vella Lavella:

> On several of the beaches therefore along the eastern strip of Vella, solid mahogany blocks 18 inches in diameter were sunk to a depth of four feet, six inches into coral on the foreshore bottom. The use of these made it less likely that a bulldozer would be called upon to push off an LCT which had buried its nose too deeply in the margin of the bay. It was also found necessary to call in an engineer to do the diving necessary at some of the Biloa jetties on Vella. To blow up underwater coral, with or without a diving helmet, by engineering one's way underneath coral mushrooms to fix electrically fired charges was a job worth mentioning in despatches.[50]

For the supply personnel, life was unpleasant:

> On Vella Lavella forward ordnance depot men, including Warrant-Officer J. Badham and Sergeant Harrison, worked in a sea of liquid mud, which never dried out

because the heavy jungle trees, keeping all sunlight out had to be left as natural camouflage against the constant air attacks. Ordnance supplies were spread over an unloading area of about three acres of jungle, from which they had to be transported eight miles to a number of tarpaulin shelters where the stocks were sorted ready for issue to units. Trucks, fitted with four-wheel drive, were frequently bogged down to the running boards as they tried to get through the roadless jungle, crashing a track between the closely packed growth and trees. As one truck managed to extricate itself and assist another by towing it, the vehicle in front would become stuck in the deep mud, and would itself have to be assisted. For mile after mile the trucks were inched along the route, and the difficult task of landing and distributing supplies under such appalling conditions brought the men close to exhaustion.[51]

Even the geography of the island seemed to conspire against the supply men. The dense jungle forced them to stick to the coastal areas, which meant vehicles had to cross saltwater areas that played havoc with vehicle parts and equipment.

Dampness and mould appeared on accumulators. Rubber insulation disintegrated. Slip-rings in the electrical equipment of Bofors guns rotted almost completely away giving off an offensive acrid, sulphurous odour. Axles and rear assemblies of trucks were fractured when tyre chains, after churning through the mud topsoil, caught suddenly on hard coral outcrops beneath the surface soil.[52]

The need to keep trucks and jeeps functioning increased as the tempo of combat increased.

Men of the 20th and 37th Light Aid Detachments, the No.2 recovery and armament section and the 29th Light Anti-aircraft workshops could usually be seen lying on their backs in the mud, in a bath of sweat, working at vitally needed vehicles, or toiling beneath canvas shelters repairing fighting equipment damaged in battle or affected by tropical conditions. When these units were required to move their camp and equipment, they had often to winch their heavy equipment trucks along by means of trees, so difficult were travelling conditions and the mud.[53]

Yanks and Kiwis—Getting Along with Each Other

Part of being in charge of all units on Vella Lavella, for Barrowclough, included taking command responsibility for both his own New Zealand units

Opposite top: **Heavy logs being manhandled on jetty by 20th Field Company at Maravari (official photographer; courtesy Archives New Zealand/Te Rua Mahara o te Kāwanatanga, Wellington Office, WAII, 7 3, Official Photograph Album).** *Bottom:* **View of jetty at Maravari (official photographer; courtesy Archives New Zealand/Te Rua Mahara o te Kāwanatanga, Wellington Office, WAII, 7 3).**

and American units. Barrowclough had the services of an American officer, Lt. Hutchins, USN, as the island radio and communication officer. This was just as well, since Barrowclough faced difficulties in dealing with the unfamiliar American military cultures. On 24 October he had a conference with Lt. Hutchins with regard to Hutchins' duties. Radio signals were vitally important to the security of the island. Despite this, Barrowclough found the meeting "a rather complicated affair in view of our unfamiliarity with U.S. ideas on the control of communications in these various Islands where Army, Navy and Marine Corps and Air Forces organizations are so independent of each other."[54]

The American logistical network was the dominant one, so when the 3NZ Division Army Service Corps became responsible for the island quartermaster duties, it had to adapt itself to American usages, modifying American systems for the operation of supply, petrol, oil and lubricant dumps. Although American units were cooperative, it was thought sensible to appoint

At Biloa village, Vella Lavella, Major General Griswold, Commander 14 Corps, U.S. Army, and Major General Barrowclough, Commanding General, Vella Lavella Command, 20 September 1943 (U.S. Signal Corps; courtesy Archives New Zealand/Te Rua Mahara o te Kāwanatanga, Wellington Office, WAII, 7 3, Official Photograph Album).

a New Zealand supply liaison officer to the American supply (G4) system.[55] Goodwill on both sides was required to overcome each nationality's idiosyncrasies; fortunately, this was forthcoming.

The New Zealanders formally took over the quartermaster role on 1 October 1943. Supplies were funneled through the South Pacific command, but it was the New Zealanders who issued supplies of petrol, rations and numerous other items to the 17,000 soldiers on Vella Lavella. There were American ration dumps at Barakoma and Biloa, and a new one was created at Maimoa. Because of the tropical conditions, special care had to be taken that items were stored properly and safely. This required considerable adaptability. The Commander Royal Army Service Corps commented, "We had no manuals, we just had to say to ourselves, now what's the best way to do this? If it worked that was fine. If it didn't we said, well that was a lousy idea and we'd think up another way."[56]

There was always the potential for friction between the Americans and New Zealanders, particularly when they had different agendas. Barrowclough's primary mission was the defense of Vella Lavella. This brought him into conflict with General Archer Vandegrift, USMC. Barrowclough ordered part of the USMC Parachute Regiment to occupy defensive positions on the north coast of Vella Lavella. On the face of it, this decision made good sense. However, this was anathema to General Vandegrift. Marines were intended for offensive operations, not digging foxholes and static garrison duty. He protested vigorously, and Barrowclough acceded to his earlier order being overridden, with the reservation that, in the event of an invasion, he could order the Marines back.[57]

Although the Americans and New Zealanders generally worked in harmony, there were differences in culture and expectations. Barrowclough came from a small country that had been hard hit by the Great Depression. He was acutely conscious of the cost of ammunition and did not understand that the same principles of accounting and conservation that governed his army did not apply to the burgeoning American arsenal. On 1 November, he visited the American P.T. boat base at Lambu Lambu and was shocked to discover that "it was a very untidy state and a very considerable lack of discipline on the part of the American troops stationed there. A new Squadron had just moved in and I spoke to the Commander of it, particularly with regard to the indiscriminate waste of ammunition. The whole time I was there American Navy personnel were blazing away at the sea and hitting it every time. There was no sign of careful marksmanship. Sanitary arrangements were primitive."[58]

Another issue was the returning of salutes. The American practice was for officers to return the salutes of subordinates. The New Zealand Army, following the British Army, did not have this practice. Recognizing, however, that adhering to the British practice could be interpreted as an act of discourtesy, orders were issued instructing New Zealand officers to return such salutes.[59]

The New Zealand soldiers invariably recognized that they were the junior partners in the war against the Japanese. This often engendered an attitude of "we will show them," an attempt to prove the New Zealanders worthy as Allies. On Vella Lavella there was a manifestation of this mind-set in regard to signals. An American general asked Barrowclough if he had experienced any problems in sending signals, and Barrowclough replied that he had not. He and the American general decided to secretly test their respective signal establishments. A signal was devised: "Most Immediate, Most Secret." The signal would be enciphered, sent, and then deciphered by the receiver. Barrowclough's signalmen had an advantage, however. The New Zealand signalers had a system in which, while the signal was being enciphered, a preceding warning signal was sent to the New Zealand receiving station so that they would have their most competent operators and cipher specialists available to handle it. A dispatch rider would also be available to deliver the message promptly. The New Zealand message was sent and an acknowledgment received within 15 minutes. Barrowclough and the American general then visited the American signalers and inquired how matters were going. To Barrowclough's satisfaction, the American signals master sergeant replied, "It is almost coded up and ready for transmission, Sir."[60]

The different nationalities on the island generally got on well:

Friendships had been struck up by boys of the battalion [30th Battalion] with servicemen among the American units on the island, notably the 77th Seabees and the paratroopers. After tea at night, trucks crowded with servicemen not only from the American units but also from the 35th and 37th New Zealand Battalions passed the company areas going to the pictures at Joreveto, Biloa boat pool or Acorn 10. Rain had fallen every day for over 50 consecutive days and very often, as at Joreveto, it meant sitting on a hard coconut log, with a cape over one's head trying to watch a picture that one wouldn't cross the road to see at home. However, it was something to do to relieve the monotony and the cinema had become a common meeting ground for New Zealand units in the area, where mates from the same town could swap news. One evening two inebriated sappers climbed on to the stage and started making love to the lovely ladies on the screen, until they were howled off by the audience. If you ignored the mud under foot, Joreveto, at dusk, was a pretty spot with its orderly rows of coconut palms, parakeets and bats wheeling overhead, and the smoke from the neighbouring cookhouses drifting round the palm trunks.

When better programmes [were] offered at the American units' cinema at Biloa or the indoor one at Acorn 10, the men hitchhiked along. It was the experience of the 30th Battalion throughout its stay in the Pacific theatre of war that American units were always happy to make New Zealanders welcome to their entertainments, which included pictures and concerts given by celebrity artists. Not only this but from the time the division reached the combat area a free comforts issue of 200 cigarettes and toilet necessities was made weekly by the Americans.[61] New Zealanders were welcomed at American film shows and there was a degree of camaraderie among the young men.

The New Zealanders were also introduced to the American tradition of Thanksgiving. A New Zealander wrote:

For the first time in our lives, we had a share in the celebration of the American Thanksgiving Day. Turkey dinner is traditional with Thanksgiving, but this year people all over the States went without their gobblers so that the men in the South Pacific could be given a special treat. We had ours for mess tonight, and what a meal. Helpings were liberal and with fresh potatoes it was the best feed in months.[62]

One American practice did, however, raise alarm. When the Kiwi signalers became aware of a radio on Vella Lavella transmitting in a foreign tongue, a continuous listening watch was set up and directional signal-finding equipment used to locate the source of the signals. After several days the Kiwis discovered the source—an American station that was using Native American soldiers, the now famous "Windtalkers," to send messages in their own language, thereby avoiding the time-consuming tasks of coding and decoding messages.[63]

One sad aspect was that the bodies of dead New Zealanders were recovered from Boro and Warambari Bay and were interred at an Allied cemetery at Maravari. This cemetery contained the remains of not only the New Zealand dead but also Americans killed in air raids. An Honor Guard was provided by soldiers from 14 Brigade and 58th Naval Construction Battalion when the cemetery was dedicated on Sunday, 19 December 1943. An American padre and the senior New Zealand chaplain Bishop Gerard conducted the service.[64] The white crosses at the head of coral mounds made for a somber sight, particularly as some were marked "Known only to God." A memorial chapel was created by the Islanders and was dedicated on 30 January 1944. (Later, as the New Zealanders withdrew from the Solomon Islands, the remains were disinterred and reinterred at the cemetery at Bourail in New Caledonia,[65] and American remains were moved to Hawaii.)

The 58th N.C.B. band was in attendance and before proceedings commenced played music symbolical of the two nations whose dead were buried there. "The

White Cliffs of Dover" however was apparently the nearest they could play to a true British tune. The band led the singing of hymns and the service was completed with addresses by an American chaplain and Bishop General who paid worthy tributes to those who were buried under the palms. A male native choir under the control of Padre A.H. Voyce (NZ) sang beautifully and an American Cornetist played "Taps" followed by a New Zealand bugler sounding the "Last Post" while both Guards of Honour presented arms.

This solemn, yet somberly colourful ceremony was concluded by the band rising and turning to face "Old Glory" and play "Star Spangled Banner" and then to face our ensign to play the "National Anthem"![66]

A happier event was the celebration of Christmas 1943. Barrowclough commented, "The American Supply Service performed another miracle in getting turkeys issued to all troops in Treasury [Islands] and Vella. Shipping delays at rear of us prevented the arrival of the Christmas decorations and a number of Christmas delicacies."[67]

As mentioned, Christmas Day 1943 had also been marked by the Islanders making their way through the New Zealanders' tent lines near divisional headquarters while singing carols. The New Zealanders tried to celebrate the holiday in their own ways. Additional rations had been received so that plum puddings and fruit cake were supplied to the troops. An issue of seven bottles of beer was made over the Christmas–New Year period, a rare event for those in the combat zone. Christmas Day was also marked by the arrival of Father Christmas, transported in a jeep of E Section, New Zealand Corps of Signals, "who distributed balloons (local pattern) to his 'children.'"[68]

Halsey joined in the spirit of things by sending one of his inimitable messages:

> To all hands in my South Pacific jungle—smashing, sea-sweeping, sky-blazing crew I send best wishes for a Merry Christmas. Though your hardships and sturdy efforts may be required on that day as on all others, you may take pride in the knowledge that your magnificent performance is hastening the brighter days that lie ahead for us all. On this day, with due reverence, let us pay homage to those stout hearts who have made the supreme sacrifice, that our cause may victoriously march on.[69]

Naval Bases

A small Naval Advance Base, Vella Lavella was established at Barakoma on 8 October taking over from the Marine Corps Staging Base but the Marines still used it as a staging base. A P.T. boat base operated temporarily from Lambu Lambu Cove on the north east coast of the island between September and December 1943. The naval base and airfield supported the Treasury Islands operation in October and the Bougainville operation from November 1943 to June 1944. Airfield operations ceased on 19 June 1944 and the naval base was closed in September.[70]

JFK and PT-59

The base at Lambu Lambu Cove became the home of one of the most famous P.T. boat commanders of World War II: John Fitzgerald Kennedy, a future president of the United States. The P.T. boats had to cross a narrow entrance through the reef in order to enter the four-hundred-yards-long and one-hundred-yards-wide cove. About fifteen miles to the north of Barakoma, the primitive PT base boasted only tents and a repair dock. Squadron Eleven under Lieutenant Commander LeRoy T. Taylor took up residence with seven P.T. boats and an APc, a small coastal transport vessel. Taylor later described how the vessels were moored on the left bank of the cove "under the overhanging trees. The APc carried the base force, equipment and supplies. Our radio equipment was placed in a dry cave. Fuel was supplied in 55 gallon drums brought up by LSTs and stored on the right bank. Fuelling was entirely by hand—one barrel at a time."[71]

The base at Lambu Lambu was no Pacific paradise. It was "rat infested," with high humidity, and the living conditions on the boats were cramped. Kennedy's chief petty officer, Glen Christiansen, recalled, "As the war progressed up the Solomons, we were getting extended further, which meant supplies were difficult to come by and we went without food for instance at Vella Lavella for like three weeks. They sunk one of our small ships bringing our supplies up there, and by the time they got the supplies through it was three weeks later, so we were living on dill pickles and cheese."[72]

Kennedy's vessel, PT-109, had been destroyed in a collision with a Japanese destroyer. In an epic story of survival, Kennedy and his remaining crew made it back to Allied lines with the help of Solomon Islanders and Coastwatchers. Kennedy then took command of the old seventy-foot Elco PT-59, which was converted into a heavily armed gunboat, *Gunboat One*, and based at Lambu Lambu to carry out sorties against Japanese barge traffic around Choiseul Island.

PT-59 was involved in the rescue of Paramarines of the 2nd Parachute Battalion on Choiseul. The Paramarines had been sent to Choiseul to create a diversion and draw Japanese attention away from Empress Augusta Bay, Bougainville, the projected invasion site. The Paramarines were successful but faced annihilation if not withdrawn. An urgent request for help was received at Lambu Lambu on 2 November. Kennedy's boat had just returned from an all-night patrol and was not completely refueled. However, it set out with PT-236. They arrived off the aptly named "Warrior River," taking on Marines from two disabled landing craft and escorting two other landing craft to safety. The following night four P.T. boats escorted three LCIs to Choiseul to evacuate more of the Paramarines. Thereafter the P.T. boats carried out anti-barge patrols with diminishing returns, as the Japanese withdrew their troops from the Central Solomons. However, Kennedy's combat days were numbered. He suffered from a duodenal ulcer and back pain and was sent home.[73]

Nixon and "Murder Incorporated"

There was one other future American president on Vella Lavella, and he was to be one of Kennedy's main rivals—Richard Milhouse Nixon was a lieutenant posted to base Pyre, Barakoma airstrip, on Vella Lavella on 10 December 1943, and in the postwar years he commented that they might have met on Vella Lavella.[74] Kennedy and Nixon themselves discussed the possibility, but neither could remember the other. Nixon went on board a number of P.T. boats and said he knew most of the crews. Both men were lieutenants, and it seems if they did meet, they did not make an impression on each other.

Nixon was an operations officer, and his administrative position involved organizing cargo and transport handling for SCAT (South Pacific Combat Air Transport) Command, jokingly referred to as "Murder Incorporated" because of the number of planes and crews that disappeared without a trace. This was due to the lack of navigational aids, weather conditions and enemy action.

Nixon's job was not without danger. In addition to being exposed to Japanese air raids, he recalled Vella Lavella's potentially lethal centipedes. One night a centipede got under Nixon's mosquito netting, and he felt something on his hand. Waking up, he flipped his hand; the centipede landed on his roommate Hollis Dole and bit him. Blood was streaming out, and Dole spent the next three days in the hospital.[75]

Nixon also developed quite a reputation as a poker shark, something quite at odds with his Quaker upbringing.

Nixon's sojourn on Vella Lavella was brief. By 1 January 1944, he was posted to Bougainville.[76]

Fire at Lambu Lambu

As the war in the Solomons moved northward, bases were rolled up and new ones established. On 14 December 1943, the order was given to disestablish the P.T. boat base at Lambu Lambu. Unfortunately, on that date a fire broke out in the fuel dump and rapidly spread to the dock area and ammunition dump. The ammunition began cooking off, and conditions were hellish. Two P.T. boats were tied up to the dock. One, PT-238, managed to get away. The other, PT-239, was less fortunate. The boat was engulfed in flames, which blocked the exit to the cove and prevented seven other P.T. boats and the APc from escaping. All they could do was idle their engines and run fire hoses on their decks. The following day the fire had burned itself out, and the bodies of two sailors were recovered.[77]

As the general officer commanding, Barrowclough had to call for an investigation. This posed a weighty problem. He was a lawyer in civilian life and only too aware of the different legal systems operated by New Zealand and America, not to mention the complexities of the different systems of military justice. Barrowclough neatly resolved the issue by instituting a Court of Inquiry and appointed a legally qualified New Zealand officer as president, assisted by U.S. Navy and Marine Corps officers. Barrowclough eventually reported back to the Commanding General, Forward Area, that the base commander could have prevented the accident. He was careful, however, to draw back from a finding of negligence and simply recommended that no further action be taken.[78]

The naval bases and airfield on Vella Lavella would play a key role as both a staging area and a source of support for Operation Goodtime (the retaking of the Treasury Islands, 27 October 1943) and the invasion of Empress Augusta Bay, Bougainville, on November 1943. It would also be a base for Operation Squarepeg (the invasion of the Green Islands in February 1944).

Airfields

An airstrip was built at Barakoma within six weeks of the American landing. Two months later it was fully operational, with space for one hundred aircraft. The existence of this airfield provided a haven for damaged aircraft returning from bombing Rabaul. On 18 October, a squadron of F4-U Corsair fighters took up residence at Barakoma and began offensive operations. Strikes against Japanese airfields at Kahili, Kara and Ballale suppressed Japanese airpower and enabled fighter cover to be mounted over the invasion beaches on the Treasury Islands and Bougainville during the critical daylight period.

The prime significance of the Allied victory on Vella Lavella lay in the Allied ability to project air power. As noted in the RNZAF Operational Narrative:

> The capture of Vella Lavella and the construction of an airfield on that island out-flanked the enemy outposts on Choiseul and exposed the Kahili-Kara airfields to continuous air attack from an Allied air base only 65 miles away. Ballae airfield, the remaining enemy air base in the South Bougainville area was bombed out of commission by the beginning of October. In Northern Bougainville the airstrips at Buka and Bonis also came within effective range for Allied fighters based at Barakoma.[79]

The construction of new airfields at Munda, Segi and Barakoma moved Allied airpower two hundred miles closer to Rabaul, thus enabling Allied airpower to strike at the main Japanese base with greater force, and it also allowed Allied fighters to intercept Japanese airstrikes against Guadalcanal and the Russell Islands. This in turn conferred on Allied commanders the ability to gather shipping and material together relatively unhindered by Japanese airpower and to maintain the strategic initiative. Eric Bergerud has written, "Vella Lavella became a valuable air base, and the immediate target then became the complex of bases built by the Japanese on and near the island of Bougainville. They included Buin and Kahili on Bougainville proper, as well as the Shortland Islands to the south and Buka to the north. Within this complex rested much of Rabaul's airfleet."[80]

Various units would be based at Barakoma Airfield. The famous "Black Sheep" of Marine Fighting Squadron 214 spent six weeks based there[81] before moving to the airfield at Torokina, Bougainville. Prior to their sojourn on Vella Lavella, various members of the squadron, including the ace Greg Boyington, had made emergency landings on Vella Lavella. As Bruce Gamble notes, the Black Sheep found that "it was hot and steamy—and they would live in yet another tent city—but the unspoiled condition of the picturesque island was a vast improvement over the wretched conditions they had endured during their last tour on Munda."[82]

The Development of Vella Lavella

In order to develop the island as a base, roads linking all the various units and supply depots together were necessary. The rough jungle track had to be converted into a two-way, all-weather road capable of sustaining heavy traffic. The New Zealand engineers pitched into this task with gusto:

> On Vella Lavella we got going. At last we had some bulldozers. The 58th Seabees had done the road from the Barakoma airstrip to Uzamba. We therefore tackled the five mile stretch from Uzamba to Joroveto for a start. Coconut trees lining the coast crashed into the ocean or over the sigs' telephone wires. Then they were bulldozed into breakwaters. The existing tortuous jeep trail through jungle night and creepers became within a few weeks a surfaced two lane highway with provision for temporary one way bridges at all river crossings. Difficulties of heavy equipment, of heavy daily rainstorms and of extremely heavy traffic caused by the necessity of unloading LST convoys under heavy ack-ack protection at the southern end of the island, meant that the progress on the road was not so fast as it might have been. By the end of November, 1943, however, an additional four miles from Joroveto to Juno had been added, thanks to the help of the 77th Seabees, so that problems of maintenance now began to come to the fore. The roadways were given a preliminary road improved by fillings and providing in its very nature a good drainage medium it soon developed into a fine roadway. Speeds were kept down by Div orders to 20 mph for trucks and 25 mph for jeeps but difficulty soon arose in restricting the speeds to these limits.
>
> This experience of roading, which clearly demonstrated the need for heavy equipment and plenty of it, led to the establishment of the 26th Field as the heavy equipment company. Their prentice hand in Vella was given full scope in the stretch from Ruravai to Lambu Lambu Cove, a stretch which involved several bridges and of which time prevented the finishing. Extensions to the Barakoma airfield also developed the latent talent of 26th's dozer drivers and gave them pleasant associations with the Seabees there.[83] ... Coral and rock had to be quarried and a coral pit at Maravari produced 6,000 yards of crushed coral per month.[84] ... Foxholes and dugouts were very attractive to the local snakes and land crabs. One tough sapper, sleeping nude beneath his tent, woke to the din of ack-ack guns and the crump of bombs. He dived for his hole only to be bitten amidships by a snake. They say the snake died. But generally in spite of the hovering noises overhead we preferred to cuddle up in bed and hope for the best. We could, if the swishing noises got too near, always roll off the camp stretcher and underneath it.[85]

The road from Barakoma to Joroveto was transformed by the 26th Field Company from muddy ruts to "a smooth coral highway which followed the coast for many miles."[86]

The New Zealand Engineers (20th Field Company) built two bridges at Joroveto using timber from the jungle. The work was difficult, not least because of the engineering challenges of construction, the need for the bridges to take heavy vehicles, and the local environment that threatened to wash them away.

The second bridge gained notoriety as "the million dollar bridge" because of its construction using mahogany, a particularly valuable form of timber. The engineers' history comments:

> The glory of the second Joroveto Bridge excelled that of the first by reason of the quality of timber used in its construction and the ingenious devices adopted for pile driving in the absence of proper equipment. Mahogany from beautiful big trees was used for piles and bank seats—logs measured up to 60 feet long and 30 inches diameter. Being near the site they were readily hauled into position.[87]

The storm that destroyed the first bridge thwarted the plans of two senior New Zealand commanders. They had selected two mahogany logs for shipment back to New Zealand, no doubt to be transformed into exquisite furniture, and their names were printed on the logs in bold white paint. The logs had been dropped near the bridge, to be rolled into the river and floated out to sea, and then picked up by a Navy vessel returning to New Zealand. The logs stayed where they were dropped in full view until one day a tropical storm washed out the bridge. The engineers who came to restore the bridge found these two logs extremely useful, and the names remained on the bridge![88]

Bulldozers were essential construction equipment. Particularly useful were the heavy D-8 bulldozers for heavy jungle clearance work. "There were complications when the difficulty of maneuvering big dozers on and off little landing craft led to the dozer, as at Pakoi on Vella Lavella, diving off into the drink. No Moindah [New Caledonia, where the New Zealand engineers had been based] course of instruction had educated for such a contingency and when it was a borrowed dozer too, the salt water in the works rather injured our chances of further borrowings."[89]

Boredom and Its Cures

For the New Zealand soldiers, boredom was a constant problem. One veteran recorded, "If you didn't play cards, write, read or 'mag' you devoted your time to resting—the most popular pastime in the Third Division, irrespective of rank, commonly called 'cot bashing,' 'Maori P.T.,' 'ceiling inspection,' or 'spinal exercise'—all sooner or later succumbed to its wiles."[90]

Some solved this problem by creating handicrafts. For them, the wrecked Allied aircraft at Barakoma, as a source of raw materials, were an irresistible attraction. This led one exasperated American groundcrewman to exclaim, "You Noo Zealanders are worse than a pack of Boston Bums."[91] The Seabees were among those who turned to handicrafts—the Cruisebook of the 77th NCB noted:

We are souvenir hunters first and last and always we were hard at it on Vella Lavella. No Jap aircraft crashed but what we quickly dismantled it and set to work making aluminium crosses and hearts—native wood could be polished and carved into wonderful gifts, and what could be better than ashtrays, lamps and letter openers made from empty shell casings? Sea shells were collected from the reefs and strung for necklaces and bracelets or turned into brooches.[92]

Sometimes attempts to relieve boredom took dangerous turns. For signalman Ralph Williams, Divisional Signals, this involved an unsanctioned aerial combat mission over Japanese territory:

One of my highlights was a flight on a *Liberator* bomber. The Americans were very generous. You had to sign a form to take all responsibility off the flyers in case anything happened. You had to sit in an air gunner's position, a waist gunner on a *Liberator* bomber. They're a big four engine aircraft.... I was determined to get a flight so I drove along to the American flight headquarters, being a cheeky, scrounging Kiwi and asked the Americans, any chance of a flight? He said in his American accent "Yeah, Ok. You sign the paper." So I did. In a *Liberator* bomber, B-24.

The two American pilots were half naked, only shorts on. They were both smoking cigars flying the goddam thing. It went over Truk Island in the Pacific and it was loaded with bombs. I had a wonderful experience. Came back safely ... I hoped and prayed no blimmin *Zeros* poked their noses in.[93]

Williams' experience was by no means an isolated incident. Soldiers and groundcrew would occasionally fly in combat missions in a completely unofficial and unauthorized way. For the aircrew, it meant an extra pair of eyes and trigger fingers on the aircraft's guns; for the passengers, it was an adventure.[94]

Alcohol was in short supply, and the New Zealanders ran illegal whisky-stills in the jungle. Tins of fruit, raisins, sugar and other materials were used. Rob McLean recalled that "they used to make very good quality whisky, but sometimes, if they didn't allow it to go right through the whole process, it ended up as sort of jungle juice. I remember some Americans went blind when they drank it. Somebody or other made it badly."[95] The moonshiners produced a weird kind of "plonk." Although not officially encouraged their output of proofed spirit found a ready market among Allied servicemen at 15 to 20 dollars a bottle.[96] The padre for the 35th Battalion recalled the Kiwis' manufacture of "plonk." He "happened upon quite a goodly collection of coconuts in which there was a seething, gurgling mass which, apparently by the judicious addition of mosquito repellent, became quite a stimulating beverage. It seemed to be quite a strong potion too, judging from some of its results."[97]

One of the finest engineering feats of 20th Field Company was the creation of a jungle theater at the coconut plantation of Joroveto. Coconut logs provided seating for 3,000 men, many of whom waited patiently in the rain for 7:15 p.m. and the shows to begin.

> The effective staging of band concerts here as well as of native shows, of 26th Field concerts with the "Rhythm Rascals" or church parades with carol choirs, was greatly enhanced by the provision, by the 20th Field carpenters of an elegant sound-shell in redwood. The whole thing was built up in strips and effectively threw out the sound to the 22nd Field Ambulance personnel seated up in the "gods" behind the gonophones....
>
> The bats wheeled overhead with short shrill shrieks; around our socks, trouser legs neatly tucked in, the mozzies whispered. Between films we played a hand of bridge or chased up a match up one side of the crib board, read the latest [Turf] Digest, tested each others quiz capacities or took a surreptitious swig.[98]

On Saturday, 8 January 1944, "showery weather throughout the evening did not prevent a large crowd from seeing Judy Garland, featured in 'Lily Mars' at the Joroveto Theatre. It was rather unusual to see hundreds of heads peering at the screen from under cover of capes and ground sheets. Two 'dead-

Troops of 14 Brigade on Vella Lavella take a break in the jungle (photographer unknown; courtesy Alexander Turnbull Library, Wellington, New Zealand, reference number WH-0213).

beats' presumably under the influence of 'jungle juice' provided the entertainment before the show started. They were promptly booed off when the show started."[99]

The New Zealand Army tried in its own inimitable way to keep the troops occupied. Working parties and camp maintenance occupied a slice of time, as did marches across Vella Lavella. The troops were creative in how they filled the rest of their time: A Company, 30th Battalion, acquired a launch with a small inboard motor, which was used for fishing trips, albeit with the need for frequent bailing.[100] A swimming carnival was held at Mumia Beach with a captured Japanese barge as the flagship. Another swimming carnival was held at Joroveto on Boxing Day. A traditional native canoe race was also held. In the inter-unit canoe race the engineers used their shovels as paddles. *Confident* was used as the flagship for the festivities, and Barrowclough, Potter and Duff were taken to it.[101]

War Art and Christmas Cards

The New Zealand government had commissioned two official war artists. One of these, Lieutenant Allan Barnes-Graham, produced a Christmas card of sorts showing a Kiwi jungle soldier. This was distributed to the soldiers at no cost and was intended to be posted back to New Zealand to friends and relations. Sadly, it did little to dispel the erroneous notion that the troops in the South Pacific were living in some luxurious Pacific idyll. For his part, Barnes-Graham did not see much of the fighting. At one point he arrived just as there was some fighting at an estuary: "We picked up a man who was coming down for help. He was in the sea up to his waist and was carrying a grenade in his hands not only for the Japanese but also for the crocodiles."[102]

Barnes-Graham found that even the elements seemed to conspire against his work: "Watercolours melt in their pans and ooze through the paper wrappings of the new pans. Even pencil sketching is hedged around with unthought-of difficulties."[103]

Anti-Malaria Precautions

The struggle for Vella Lavella was the first experience of infantry combat for the Kiwis in the South Pacific. It impressed on them the difficulties of amphibious and jungle warfare; most of those at the sharp end were physically exhausted by the time the Japanese withdrew. Some of the soldiers had sub-

The New Zealand National Patriotic Fund provided postcards that soldiers could send to their families. This 1943 Christmas postcard depicts an New Zealand soldier in a jungle uniform worn in the Pacific theater. The artist was A. Barnes Graham (courtesy Alexander Turnbull Library, Wellington, New Zealand, reference number Eph-A-CARDS-Christmas-WWII-1943-02).

sisted on field rations and had not eaten a cooked hot meal for nearly a month, nor had they been able to change their clothing.

Vella Lavella was regarded as "a highly malarial island."[104] Malaria was a much feared disease, and troops were provided with a malaria suppressant—Atabrine. The problem was that the synthetic drug was new, and it was uncertain what dosage was effective. In addition, the yellow tablets were bitter. "For those with a slow swallow, the taste of the pills was anything but pleasant, and there were few who did not afterwards help them down with a sip of water."[105] Atabrine also had an undeserved reputation for causing sterility and impotence. These rumors led to a certain amount of consumer resistance, particularly in some American units.

The prescribed dose of Atabrine was half a tablet per day, with a full tablet on Sundays. It was considered that in combat conditions, where mosquito nets were not available, the dosage should have been a tablet a day.[106]

Anti-malaria precautions were thrown to the winds when the soldiers of the Battalion Combat Teams became fatalistic and stopped taking their Atabrine anti-malaria tablets. Their attitude was that "since they had been exposed in combat it was now too late to take precautions."[107] The soldiers had been 3–4 weeks without anti-mosquito nets, and Atabrine distribution had not been regular. One wounded man had his recovery delayed because of the onset of malaria; he had not had Atabrine for a week prior to being wounded. Many would suffer for this lapse later.

Appreciating the deadly effects of malaria, the troops of 1(NZ) Malaria Control Unit swung into action, attempting to tighten up anti-malaria precautions, providing lectures and organizing work parties for clearing, draining and filling malaria-carrying-mosquito breeding grounds. The area around Marquana Bay, with its low boggy ground, and mosquito breeding areas in slit trenches, bomb and shell holes, and pools in the vacated Japanese bivouac area were identified as danger areas. Overall, dress discipline was "noticeably lax," but this did tend to improve once lectures had taken place emphasizing the need. Troops were reminded that "Vella Lavella is a highly malarial Island. Shorts are not [to] be worn. Long sleeved shirts must be worn between 1730hrs and 0700hrs. Men on duty in listening posts, etc., must use mosquito repellant."[108] However, with the heat and humidity, these orders were a vain hope.

Given the heat, humidity and discomfort of the troops, the need for vigilance in anti-malarial precautions was imperative. Troops that failed to take such measures invariably paid the price—one soldier avoided taking Atabrine for 7 days in October 1943, and within a week he was in the hospital with malaria. "Six others failed to use their mosquito nets and were struck down. Some were even found bathing at night, an almost certain way of contacting malaria. Thus gross carelessness is responsible for over 60 percent of the hospital malaria cases to date, and poor discipline is the cause of probably as high as over 90 percent of cases."[109] In fairness to the troops, most were strangers to the tropics and had no prior experience of malaria, or, for that matter, other tropical diseases.

One of the triumphs of 3NZ Division is that the health of most of the troops was preserved, and the feared horrendous casualty rates did not occur. Robust anti-malaria precautions, discipline and preventive measures all contributed to this success.

Tropical Hygiene and Health

The commander of 37th BCT reported:

The health of the troops was generally good despite the trying conditions and grueling patrols that had to be undertaken. After leaving DOVELLI COVE all water had to be obtained from holes dug in the ground, there being no running water at the landing places at TAMBAMA, SUNUSUKURU and WARAMBARI. Water at WARAMBARI was supplied by boat from TAMBAMA. The water was brackish and full of sediment and caused diarrhea and some cases of dysentery. These all responded to treatment.

The R.A.P. moved throughout with Adv H.Q. The wounded were dealt with and evacuated as expeditiously as possible under the circumstances.[110]

The quality of battlefield medical care is indicated by the fact that only one battle casualty that arrived at a New Zealand MDS proved fatal.[111] However, the New Zealand medical personnel faced huge challenges—cots, mattresses and linen proved impossible to keep dry and sterile, and many of the orderlies were undergoing their first experience of dealing with seriously wounded men. What proved to be a surprise was the vigor of the wounded: "They were filthy, unshaven, possibly starved and with flies crawling over their bloodstained dressing. Despite this they frequently walked or hopped to the ward, stood any amount of handling, took an active share in looking after themselves, rarely complained of pain and made a rapid recovery."[112]

In the tropics, field hygiene is vital. In spite of training, a breakdown in field hygiene practices occurred, particularly in the disposal of human waste and the treatment of water for drinking. Dysentery outbreaks plagued operations. The Field Hygiene Section tried to have its personnel accompany troops making beach landings or moving to new camp sites. Their role was twofold—establish latrines and set up rubbish dumps to avoid the fouling of living areas.

The 6th Field Hygiene section supervised the creation of rubbish dumps along the lines of the Bradford system. A bulldozer would cut a hole in the coral 50 yards long and 10–12 feet deep. Trucks would then deposit rubbish at one end, and this would be burned and covered with coral by the bulldozer.[113]

On one occasion the use of the rubbish dumps produced explosive results: In October 1943, two American privates, Robert Brutinel and Don Carpenter from the 2nd Marine Corps Parachute Battalion, drove their truck into a New Zealand–run rubbish dump. The procedure was that the rubbish was to be burned, and then a bulldozer would bury the ashes. After they had dumped their rubbish, the Americans noticed that a New Zealander could not get the rubbish to light because it was too wet. Brutinel helpfully suggested that the New Zealander use some of the aviation fuel from a nearby dump. He replied, "I would if I could." Brutinel produced a big wrench from the truck and used it to unscrew the top of one of the aviation fuel barrels. The New Zealander grabbed one of the discarded five-gallon cans that was in the

Marines' rubbish and proceeded to immerse it in the barrel and fill it. He then quickly returned to the rubbish dump, where he threw the fuel on the rubbish and lit it. To everyone's horror, a line of flame arced from the rubbish to the aviation fuel dump. The resultant explosion destroyed the aviation fuel dump and the truck. Fortunately, the three soldiers had sprinted for the surf and were unhurt by the fireball. What the New Zealander had not known was that Marines had developed the practice of punching a hole in fuel cans when at sea so that rubbish would sink to the bottom and not betray their trail to Japanese submarines. Even though they were now on land, the Marines' standard practice had been followed, probably through force of habit. The explosion had been the result of international error. The fuel dump burned for days, and the rumor was that the Japanese had bombed it.[114]

An official history was critical of the Kiwis' attention to tropical hygiene: "The general health of the troops, however, deteriorated and they became listless due to the climatic conditions and unsatisfactory food. There seems little doubt that insufficient attention was paid to hygiene by combatant officers."[115] Particularly concerning was the outbreak of Bacillary Dysentery within the 37th Battalion's Combat Team in September and October 1943. The troops had moved into Boro, and the troops had dug slit trenches. They had been obligated to remain in these trenches for extended periods. Latrines were dug, but many of them were shallow and "an extraordinary number of men failed to cover their feces deposits with earth after using these latrines." The predictable result was an outbreak of dysentery in the last week of September that affected an average of 50 soldiers a day, creating "a very serious problem in the conduct of offensive actions against the enemy." The symptoms were far from pleasant.[116] "Usually, the men affected commenced vomiting and diarrhea at night, would have repeated loose motions about one an hour and by morning would be passing blood and mucus only. These men had to remain in their slit trenches during the night, as anyone moving about at night was likely to be shot." The treatment consisted of the afflicted soldiers being given rest and chlorinated water. Sulfaguanidine tablets were prescribed. Mashed-up biscuits and hot water were provided as the soldiers got better. Generally the soldiers could be expected to return to duty within 48 hours.

The tropical heat made the frequent washing of clothes a necessity. On Vella Lavella Kiwi ingenuity came to the fore. Washing machines were devised by the New Zealand engineers using the churn principle. Hot water was provided by oil-fed burners.[117] *Headquarters* records, "In addition to the heat there were deluges of rain with as much as six inches falling in one day. Clothes drying became a major problem and on one occasion on Vella Lavella, after

Kiwis Sappers of 20th Field Company with improvised washing machine made from 44-gallon drum and packing case (official photographer; courtesy Archives New Zealand/Te Rua Mahara o te Kāwanatanga, Wellington Office, WAII, 7 3).

five weeks of incessant downpours it became necessary to utilize a tent, empty petrol drums and a field cooker to provide a drying room."[118]

Vella Lavella, with its humidity, torrential rain showers and deadly flora and fauna, was no Club Med. Lawrence Baldwin recalled that he suffered acutely from skin rashes and boils. The troops tried to get some relief from the heat by going shirtless, but this simply exposed them to sunburn. Most tried to stay in the shade.[119]

After the ground combat had finished, and as part of the smartening-up process and re-imposition of discipline, the troops were told that "all ranks will shave daily." Some troops, particularly in the BCTs, had stopped shaving for reasons of practicality and were sporting luxuriant growths.[120]

There was light relief sometimes:

> This little story concerns some of the headquarters company boys who, one day after the first echelon had left for Green Island, were taking pot shots at an empty petrol drum floating about 200 yards off the shore. Someone aimed, fired, and

suddenly with a loud report and a sheet of flames the drum was no more. What was thought to have been empty was a full drum of gas. Smoke and flames billowed off the surface of the water. A jeep arrived on the scene very shortly afterwards and some American naval officers leapt out.

"Is the pilot out?" hurriedly queried one officer.

"What pilot?"

"Didn't a plane crash here?" said the officer.

Seen from afar it looked as if a plane had crashed in flames into the water and it took a good deal of explaining on the part of the boys to talk themselves out of trouble.[121]

PTSD

Although it was not yet recognized as such, Post Traumatic Stress Disorder was setting in for the soldiers who had seen combat. The clerk compiling the Historical Record of 37th Battalion for the month of October 1943 noted, "Many of the men had wild dreams at night and those awake heard frequent screams and cries from the slumberers around them."[122]

The Nat Pat

One of the more unusual organizations on Vella Lavella was the National Patriotic Fund ("Nat Pat"), which was usually represented by YMCA secretaries. The role of the Nat Pat was to provide comforts for the New Zealand soldiers such as writing materials, razors and reading material. Bob Wardlaw, the YMCA secretary attached to the 30th Battalion, earned the respect of his comrades. He acquired an India Pattern tent and set this up as his living quarters and store. "Anyone passing, Americans and New Zealanders alike were never begrudged a cup of tea (and biscuits when available). Wardlaw's tent became known as 'Teapot Corner.' Supplies of diesel for boiling water and tea sometimes were in short supply and the Americans supplied these. The oil burning boiler has made a non-stop tea service possible, operating from 0900hrs to 2100hrs daily, every day of the week. Over 100 gallons of tea are used every day." The New Zealanders were tea drinkers of some magnitude, and the supply of tea was important for maintaining their morale.[123]

Lessons Learned

As stated earlier, Vella Lavella was the first combat experience for most of the New Zealand soldiers. They were green, and it was only by experience that they learned. Signals Security was one area in which there was laxity. "Elementary signals security measures are NOT being generally observed," lamented Lt. Col. Sugden. In telephone conversations the troops discussed points in secret documents, referred to their units, and mentioned officers' names and troop movements.[124]

Important lessons had been learned about infantry-artillery cooperation and how to fight the determined Japanese defenders. A New Zealand officer, in an after-action report, commented, "Although we fully realize that no war can be fought and won without casualties, we have also learned that in this type of warfare such casualties may be minimized by the skillful use of Arty; and where possible M.M.G. & 3" mortar support. We give great credit to all three supporting arms for a good job of work." Combat operations had been undertaken during daylight hours, and a close perimeter defense was set up at night. The officer remarked, "Any movement by night created a tremendous noise and if carried out at all should only be done by specially chosen and highly trained men."[125]

The Battalion Combat Teams concept had proven flexible and sufficient to get the job done. However, there had been "a tendency by commanders of combat teams to establish separate combat headquarters in addition to battalion headquarters, instead of absorbing the extra attached units into their battalions. This was frowned upon by Barrowclough and did not happen again during the remainder of the division's service in the Solomons."[126] Arguably, given the small-scale level of combat undertaken by the New Zealanders, the combined arms approach was the only practical way of fighting: Artillery (despite the limitations of terrain) provided the necessary support for the infantry, which in turn occupied the ground. Medical services undoubtedly saved lives. It is also noteworthy that combined arms teams were an innovation for the New Zealand Army, and there were bound to be teething problems.

The next operation undertaken by 3NZ Division's 8 Brigade soldiers was, if anything, more complex than the operations on Vella Lavella because it involved an opposed amphibious assault. The Battalion Combat Teams approach was abandoned for Operation Goodtime, and the three infantry battalions involved fought on their own terms.

The New Zealanders had passed their first test of battle and were confident in their weapons, field craft and commanders. 14 Brigade would be employed in one further combat operation, Operation Squarepeg, the invasion of the Green Islands on 15 February 1944. This invasion, a part of Operation Cartwheel, was spectacularly successful, and soon after bombers from the Green Islands were battering the Japanese base at Rabaul.

The Kiwis Leave Vella Lavella

The leaving of Vella Lavella by New Zealand troops was a huge logistical exercise and entailed all the necessary packing and organization:

On the evening of Saturday, 12 February, there put into Mumia beach two LSTs with their cigar shaped blimps, used as a protection against dive bombing attacks, floating overhead. They had come from Guadalcanal and on board was a troop of tanks which were to be employed for the first time by the New Zealand Division in jungle warfare. The LSTs would load guns and equipment and together with the LCIs (landing craft, infantry), would set out on the journey to Green Island to be joined in the night by the very much faster destroyers carrying the landing assault troops. The final day on Vella Lavella was spent in packing kit bags, burying and burning the rubbish one seemed inevitably to accumulate, trying to find space in kit bags for cakes that somehow always seemed to arrive when a move was imminent, and writing a hasty letter home with its post-script—"If you don't hear from me for a while, I'll be all right." Reveille was at 2.30 am on Monday, 14 February, and after a breakfast of the much abused Vienna sausages, cots were folded and

Soldiers of 14 Brigade, 3New Zealand Division loading equipment and leaving Vella Lavella, 1944 (photographer unknown; courtesy Archives New Zealand/Te Rua Mahara o te Kāwanatanga, Wellington Office, WAII, 7 3, Official Photograph Album).

kit bags stored. The companies formed up on the road in full kit and moved off, over the "million dollar" bridge at Mumia (constructed of solid mahogany) up to Juno Beach. After a wait of several hours, assault boats took the troops out to the destroyers.[127]

For the Americans, the success of the Kiwi operations on Vella Lavella meant they knew the quality of New Zealand combat units and that they could be relied on to get the job done. If 14 Brigade had failed to secure Vella Lavella, it is likely that further New Zealand combat operations under the American aegis would have been doubtful. General Griswold sent a congratulatory message to Barrowclough that concluded, "We have shown our readiness and ability to work together as Allies, and it is with the greatest confidence that I look forward to future operations with the Third New Zealand Division!"[128]

Although the Kiwis were the land component of mopping-up operations

Soldiers of 14 Brigade, 3New Zealand Division embarking on an LCI at Juno Beach, Vella Lavella, for Nissan Island (photographer unknown; courtesy Archives New Zealand/Te Rua Mahara o te Kāwanatanga, Wellington Office, WAII, 7 3, Official Photograph Album).

on Vella Lavella, the Kiwis could have done nothing without the support of American forces who supplied shipping and logistics. The operations on Vella Lavella can be viewed as an excellent example of how a small nation can contribute to the success of a larger operation.

By mid–1944 the war had moved north toward Japan. The need to neutralize Rabaul lessened as the Japanese garrison's offensive capabilities were eviscerated by disease, lack of supplies and an abandonment by the Japanese high command. In January 1944 the Seabee units left Vella Lavella and CBMU 502 began salvage operations, including the dismantling of the aviation fuel dump. Even this unit left for Emirau on 12 July 1944. The Australians of 23 Brigade took over the garrison of Vella Lavella as part of "The Outer Islands" in late 1944, but they withdrew their men in 1945.

For the men of 14 Brigade, the completion of Operation Squarepeg meant the end of their sojourn in the South Pacific. Their division was recalled to New Zealand, and, for manpower, economic, strategic and political reasons, 3NZ Division was disbanded.

Casualties

The New Zealand casualties from Vella Lavella were blessedly light, considering the determined resistance of the Japanese defenders and the truly appalling conditions under which the New Zealanders had to fight. Barrowclough reported to his prime minister on 31 December that "the whole operation cost us forty seven killed and thirty six wounded. A conservative estimate of enemy casualties was two hundred killed."[129] *The Pacific* records, "Four officers and twenty eight other ranks were killed and one officer and thirty one other ranks were wounded."[130] However, another official medical history describes forty-four New Zealand soldiers killed, with a further three dying of wounds. It also indicates that thirty-six were wounded.[131]

This makes Vella Lavella the costliest land engagement in New Zealand's Pacific War.

Twelve

Resonance and Memory

Echoes

Echoes of the struggle for Vella Lavella continue to resonate. The Islanders have not forgotten what occurred on Vella Lavella and are still grateful for their liberation from the Japanese. In the late twentieth century the Solomon Islands fell into the thrall of warlordism, gangsterism and corruption, and it became "a failed state." At the request of the Solomon Islands government, a Regional Assistance Mission Solomon Islands (RAMSI), consisting of soldiers, police and aid workers from Australia, New Zealand and other Pacific Islands, was sent to the Solomons to stabilize the situation. Goodwill earned by the soldiers of 14 Brigade became an asset of considerable value to the New Zealand soldiers of RAMSI.

A concrete memorial cairn to the fifteen New Zealanders killed in the air attack of 1 October 1943 was erected by their comrades of the 209th Light Anti-Aircraft Battery.[1] In the postwar years the cairn fell into disrepair, and in the course of stripping timber from the jungle Asian workers dumped the cairn to one side. This was discovered by New Zealand soldiers patrolling the area as part of the RAMSI deployment in 2006. The plaque on the cairn, which had become corroded, was sent to the NZ Army Museum at Waiouru, New Zealand. The New Zealand High Commission in the Solomon Islands and the New Zealand Defence Force set about having a replacement plaque erected on the site. The HMNZS *Resolution* delivered the new plaque, and a dedication service was held in 2011.[2]

At Boro, Harry Savekana has become the unofficial caretaker of a memorial plaque to the New Zealanders who were killed on Vella Lavella. Their bodies were originally buried at Boro but later reinterred at Bourail Cemetery, New Caledonia, along with other New Zealand war dead from the Pacific.

As Savekana commented, "The bones may have been removed but the flesh and blood of the New Zealand soldiers remains here."[3]

The bond between Trevor Ganley and his rescuers was deep. The Islanders remembered him fondly and named the place where he had come ashore "Ganley Point." In 1980 Ganley visited the island, determined to repay in some measure the Islanders' kindness to him. He asked Kisine Zoro how he could help him, and Zora responded that the whole community should benefit, so Ganley provided Supato School with a classroom building and helped with its construction. Kisine's son, Kevin Zora, has named his son after Trevor Ganley. The link forged in 1943 between two warriors of the Pacific endures.

Most of the soldiers who fought on Vella Lavella were content never to return. Some, however, did travel back in the postwar years. One was Rex Gregor, who wanted to retrace his wartime steps. Vella Lavella is not an easy place to get to, and the insurgency on Bougainville did not make it any easier. But after some difficulties, Gregor and his wife made it to Vella Lavella, where the Islanders welcomed them. He recalled:

In the foreground: Supato School on Vella Lavella, built postwar with the help of Trevor Ganley and his family. Supato Church is in the background (courtesy Les Dawson).

I suddenly noticed this native who had on a bright orange T-shirt. He was pushing his way through the crowd and walking with a bad limp. He came up to me and threw his arms around me and hugged me. "You saved my life" he said. "I would not be able to walk if it weren't for you." I had nearly forgotten the incident he was talking about, and frankly I had never considered it a life saving effort. About two weeks after we had landed some natives had brought this eight year old boy to my First Aid Station. He had apparently stepped on a Japanese land mine or possibly accidentally detonated an unexploded shell. At any rate the calf of his leg and his foot was badly mangled. I cleaned his wounds and sprinkled them with sulfanilamide powder and bandaged his legs with splints. Later when the 77th Seabee Battalion landed to build an airstrip at Pusisama I took him down to their camp and the doctor with the Seabees (Dr J.J. Korn) treated and cared for his leg.[4]

The Islander, Leashe Magila, had walked for two hours through the jungle to greet Gregor. The reunion was intensely emotional for both men.

For many soldiers, their time on Vella Lavella would affect their health in the postwar years. Gordon Graham contracted malaria on Vella Lavella:

The first time I had it I did not know what was happening. I had to be sent off to Auckland Hospital. The chap who was my platoon commander had also contracted malaria. The medical people were unfamiliar with the disease. On one occasion I had a high fever and chills and the farmer I was working for got very alarmed, not knowing what was ailing me. The malaria bouts gradually eased over the years.[5]

For the American soldiers who fought on Vella Lavella, or even in the New Georgia campaign, their efforts were overshadowed by the battles of the Central Pacific Drive. They are truly forgotten soldiers. The 35th Infantry Regiment was engaged in the brutal slog to take Luzon in the Philippines, a similarly overlooked campaign.

The Japanese soldiers embroiled in the battle for New Georgia were also swept into obscurity. The battles of the Great Pacific War were of a titanic nature, and major events overshadowed those on Vella Lavella. The survivors who were lifted off Vella Lavella would in all likelihood have been caught up in the battles for Bougainville.

Sadly, the operations on Vella Lavella are all but forgotten in New Zealand. There is simply no popular memory of Vella Lavella, no doubt because of the limited duration of combat operations, the almost nonexistent press coverage, the lack of public awareness of where Vella Lavella is located (and an associated ignorance of the strategic importance to New Zealand of the Solomon Islands) and the low number of battle casualties. The New Zealand Army has a "Vella Lavella Barracks" at Waiouru Military Camp, but there is no significant institutional awareness of what was accomplished on Vella

Lavella. New Zealand forces deployed with RAMSI were generally ignorant of their predecessors' footprints.

Reflection and Significance

Major (later Brigadier General) Donald M. Schmuck, USMC, wrote of the American invasion:

> I am convinced that a proper account of this operation could be a text book example of how the war was sometimes waged during the early days in the South Pacific—of a hastily contrived amphibious operation launched without proper enemy intelligence or reconnaissance, with a confusing chain of command (they neglected to inform me that the 1st Amphibious Corps on New Caledonia was in charge—not the 3rd Marine Division on Guadalcanal), with inadequate medical personnel, communications, anti-aircraft capabilities, as well as little if any air and naval cover. The young Navy Captain in command of the amphibious task force knew even less than I did about the situation except that the "Slot" was a deadly, dangerous place for his group of slow moving vessels and he wanted me and my troops off his ships ASAP![6]

Although Schmuck's judgment is harsh, it does reflect the fact that the Americans were still on a steep learning curve in August 1943. Things had come a long way since Operation Watchtower, the invasion of Guadalcanal a year before. Nonetheless, lessons such as efficient combat loading, the need to land troops in suitable designated areas and get troops away from the beachhead as soon as possible, and the need to get supplies ashore and ships away from the reach of Japanese airpower were all lessons painfully learned. It should also be appreciated that even though the American landing on Vella Lavella was unopposed, it was still a high-stakes gamble, given the threat of Japanese air and naval power. That gamble did, however, pay off.

Amphibious operations are incredibly complex, and thorough planning and preparation are the keys to success. There is no denying that things did go wrong with landing operations (troops landed at the wrong beach, ships lined up to unload, porous air cover), but that was all part of the learning process. For Schmuck, the personal learning curve was a traumatic one:

> I can never forget the gut-wrenching experience of standing there on the open bridge with the Captain at dawn midst those enemy held islands, I in full Marine combat gear armed to the teeth, he in gold braid and starched khaki, both of us searching desperately for a beach suitable for landing on that dense jungle shore— and me steadfastly insisting that it was his responsibility to say "land the landing force" as well as where and when—just as I had been instructed in Basic School.

History should record that the Marines did land and although the enemy gave them a warm welcome, we got the job done.[7]

A Kiwi veteran, Lindsay Adams, pondered the significance of his time on Vella Lavella:

It is impossible to reflect on the Vella Lavella operation which was all over in 3 weeks, without wondering if it made any difference to the war as a whole, whether the rescue of 500 or 600 Japanese benefited the enemy in any way, and whether the loss of a mere three score or so of our troops in the process had any military significance at all.

The answer, on further reflection is that the Vella Lavella operation by elements of the 3rd NZ Division, if put under the microscope and magnified greatly in terms of numbers and time, would reveal every aspect of war at its best and at its worst. Everything that happened over that short period, was, in miniature, representative of everything that could possibly happen to any serviceman or servicewoman in any war. There were links with the navy and the airforce and with the American Allies, as seen in the naval battles and air skirmishes going on around all the islands including Vella Lavella. There was military significance from many angles in what our troops accomplished through the intensity of what they endured and surmounted, however small the scale.

Every kind of apprehension and terror came to those few at the sharp end of this jungle war and there were many instances of great courage and determination. The few who gave their lives gave them in extremely daunting circumstances, alone and carrying the burden for hundreds of others lucky enough not to be put to the same test.[8]

Adams' sentiment equally applies to all nationalities that fought on Vella Lavella. Yet there were beneficial aspects to the struggle for Vella Lavella. Among other things, the seizure of Vella Lavella brought the campaign for the Central Solomon Islands to an end. It also paid the Allies three strategic dividends: First, it enabled the Allies to dominate the Vella Gulf and the islands that had been bypassed. An airfield and naval base were rapidly established on Vella Lavella, and the Japanese garrisons to the south began to wither through lack of supplies. Second, the concept of bypassing Japanese positions rather than confronting them head-on minimized Allied casualties and validated the bypass concept. The technique would be repeated many times in the South Pacific. "The success of the Vella Lavella operation, which by-passed Kolombangara and in a few weeks forced its evacuation without a fight, led to a further re-examination of Solomon's strategy."[9] Ultimately, this strategy would save many Allied and Japanese lives, as well as those of the Islanders.

The third strategic dividend was that it allowed the momentum of the Allied advance in the South Pacific to continue apace. As Eric Bergerud has commented, "New Georgia was a U.S. defeat in all but name. Halsey quickly redeemed the situation by landing New Zealand and U.S. troops on the nearly undefended island of Vella Lavella weeks later. This brilliant move cut off the remaining Japanese garrisons in the middle Solomons and forced another Guadalcanal-style evacuation. Once Vella Lavella had solved the problems of the middle Solomons, Bougainville was obviously the next target."[10] *The Pacific* noted that "the capture of Vella Lavella paved the way for the next thrust forward—the occupation of the Treasury Group, 73 miles away and the landing on Bougainville."[11] An RNZAF analysis likewise concluded:

> The capture of Vella Lavella and the construction of the Allied airfield at Barakoma on that island, outflanked the enemy outposts on Choiseul and exposed the Kahili-Kara airfields to continuous air attack from an Allied air base only 65 miles away. The Japanese strips in the north at Buka and Bonis were within effective range for Allied fighters from Barakoma. Ballale airfield, the remaining enemy air base in the south Bougainville area, was bombed out of commission by the beginning of October and was no longer "of any importance." The Japanese air force was unable to protect its bases on Bougainville and its supply lines from Rabaul to the north Solomons. Consequently the enemy forces on Bougainville were exposed to an overwhelming amphibious assault by the superior Allied air force.
>
> The complex interplay between air, naval and land forces was very much in evidence during the struggle for Vella Lavella. Air support was given to land and naval forces and disrupted the flow of Japanese barges shifting supplies to their island garrisons. Land forces provided security for the air base at Barakoma. Naval power enabled the essential fuels, ammunition, and myriad other supplies to be brought forward so that all fighting services could operate.[12]

USMC historians Jeter Isley and Philip Crowl saw significance in the contrasting grind of taking New Georgia as opposed to the relative ease with which Vella Lavella was taken. They believe that "these two mid 1943 operations were of great importance not only to the winning of the Pacific War but also to the development of amphibian techniques." They point to the increasing skill and professionalism of the U.S. Navy and the evisceration of Japanese airpower. The availability of new mass-produced amphibious craft meant that it was possible to take men and supplies from one area and deposit them at a point where the enemy was weak. The bypass concept was shown to be not only feasible but also the preferred strategy.[13]

John Miller, the U.S. Army official historian, concluded that

> the bypassing of Kolombangara[,] though overshadowed by later bypasses and clouded by the fact that the bypassed troops escaped, was a satisfactory demonstration of the technique; the seizure of Vella Lavella provided Halsey's forces with a good airfield for a much lower price in blood than an assault on Kolombangara. The Allies swiftly built another airfield at Ondonga Peninsula on New Georgia. This gave them four—Munda, Barakoma, Ondonga and Segi. The first three, the

BUT NOW YOU KNOW
Vella Lavella 22 Dec. 1943

You have heard no doubt, of tropical Isles,
Where sun-tanned maidens, with lovely smiles,
Lie on the beaches, 'neath spreading palms,
And welcome newcomers, with outstretched arms.

You have heard of gentle breezes that blow,
And luscious fruits, that the natives grow,
While, in shimmering waters of azure blue,
Swim tropical fishes of every hue.

You have heard of romance by sandy shores,
And freedom unlimbered by white man's laws,
Where drinks are ample, and tasty and cool,
And the white man, who works is a ruddy fool.

BUT NOW YOU KNOW!!!

But now you know, if you used your eyes,
That the stories you've heard, are nothing but lies,
What women there are, are big and fat,
If you look at others, you're on the mat.

Your only fruit, comes out of a tin,
Mosquitoes feed on your tender skin,
The gentle breeze, is a stormy gale,
And the tents must be struck - you know the tale.

The only beaches are miles away,
There's nothing to do, when you get your pay,
As for the men, who never do work,
They're only the experts who've learnt to shirk.

They've rationed our beer, we can't get a drink,
If you want to write home, you'll find no ink,
You wait every day, to see if there's mail,
But they must have a houseful, down at Bourail.

So when you go home, let's hope it's soon,
If songs of the South Seas, New Zealanders croon,
Just tell them the truth, as you've seen it like me,
In Pacific Defence, in the '43.

"But Now You Know," a poem by an anonymous New Zealand soldier, Third New Zealand Division Association Newsletter (author's collection).

most used, brought all Bougainville within range of Allied fighters. When South Pacific forces invaded the island, they could pick an undefended place and frustrate the Japanese efforts to build up Bougainville's defenses and delay the Allies in New Georgia.[14]

The seizure of Vella Lavella was a small part of a gigantic war the Japanese have called "The Great Pacific War." Nonetheless, small battles on obscure islands would often mark the progress of the Allied advance, which would ultimately lead to the Japanese surrender on the USS *Missouri* in Tokyo Bay. The American historian Harry A. Gailey considered:

> Japan lost the war because of a series of complex strategic and tactical defeats, among which the Solomon Islands campaigns played a significant part. It would be an exaggeration to maintain that Japan lost the war in the Solomons, but it would be equally wrong to ignore the effects on the Japanese of attempts to defend Munda, Kolombangara and Bougainville after their defeat at Guadalcanal. The various battles on and around this long string of fetid, jungle-covered islands took a toll in ships, planes and men that the Japanese in attempting to meet the demands of other theatres could never replace.[15]

However, another American historian, John Prados, takes a broader view. He considers the Solomon Islands campaign pivotal to the defeat of Japan, pointing out that even after the Battle of Midway the Japanese were militarily stronger in the Pacific than the Allies. He contends that "the Solomons became the grave of Japan's dream. Here the pendulum of the Pacific War began to swing against Tokyo." He argues, "In the Solomons the war was fought to a decision."[16]

Vella Lavella was an Allied victory in the absolute, truest sense. It was a victory that wrong-footed the Japanese strategically, and that victory was the result of cooperation between American naval, land and air forces; New Zealand land and air forces; Australian, English and New Zealand Coastwatchers; and Fijian, Tongan, Samoan and Solomon Island soldiers. The contribution of the Islanders of Vella Lavella likewise set the capstone on Allied victory.

Chronology

1943

6 July—Battle of Kula Gulf; USS *Helena* hit by 3 Japanese torpedoes and sinks off Vella Lavella Island.

21–22 July—Beadle's reconnaissance party travels to Vella Lavella.

24 July—Sgt. Trevor Ganley's Hudson is shot down by Japanese fighters.

6–7 August—Battle of Vella Gulf.

11 August—Admiral Halsey, Rear Admiral T. S. Wilkinson and Brigadier General Robert B. McClure issue orders for the invasion of Vella Lavella.

12–13 August—A 25-man reconnaissance party lands at Barakoma, Vella Lavella.

13 August—Imperial Japanese Headquarters issues order abandoning the Central Solomons.

14 August—Brigadier General Francis P. Mulcahy, USMC, opens his command post as COMAIR New Georgia at Munda Point.

15 August—First Echelon arrives at Barakoma; 35th Infantry Regiment lands on Vella Lavella unopposed. Lt. Kenneth Walsh, USMC, downs two Japanese aircraft.

17–18 August—Second Echelon arrives at Barakoma. USN destroyers fail to stop Japanese troops landing on northern Vella Lavella. Naval Battle of Horaniu.

21 August—Third Echelon arrives at Barakoma.

25 August—Japanese set up a barge staging base on Horaniu to assist their evacuation of Japanese forces trapped in the Central Solomons. All organized Japanese resistance on New Georgia ceases.

26 August—Fourth Echelon arrives at Barakoma.

30 August—Lt. Kenneth Walsh battles fifty Japanese aircraft, shooting down four before being forced to ditch off Vella Lavella.

2 September—Major Tripp's South Seas Scouts depart from Barakoma to carry out reconnaissance patrols.

3 September—Rear Admiral T.S. Wilkinson formally hands command of American forces ashore on Vella Lavella to General Griswold.

13 September—Advanced party from 14 Brigade attacked by Japanese aircraft at Maravari.

14 September—U.S. artillery and infantry attack Horaniu.

14–16 September—American bombers strike at Japanese bases at Kahili and Balale escorted by Nos. 15 and 17 Squadrons, RNZAF.

18 September—14 Brigade lands at Barakoma. Barrowclough assumes command of Allied forces on Vella Lavella under the title of "Northern Landing Force."

20 September—Munda is cleared of Japanese troops.

21 September—35th and 37th Battalion Combat Teams begin pincer movement around Vella Lavella. A reconnaissance group in platoon strength from each BCT leaves the HQ of 14 Brigade Group at Maravari for Mundi Mundi and Paraso Bay.

22 September—Lt. W.J. McNeight, with a platoon of five picked men, makes an unopposed landing at Mundi Mundi, which is found unsuitable as a base for future operations.

23 September—A utility aircraft and four fighters land at Barakoma airfield.

25 September—A small patrol of the 35th BCT observes Japanese troops around Bangarangara but, following orders, withdraws without being seen. 30th Battalion disembarks at Mumia beach. A Japanese air raid hits Advanced Brigade Headquarters at Matu Suroto, killing five and wounding fifteen soldiers. Japanese aircraft hit LST-167 at Ruravai Beach. Nine hundred Marines of 1 Marine Amphibious Corps land on east-central coast of Vella Lavella. New Zealand soldiers commence active operations to clear the Japanese off Vella Lavella.

26 September—"D" Company, 35th BCT, moves to Etupeka, detaching two sections halfway between Tambala and Etupeka.

27 September—U.S. planes land at Barakoma airstrip courtesy of the 58th NCB. Capture of Japanese *Daihatsu* landing barge, renamed HMS *Confident* by a patrol from the 37th Battalion. Albon/Beaumont patrol is ambushed at Marquana Bay.

28–29 September—The Japanese begin the evacuation of Kolombangara.

1 October—Eighth Echelon arrives at Vella Lavella at Narguai. Japanese planes bomb LST-448, destroying it and killing NZ AA gun crews. New Zealand forces take over quartermaster duties on Vella Lavella.

2 October—Barrowclough establishes Divisional HQ at Gill's Plantation, Joroveto. 3NZ Division Field Battery arrives on Vella Lavella.

3 October—A and B Companies clear Machine Gun Gully.

4 October—37th Battalion Combat Team moves to Susulautolo Bay.

5 October—37th Battalion lands at Warambari Bay, where it encounters serious opposition and the Japanese have to be driven back so that a defensive perimeter can be established.

5–6 October—Pocketing of Japanese complete.

6 October—Naval battle off Vella Lavella.

6–7 October Japanese evacuate Vella Lavella.

7 October—A battalion of U.S. 27th Infantry Regiment occupies Vila, Kolombangara.

8 October—USN establishes a small Naval Advance Base at Barakoma, Vella Lavella.

9 October—Vella Lavella declared secure. Brigadier Potter at 10 a.m. declares 14 Brigade's task completed. Air and naval bombardments force the Japanese to evacuate Kolombangara.

10 October—Gizo Island is searched by two platoons from 30th Battalion.

16 October—U.S. Corsairs strafe barge K51–5.

17 October—After the completion of dispersal areas and arrival of ground crew, Barakoma Airfield is declared operational by 58th NCB.

19 October—Ganongga Island is searched by a patrol from 4 Field Security.

20 October—12th Echelon arrives at Vella Lavella. 35th Regimental Combat Team leaves Vella Lavella by LST for Guadalcanal.

10 November—35th Infantry Regiment arrives in New Zealand for a rest period.

26 November—Seaward relinquishes command of the 35th Battalion.

28 November—A church service is held to dedicate a memorial cairn to the men of 209th Light Anti-Aircraft Battery killed on 1 October 1943.

14 December—Fire at P.T. boat base at Lambu Lambu (2 dead).

19 December—An Allied cemetery at Maravari is dedicated.

24 December—An earthquake hits Vella Lavella.

1944

5 January—Divisional HQ of 3NZ Division closes on Vella Lavella and moves to Guadalcanal.

19 January—Command on Vella Lavella passes to Sixth (U.S.) Island Command.

15 February—Operation Squarepeg; 14 Brigade takes part in the capture of the Green Islands.

15 June—Airfield operations cease on Vella Lavella.

12 July—CBMU 502 leaves Vella Lavella.

September—Naval base is closed.

20 October—3NZ Division ceases to exist. Elements of 23 Brigade, Royal Australian Army, under Brigadier Arnold Potts take over garrison duties on Vella Lavella.

25 December—35th Infantry Regiment, 25th Division, U.S. Army, lands on Luzon, Philippine Islands.

1945

2 September—Surrender documents are signed by Japanese representatives on the USS *Missouri*.

Appendices

A: Naval Order of Battle, 15 August 1943

DESTROYERS

USS *Nicholas*, USS *O'Bannon*, USS *Taylor*, USS *Chevalier*, USS *Waller*, USS *Saufley*, USS *Philip*, USS *Renshaw*, USS *Conway*, USS *Eaton*, USS *Pringle*, USS *Cony*

AUXILIARY PERSONNEL DESTROYERS (APDs)

USS *Stringham*, USS *Waters*, USS *Dent*, USS *Talbot*, USS *Wade*, USS *McKean*

LANDING CRAFT, INFANTRY (LCI)

21, 22, 61, 64, 67, 68, 222, 330, 331, 332, 333, 334

LAND SHIP, TANK (LST)

354, 395 and 399

SUB-CHASERS

760 and 761

P.T. BOATS

26 from Rendova and Lever Harbour

Composition of the III Amphibious Force Task Units for the Occupation of Vella Lavella, 15 August 1943

III AMPHIBIOUS FORCE

R.Adm. Theodore S. Wilkinson, in *Cony*
TransDiv 22, L.Cmdr. Robert H. Wilkinson

TASK UNIT 31.5.1

Advanced Transport Group, Capt. Thomas J. Ryan Jr.

TransDiv 12, Cmdr. John D. Sweeney
Stringham, Waters, Dent, Talbot
TransDiv 22, L.Cmdr. Robert H. Wilkinson
Kilty (F), McKean, Ward
Destroyer Screen, Capt. Ryan (ComDesDiv 41)
Nicholas, O'Bannon, Taylor, Chevalier, Cony, Pringle

TASK UNIT 31.5.2

Second Transport Group, Capt. William R. Cooke Jr.
LCI Unit, Cmdr. James M. Smith
LCIs 21, 22, 23, 61, 67, 68, 222 (F), 322, 330, 331, 333, 334
Destroyer Screen, Capt. Cooke (ComDesDiv 43)
Waller, Philip, Saufley, Renshaw

TASK UNIT 31.5.3

Third Transport Group, Capt. Grayson B. Carter
LSTs 354, 395, 399
Screen, Cmdr. James R. Pahl (ComDesDiv 44)
Conway (F), Eaton, SCs 760, 761

SCREEN

DesDiv 41, 43 and 44*
MTB Flotilla CAST, Cmdr. Allen P. Calvert
New Georgia MTBs Kolombangara MTBs: 8 MTBs

Northern Landing Force, Brigadier Gen. Robert B. McClure, USA

Troops
Headquarters Detachment
4th Marine Defense Battalion (less certain detachments)
35th Regimental Combat Team, USA (less certain detachments)

Naval Base Force, Capt. George C. Kriner
58th Naval Construction Battalion (less rear echelon)
Naval Base Units, including Boat Pool No. 9

Total: About 4,600 officers and men

After performing convoy duty to Barakoma beach, these destroyers were to form a screen for landing operations. (See William L. McGee, Amphibious Operations in the South Pacific in World War II, vol. 2 [Santa Barbara, California: BMC Publications 2002], 591.)

B: U.S. Order of Battle, 15 August 1943, Ground Units (Brigadier General McClure, U.S. Army)

a. 35th Infantry Regiment Combat Team, 25th U.S. Division (less certain detachments)

b. 58th NCB (less rear echelon)

c. Military Intelligence Service

d. Headquarters Detachment, Northern Landing Force

e. 4th Marine Defence Battalion (less certain detachments)

f. Naval Base Group, including Boat Pool No. 8

g. Reconnaissance Troop, 25th U.S. Division

h. 64th Field Artillery Battalion

i. Company C, 65th Combat Engineers Battalion

j. Company B, 25th Medical Battalion

C: U.S. Forces on Vella Lavella—1943

a. Seabees
58th Naval Construction Battalion
77th Naval Construction Battalion
6th Special Naval Construction Battalion
CBMU 502

b. U.S. Army
35th Regiment (The Cacti), 25th Infantry Division
Military Intelligence Service
64th Field Artillery Battalion
65th Combat Engineer Battalion
25th Medical Battalion

c. USMC
Paramarines
4th Base Depot Supply Service
Provisional Force 3rd Marine Division

D: NZ Battalion Combat Teams

14 Brigade, 3NZ Division (Brigadier Leslie Potter)

35TH BATTALION COMBAT TEAM

a. 12 Field Battery (Major L.J. Fahey), 17 Field Regiment

b. C Troop, 207 Light Anti-Aircraft Battery (Lieutenant J.C. Hutchison)

c. C Troop, 53 Anti-Tank Battery (Lieutenant D. Taylor)

d. Detachment of 20 Field Company Engineers (Second Lieutenant A.R. Garry)

e. Detachment of 16 MT Company ASC (Captain T.P. Revell)

f. No. 3 Platoon, 14 Infantry Brigade Medium Machine Gun Company (Lieutenant R.B. Lockett)

g. K Section Signals (Lieutenant E.G. Harris)

h. D and E Platoon, 14 Infantry Brigade

37TH BATTALION COMBAT TEAM

a. 35 Field Battery (Major A.G. Coulam)

b. A Troop, 207 Light Anti-Aircraft Battery (Lieutenant O.W. MacDonald)

c. A Troop, 53 Anti-tank Battery (Lieutenant C.E. Kerr)

d. Detachment of 16 MT Company ASC (Captain J.F. Wilson)

e. Headquarters Company, 22 Field Ambulance (Captain B.W. Clouston)

f. 3rd Platoon, 14 Brigade, Medium Machine Gun Company (Lieutenant K.A. Wills)

g. E Section, Signals (Lieutenant L.C. Stewart)

h. Detachment of 20 Field Company Engineers (Lieutenant R.W. Syme)

(See Oliver A. Gillespie, *The Pacific* [Wellington: Historical Publications Branch, 1952], 130.)

E: Japanese Order of Battle

a. Survivors from 6th and 38th Division (estimated at 300)

b. Special Naval Landing Force

c. Downed aircrew

d. Survivors of IJN ships sunk near Vella Lavella

The precise numbers of Japanese defenders are unknown but are estimated at 500–700. Contemporary NZ Army documents refer to the following:

• Sawayama Unit

• Kajiwara Unit

• Tashiro Unit

• 41st Infantry Unit; Regimental Commander Col. Kiyomi Yazawa, Rear Echelon Battalion Commander

• Major Kanzo Iizuka, Battalion Commander

• 1st Lt. Sakae Okazaki

Glossary

AA—Anti-aircraft guns

Ack-Ack—Anti-aircraft fire

Acorn Unit—An American unit specializing in supplies and administration

AIRSOLS—Aircraft Solomon Islands Command

Angel—Friendly aircraft

APc—Small coastal transport vessel

APDs—Fast Transport, Destroyers (special destroyers of the USN adapted for troop-carrying purposes). Originally intended to carry raiders, the APDs performed yeoman service in the Pacific War, delivering troops. In U.S. Naval terminology, "AP" designates a transport vessel and "D" designates a destroyer.

Arty—Artillery

Ash—Allied codename for Vella Lavella

B-24 Liberator—USAAF four-engine bomber

Bandit—Enemy aircraft

BAR—Browning Automatic Rifle (American rifle that could be fired at a rate of up to 650 rounds per minute). Usually 2 soldiers operated it, one to fire and one to carry the ammunition. Although a rifle, it had many of the characteristics of a light machine gun.

BCT—Battalion Combat Team (NZ) (a battalion augmented by smaller support units)

BHQ—Battalion Headquarters

Black Sheep Squadron—A squadron of USMC Corsair fighters, at one point led by the legendary ace "Pappy" Boyington until he was shot down and captured

BN—Battalion

Bogey or Bogie—Unidentified aircraft

Bren—Bren Light Machine Gun

Bure—Native hut made out of local materials

Canal, the—Guadalcanal

CAP—Combat Air Patrol (a group of airborne aircraft, usually fighters, tasked with defending a particular locality or asset)

CBMU—Construction Battalion Maintenance Unit

CDR—Commander

CO—Commanding Officer

Coastwatcher—Both Allied and Japanese forces used personnel to watch air and naval movements on the islands of the South Pacific. The Allied Coastwatching system had been set up in 1939 and was reasonably sophisticated.

COMAIRSOPAC—Commander Air South Pacific Area

Combat Air Patrol—A standing aerial patrol, usually fighter planes, designated to protect a particular target

Combat Loaded—Ships would be loaded in such a way that the items necessary for combat could be unloaded first. (This is not the most efficient way of loading a ship.)

COMSOPAC—Commander South Pacific Area

Condition Green—All clear (no enemy aircraft nearby)

Condition Red—Enemy air raid in progress

Daihatsu—Wooden motorized vessel used by the Japanese for transporting troops and supplies, often formidably armed

DFC—Distinguished Flying Cross (British Commonwealth award)

Dog-Day—D–Day, the Allied code phrase for the first day of an amphibious landing

Dogeared—The U.S. codename for Vella Lavella

Dog Tags—Metal identification discs worn by Allied personnel

Doxology—A short hymn of praise to God sung in Christian worship

DSO—Distinguished Service Order (British military decoration)

F4U Corsair—a bent-winged U.S. fighter plane

FA—Field Artillery

G3—U.S. Staff Officer (Operations and Plans)

Hvy AA—Heavy anti-aircraft guns

I.F.F.—Identification Friend or Foe (a device attached to Allied planes that emitted a coded signal identifying the plane as Allied; a plane giving an improper signal or none at all was presumed to be an enemy)

IJA—Imperial Japanese Army

IJN—Imperial Japanese Navy

I Section—Intelligence Section

Kate—Allied code name for Nakajima torpedo bomber

Kiwi—The national flightless bird of New Zealand, and the name by which New Zealanders refer to themselves (pronounced "Kee-Wee")

Kts—Knots

LCI—Landing Craft, Infantry (an amphibious craft capable of carrying 30 tons and about 200 men; its distinctive feature is twin ladders on either side of the bows, so that men and equipment can be landed directly onto the beach)

LCM—Landing Craft, Mechanized

LCT—Landing Craft, Tank

LCVP—Landing Craft, Vehicle, Personnel

Light Aid Detachment (LAD)—New Zealand engineering unit

Long Lance Torpedoes—Japanese Type 93 torpedoes of devastating lethality, powered by oxygen and virtually undetectable once launched

LST—Landing Ship, Tank

Mae West—An inflatable lifejacket named after the buxom Hollywood starlet

Merrill's Marauders—An American unit formed to do long-range penetration of Japanese lines, similar to the British Chindits. The unit fought in Burma and became burned out.

Nat Pat—National Patriotic Fund (a New Zealand organization set up to coordinate the supply of comforts to the soldiers; YMCA secretaries usually acted as representatives in the frontline areas)

NCB—Naval Construction Battalion (Seabees)

NCO—Non-Commissioned Officer (e.g., Sergeant)

NZ—New Zealand

OO—Operations Order

OP—Observation Post

Paramarines—USMC-trained parachutists (generally, however, used as infantry on Guadalcanal and Choiseul)

Permanent Force—Full-time, regular NZ Army soldiers

PFC—Private, First Class (American rank—basic soldier)

Pidgin—A language developed in the South Pacific by local peoples, made up of composite words and phrases

PT—Physical Training

P.T. Boat—Patrol Torpedo boat

Pub—New Zealand slang, short for "Public House" (establishment that sold liquor)

Pyre—U.S. codename for Barakoma Airfield

R & R—Rest and Recreation

RAAF—Royal Australian Air Force

RAMSI—Regional Assistance Mission Solomon Islands

RAN—Royal Australian Navy

RANVR—Royal Australian Naval Volunteer Reserve. Coastwatchers were generally enrolled in the RANVR to give them rank and hopefully avoid their execution as spies in the event of capture by the Japanese—a vain hope, in most instances.

RAP—Regimental Aid Post

RCT—Regimental Combat Team (U.S.) (an infantry regiment augmented by smaller support units)

Red Meatball—American slang for the round, red insignia on Japanese aircraft

RNZAF—Royal New Zealand Air Force

RNZN—Royal New Zealand Navy

SC—Sub-chaser

SCAT—South Pacific Combat Air Transport Command

Scramble—A rapid takeoff of aircraft in response to an alert or enemy attack

Slot, the—The passage between Bougainville and Guadalcanal (a heavily contested piece of water during the Solomons Campaign)

SOPAC—South Pacific Area (an American command zone). Admirals Ghormley, Halsey and Carney commanded this area at various times between 1942 and 1945.

Stonk—Concentrated artillery barrage

Stretcher Bearer—British term for a soldier trained to provide first aid medical treatment and evacuate the wounded from the battlefield (equivalent to the U.S. "corpsman/medic")

Territorial—A part-time NZ military force; a militia

Thirteenth Air Force (13th USAAF)—The U.S. Army Air Force that flew in the Solomons. Confusingly, it had previously been known as the Fifth Air Force.

Tokyo Express—Japanese naval resupply and reinforcement convoy, usually undertaken at high speed by destroyers

Tommy Gun—Thompson Sub-Machine Gun

TransDiv—Transport Division

Units of Fire—Ammunition calculated to be sufficient for a day's fighting

USMC—United States Marine Corps

USNR—United States Naval Reserve

Val—Allied codename for the Aichi Type 99 Dive-bomber

Ventura—Allied twin-engine light bomber produced by Lockheed. A variant of the Hudson. The Ventura was supplied to the RNZAF by the Americans. Used mainly as a patrol bomber for reconnaissance work and anti-submarine patrols.

VMF—Marine Fighter Squadron. In U.S. terminology, "V" designates a fixed-wing aircraft, "M" designates Marine Corps, and "F" designates the squadron as being equipped with fighters.

Washing Machine Charlie—An Allied nickname for Japanese planes that carried out nocturnal harassing raids on Allied positions. They rarely inflicted damage or casualties, but they were very successful in depriving the soldiers of sleep. The engines of the Japanese planes were de-synchronized, producing a distinctive noise similar to that of an agitator in an old-fashioned washing machine.

William—Codename for III Amphibious Force Task Units

YB—Yellow Belly (American term of abuse referring to the Japanese)

Zeke or Zero—Allied names for the Mitsubishi A6M Fighter, a single-engine Japanese aircraft that was one of the most maneuverable and successful fighter planes of the Pacific War

ZL—Zone of Lethality (artillery term for an area where fatal casualties will occur)

Chapter Notes

Introduction

1. A flightless bird, a national symbol of New Zealand. New Zealanders refer to themselves as "Kiwis."

2. A recent study of the New Georgia Campaign by Brian Altobello, *Into the Shadows Furious: The Brutal Battle for New Georgia* (Novato, CA: Presidio Press, 2000) does not cover the fighting on Vella Lavella.

3. John Miller, *Cartwheel: The Reduction of Rabaul* (Harrisburg, PA: National Historical Society, 1993), 180. This statement would have caused wry amusement to those who fought there and confirmed that their efforts were forgotten and unappreciated.

Chapter One

1. *Dictionary of American Naval Fighting Ships* (DANFS).

2. Richard Worth, *Fleets of World War II* (Cambridge, MA: Da Capo Press, 2001), 302.

3. *Ibid.*

4. The later USN inquiry established that no warship of *Helena*'s size could have survived three torpedoes. War Damage Report No 43 Bureau of Ships, 15 September 1944.

5. Burris Jenkins, Jr., "Back from Hell," *The Detroit News*, circa late 1943.

6. John Chew narrative, http://www.usshelena.org/chew.html.

7. Narrative of Frank Cellozzi, USS *Helena* website, http://www.usshelena.org.

8. Chew narrative; Chew described an ailment known as "immersion ankles," sores from being in salt water that made walking painful.

9. Narrative of James Layton, *Helena* website.

10. Cellozzi narrative.

11. Narrative of Deale Binion Cochrane, *Helena* website.

12. Chew narrative.

13. Cellozzi narrative.

14. John J. Domagalski *Sunk in Kula Gulf*, Dulles, Virginia: Potomac Books, 2012, 189.

15. Sources—Walter Lord *Lonely Vigil: Coastwatchers of the Solomons*, Annapolis, Maryland: Bluejacket Books, 2006, Chapter 12, 165 Uninvited Guests; USS *Helena* Website, http://www.usshelena.org.

16. Archives NZ, Air 118 110, 77 IX, Ganley letter to War History Board, 25 September 1946.

17. Maori Television ANZAC Day 2011, "Ng a Toa O te Moana-nui-a-kiwa. The Warriors of the Pacific, Solomon Islands."

18. Ganley letter to War History Board.

19. *Ibid.*

Chapter Two

1. Miller, 173.

2. Third Division Histories Committee *Pacific Saga*, Wellington: A.H. & A.W. Reed, 1947 67.

3. Rottman, Gordon L. *World War II Pacific Island Guide: A Geo-Military Study*, Westport, Connecticut: Greenwood Press, 2002, 127–130.

4. *Warriors of the Pacific*, Maori Television, Anzac Day, 2011.

5. Rennie, 44.

6. T. Duncan Stout, *Medical Services in*

New Zealand and the Pacific, Wellington: Historical Publications Branch, 1958 44.

7. Oliver A. Gillespie, *The Pacific* (Wellington: Historical Publications Branch, 1952), 130.

8. Army Board, *From Guadalcanal to Nissan: With the Third Division Through the Solomons* (Wellington, 1945), 15.

9. John M. Collins, *Military Geography for Professionals and the Public* (Washington, DC: Brasseys, 1998), 117.

10. *Ibid.*

11. *Ibid.*, 121.

12. Eric Bergerud, *Touched with Fire: The Land War in the South Pacific* (New York: Penguin Books, 1996), 493.

13. Correspondence with author, 23 April 2012.

14. Eric Bergerud, *Fire in the Sky* (Boulder, CO: Westview Press, 2000), 124. What Harper failed to realize was that animal tuberculosis was prevalent on Vella Lavella and New Zealand troops were prohibited from shooting cattle and were warned that the meat was unfit for human consumption. (Lt. Col. A.H. Sugden, Routine Order No. 8).

15. Narrative of Jerome J. Hendrick (Author's collection).

Chapter Three

1. Hendrick narrative.

2. Correspondence with author, 23 April 2012.

3. "Dr. J. Alfred Burden, Col.: MIS Pioneer," http://www.javadc.org/burden.htm. See also James C. McNaughton, *Nisei Linguists: Japanese Americans in the Military Intelligence Service During World War II* (Washington, DC: U.S. Government Printing Office, 2006), 176.

4. Parts of the Solomons were administered by the British and parts such as Bougainville by the Australians as mandated territory.

5. John Prados, *Islands of Destiny: The Solomons Campaign and the Eclipse of the Rising Sun* (New York: New American Library, 2012), 30.

6. Methodist Church of New Zealand Archives, Register of Ministers, *Touchstone*, July 2006, 15.

7. Walter Lord, *Lonely Vigil* (Annapolis: Naval Institute Press, 2006), 112–5.

8. D.C. Horton *New Georgia: Pattern for Victory* (London: Pan/Ballantine Books, 1972), 35.

9. Archives, NZ Air 1282. Comairsols—Patrol Squadron 54 "Black Cats." Description and analysis of operations in the Solomon Islands area March–December 1943.

10. John Crawford, "Major General Sir Harold Barrowclough: Leadership and Command in Two World Wars," Glyn Harper and Joel Hayward, eds., *Born to Lead* (Auckland: Exisle Publishing Ltd., 2003), 144–163.

11. Rennie, 38.

12. Rennie, 101.

13. Lindsay Adams narrative, authors collection.

14. Lindsay Adams interview, November 2006.

15. *Ibid.*

16. NZDF Personnel File.

17. Lindsay Adams narrative.

18. Personnel File, NZDF Records, Trentham. Sugden was mentioned in dispatches for his record in the South Pacific. He suffered dysentery in 1944, probably contracted in the Solomon Islands. In the post war world he had various administrative positions but while viewed as a competent officer, his career seemed to have been blighted because he served in 3NZ Division rather than with 2NZ Division in the Mediterranean. He died 21 March 1981.

19. NZDF Personnel File.

20. Archives NZ, WAII, 1158, 37 Bn War Diary, 20 August 1943, Meli Beach.

21. Archives NZ, WAII, 1, DAZ 158/1/21 Historical Record of 37th Bn for the month of August 1943, Entries 15 and 18 August 1943.

22. Doug Ross interview, 8 November 2006.

23. Archives NZ, EA 86/1/1 Defense of Pacific.

24. Colonial Office, *Among Those Present*, London: His Majesty's Stationery Office, 1946, 39.

25. Colin R Larsen, *Pacific Commandos—New Zealanders and Fijians in Action: A History of Southern Independent Commando and First Commando Fijian Guerrillas* (Wellington: A.H. & A.W. Reed, 1946), 100.

26. Colonial Office, *Among Those Present*, 54.

27. *Ibid.*, 55.

28. *Ibid.*, 60.

29. *Ibid.*, 61.

30. Larsen, 152.

31. *Ibid.*, 153.

32. Larsen, 149.

33. *Ibid.*, 150.

34. Samuel Eliot Morison, *History of United States Naval Operations in World War II, vol. VI Breaking the Bismarks Barrier, 22 July 1942–1 May 1944* (Edison, NJ: Castle Books, 2001), 221.

35. See Edward Drea, *Japan's Imperial Army: Its Rise and Fall, 1853–1945* (Lawrence: University of Kansas Press, 2009), 258–260; and Edward Drea, "Making Soldiers-Training, Doctrine and Culture in the Imperial Japanese Army," paper delivered at Australian War Memorial 2012 Conference "Kokoda: 'Beyond the Legend,'" 6 September 2012.

36. Archives NZ, WAII, Series 1, AD12, 28/15 vol. 1 Pacific Operations.

37. Gillespie, 127.

38. *Ibid.*

39. Horton, 34.

Chapter Four

1. John Rentz, *Marines in the Central Solomons* (Washington, DC: Historical Branch, Headquarters, U.S. Marine Corps, 1952), 9.

2. Jeter A. Isley, and Philip Crowl, *The U.S. Marines and Amphibious War* (New Jersey: Princeton University Press, 1951), 170.

3. The U.S. 25th, 37th and 43rd Divisions had been involved in the New Georgia Campaign and the 43rd in particular had suffered significant casualties.

4. Nimitz's biographer, E.B. Potter, attributes the new strategy to Nimitz: "At Nimitz's suggestion, Halsey took a leaf out of Kinkaid's Aleutian plan and bypassed the strongly defended island of Kolombangara in favor of a landing on lightly held Vella Lavella Island, further up the slot." E.B. Potter, *Nimitz* (Annapolis: Naval Institute Press, 1976), 245. Halsey, however, credits his staff with suggesting the bypass policy. William F. Halsey, and J. Bryan, *Admiral Halsey's Story* (New York: McGraw Hill, 1947), 170–171.

5. Isley and Crowl, 174.

6. "Daihatsu" is an abbreviation for "Ogata Hatsu—dokitei," which means a large landing barge. The Daihatsu was 41–44 feet long; it could carry 100–120 men for short distances, 40–50 on long trips. The sides were usually armored and it carried machine guns. Miller, 182.

7. Lt. Col. W.H. Allen, Jr., "Action at Vella Lavella," *The Field Artillery Journal*, vol. 40, May–June 1950 (Washington, DC: The United States Field Artillery Association), 120.

8. W.F. Craven, and J.L. Cate, eds., *The Army Air Forces in World War II*, vol. 4, *The Pacific: Guadalcanal to Saipan, August 1942 to July 1944* (University of Chicago Press), 236.

9. *Ibid.*, 236.

10. Report on the occupation of Vella Lavella, 12 August to 3 September 1943, Commander Third Amphibious Force, 6 October 1943.

11. Potter, 228.

12. *Ibid.*, 228.

13. E.B. Potter, *Bull Halsey* (Annapolis: Naval Institute Press), 1985.

14. Morison 227–8.

15. Prados, 302.

16. Ronald H. Spector *Eagle Against the Sun*, New York: Viking Penguin 1984, 239.

17. A "snooper" aircraft found the Japanese ships and sent off a sighting report which the Japanese overheard. This sighting was deliberately done to avoid arousing Japanese suspicions that their signal codes had been broken by the Allies. Prados, 303.

18. Prados comments that "...*Shigure's* rudder, apparently so encrusted with barnacles that the holed rudder was only slightly less efficient at turning the ship," 304.

19. Tameichi Hara *Japanese Destroyer Captain* (New York: Ballentine Books, 1961), 187–192.

20. United States Navy Combat narrative, Kolombangara and Vella Lavella, 6 August–7 October 1943.

21. Mark Stille, *USN Destroyer vs IJN Destroyer, The Pacific 1943* (Oxford: Osprey Publishing, 2012), 71.

22. Paul S. Dull, *A Battle History of the Imperial Japanese Navy 1941–1945* (Annapolis: Naval Institute Press, 1978), 278–279.

23. Hara, 191.

24. Prados, 304.

25. Archives, NZ Air 118/4 Chapter 6, 5. Comairsopac Intelligence Air H 483/6/1.

26. Wilkinson Report, 3.

27. Miller, 173–175.

28. Clarence Edward Gedeon, ed., *History of the 58th Seabees* (New York: Foxcraft Commercial Press, Incorporated, 1950).

29. He had acquired this nickname because of his aptitude for the game of table tennis.

30. FE25/A16-3(1) Operation Order No. A12-43, 11 August 1943, 3.

31. PT boats were particularly vulnerable to air attack in daylight hours.

32. Operation Order No. A12-43 Annex A.

33. Operation Order No. A12-43, 46.
34. George C. Dyer, *The Amphibians Came to Conquer*, vol. 1 (Washington, DC: Government Printing Office, 1969), 500.
35. Miller, 178.
36. Lt. Col. W.H. Allen, *Action At Vella Lavella*, 120.
37. Wilkinson Report, 3.
38. Horton, 135.

Chapter Five

1. Frank Marks narrative.
2. Private James C. Cook narrative.
3. Vella Lavella Report, 5.
4. J. Henry Doscher, Jr., *Subchaser in the South Pacific: A Saga of the USS SC-761 During World War II* (Austin, Texas: Eakin Press, 1994), 45.
5. Lt. Col. W.H. Allen, *Action at Vella Lavella*, 122.
6. Wilkinson Report, 6.
7. Department of the Navy, Bureau of Yards and Docks, *Building the Navy's Bases in World War II, History of the Bureau of Yards and Docks and Civilian Engineer Corps 1940– 1946*, vol. 2 (Washington, DC, 1947), 266.
8. *Ibid.*, 265.
9. Allen, 121.
10. Wilkinson Report, 6.
11. Historical Division, General Headquarters, S.W. A., G-3 Journal 9 October 1943, Australian War Memorial.
12. Chris Rudge, *Air-to-Air: The Story Behind the Air-to-Air Combat Claims of the RNZAF*, Lyttelton, NZ: Adventure Air, 2003), 144.
13. William Wolf, *13th Fighter Command in World War II* (Atglen, PA: Schiffer Publishing, 2004), 200.
14. Mark Styling, *Corsair Aces of World War II* (Oxford: Osprey Publishing, 1995), 11.
15. Bob Spurdle, *The Blue Arena* (London: William Kimber & Co., 1986), 134.
16. The RNZAF narrative records: (a) 0530–0900hrs ... 4 P-40s on patrol over Vella Lavella, (b) 0530–0745 hrs.... 4 P-40s on patrol over shipping, (c) 0615–0845 hrs.... 4 P-40s on patrol over shipping in Vella Gulf, (d) 1000–11320 hrs.... 4 P-40s on patrol over Vella Lavella, (e) 1000–1240 hrs ... 4 P-40s on patrol over shipping. Archives NZ, Air 118/4, Chapter 6, 8.
17. Rudge, 141–2.

18. Archives, NZ, "Air 118 Operational Narrative," 9.
19. Rudge, 144–5.
20. Miller, 180.
21. Commander Third Amphibious Force to Commander in Chief, U.S. Pacific Fleet, Action Report Covering Operations 16–19, August 1943, 20 December 1943, FE25/A16-3(3).
22. Robert B. Carney, Chief of Staff to Commander in Chief, U.S. Pacific Fleet, A16-3/(91), 5 September 1943.
23. Wilkinson Report, para 45, 14–15.
24. Wilkinson Report, para 46, 15.
25. Wilkinson Report, 7.
26. Medal Citation.
27. Eric Bergerud, *Touched with Fire*, 389.
28. Wilkinson Report, 8.
29. Rear Admiral T.S. Wilkinson, 17 September 1945, cited in Doscher, *Subchaser in the South Pacific* (Austin, TX: Eakin Press,) 101–102.
30. J.D. Ladd, *Assault from the Sea 1939– 1945: The Craft, the Landings, the Men* (New York: Hippocrene Books, 1976), 198.
31. Battle Action of USS SC-505, 31 August 1943, cited in Doscher, *Subchaser in the South Pacific*, 99–100.
32. http://www.6thcorpscombatengineers.com.
33. Wilkinson Report, 10.
34. Rudge, 146.
35. Wilkinson Report, 13.
36. *Ibid.*, 11.
37. Wheeler, 181.
38. Rentz, 133.
39. Archives, NZ, Air 118, Operational narrative, 9.
40. www.6thcorpscombatengineers.com.
41. Frank Marks narrative.
42. Correspondence with author, 23 April 2012.
43. John Dower, *War Without Mercy: Race and Power in the Pacific War* (London: Faber & Faber, 1986), 63.
44. Frank Marks narrative.
45. For SSG Marvin Gunder the transfer was fatal. He died of malaria in Burma on 23 April 1944.
46. *Ibid.*
47. Allen, 123.
48. 35th Infantry Regiment (Cacti) Association, www.cacti35th.org/regiment/14a/Kia_details.
49. Hendrick narrative.
50. *Ibid.*

51. *Ibid.*

52. Allen, 123.

53. *Ibid.*, 124.

54. *Ibid.*, 124.

55. Narrative of James C. Cook.

56. Frank Marks narrative.

57. Eric Bergerud, *Touched with Fire*, 115.

58. Miller, 182.

59. John Prados, *Islands of Destiny*, 308.

60. Historical Division, General Headquarters, S.W. A. G-3 Journal, 9 October 1943. Item #890 entry August 17, 1943, Australian War Memorial, Canberra.

61. Australian War Memorial, Combat Intelligence Center South Pacific Force Translation of captured Japanese document S-3101, Diary of a Member of the 41st Infantry Regt.

62. This is noteworthy in that it was the first land combat involving soldiers of 3NZ Division. Archives NZ, WAII, 1, DAZ 158/1/22 Copy of diary kept by Sgt H.B. Brereton while temporarily at 1 Fijian Commandos.

63. Archives NZ, WAII, 1 DAZ Copy of Diary kept by Sgt. H.B. Brereton while temporarily attached 1 Fijian Commandos, September 14, 1943.

64. Larsen, 145.

65. Gillespie, 271.

66. Larsen, 147.

67. Archives NZ, Air 118/14 RNZAF narrative, Chapter 6, 14.

68. Bruce Gamble, *The Black Sheep: The Definitive Account of Marine Fighting Squadron 214 in World War II* (New York: Random House, 2003), 250–1.

Chapter Six

1. War Diary, Major General H.E. Barrowclough, entry 4 September 1943.

2. *Ibid.*, entry 9 September 1943.

3. *Ibid.*, entry 9 September 1943.

4. *Ibid.*, entry 10 September 1943.

5. Gillespie, 25–6.

6. War Diary, 35th Battalion HQ.

7. War Diary, Barrowclough, 17 September 1943.

8. Gillespie, 126.

9. Third Division Histories Committee, *Headquarters* (Wellington: A.H. & A.W. Reed, 1947). This volume is broken into two parts, one dealing with headquarters, the second dealing with communications.

10. Historical Record of 37th Bn for the month of September, 1943, entry 17, September 1943.

11. *Communications*, 191.

12. "A Soldier Remembers," 3NZ Division Association Newsletter, 1992, 29.

13. Gillespie, 127.

14. *Ibid.*, 127–8.

15. *Pacific Pioneers: The Story of the Engineers of the New Zealand Expeditionary Force in the Pacific* (Wellington: A.H. & A.W. Reed, 1947), 657.

16. Archives, NZ AD12 28/15/1—pt 4 Operation Kiwi Report, Barrowclough to Army HQ, September 1943.

17. Historical Record of 37 Bn, entry 18 September 1943.

18. Interview J.T. Humphrey, 19 June 2000.

19. Third Division Histories Committee, *The 35th Battalion* (Wellington: A.H. & A.W. Reed, 1947), 40.

20. *A Soldier Remembers*, 29.

21. *The 35th Battalion*, 40.

22. Archives NZ, WAII, 1, DAZ 126.1 War Diary 17 Fd Regt NZA, 18 September 1943.

23. Historical Record of 37th Bn, entry 18 September 1943.

24. *The 35th Battalion*, 41.

25. Maj. Gen H.E. Barrowclough's war diary, entry 17 September 1943.

26. Conversation with Ross Templeton, 23 June 2012.

27. *A Soldier Remembers*, 29.

28. War Diary, Barrowclough, Entry 17 September 1943.

29. *Headquarters*, 192–3. Perhaps instead the bombs dropped were simply duds?

30. *The Tanks*, 113.

31. *Headquarters*, 193.

32. Lawrence Baldwin interview, 13 February 2012.

33. Frank Rennie, *Regular Soldier: A Life in the New Zealand Army* (Auckland: Endeavour Press, 1986), 44–5.

34. *Headquarters, 193.*

35. *Ibid* 29.

36. Archives NZ, WAII, 1, S28/15 vol. II, GOC NZEF IP to Army HQ 20 September 1943.

37. *Ibid.*

38. *Ibid.*, 30.

39. War Diary, Barrowclough, entry 23 September 1943.

40. *Pacific Pioneers*, 27.

41. War Diary, Barrowclough, entry 20 September 1943.

42. Correspondence with author, 23 April 2012.

43. Frank Marks narrative.

44. Hendrick narrative.

Chapter Seven

1. 14 Bde GP O.O. No.1.

2. Gillespie, 126.

3. *Ibid.*

4. War Diary, Barrowclough, Entry 19 September 1943.

5. Archives NZ, WAII, 1, DAZ 155/1/21, Appendix V).

6. 14 Bde GP Operations Order. No.1, 21 September 1943.

7. *Ibid.*

8. Archives NZ, Wellington Office, EA 28, 28/15/4 Report on Ops 3NZ Division Barrowclough to Fraser, 31 December 1943.

9. Archives NZ, Wellington Office, WAII, 1, DAZ 121/1/8 3NZ Division, Intelligence Summary No 1. Entry 2 September 1943.

10. *3rd Division Histories Committee, Pacific Saga* (Wellington: A.H. & A.W. Reed, 1947), 67.

11. Rennie, 45.

12. Report on Ops.

13. Gillespie, 131.

14. 37 BCT Operations, 21 September–10 October, 15 October 1943.

15. Gillespie, 131.

16. *Headquarters*, 78.

17. *The 35th Battalion,* 42.

Chapter Eight

1. War Diary, Barrowclough, Entry 21 September 1943.

2. *The 35th Battalion,* 42.

3. Jack Humphrey interview.

4. Lawrence Baldwin interview.

5. *The 35th Battalion,* 42.

6. *The 35th Battalion,* 43.

7. Archives NZ, WAII, 1, DAZ 157/1/21 Report of Lt. Col Seaward, undated.

8. *The 35th Battalion,* 43.

9. 3rd Divison Histories Committee, *The Gunners,* A.H. and A.W. Reed, 1948, 70.

10. Stout, 40–41.

11. *The 35th Battalion,* 43–44.

12. Army Board, 17.

13. *The 35th Battalion,* 45.

14. Lindsay Adams narrative.

15. *Ibid.*, 45.

16. The Boys anti-tank rifle was one of the least useful pieces of equipment because of its weight, bulkiness, and the lack of appropriate targets.

17. *The 35th Battalion,* 45–46.

18. Lawrence Baldwin narrative.

19. Archives NZ, WAII, 1, DAZ 126, 1/1/32 War Diary, 7 Field Regiment.

20. *The Gunners,* 74.

21. *The 35th Battalion,* 47.

22. *Ibid.*, 48.

23. *Ibid.*, 48.

24. Harry Bioletti interview, 2006.

25. *The 35th Battalion,* 49.

26. *Ibid.*, 48.

27. *Ibid.*, 48–49.

28. *Ibid.*, 48–49.

29. *The 35th Battalion,* 49.

30. Interview J.T. Humphrey, 19 June 2000.

31. *The 35th Battalion,* 51.

32. The 35th Battalion, 52.

33. *Ibid.*, 52–53.

34. *The Gunners,* 74.

35. *The 35th Battalion,* 55.

36. *Ibid.*, 55.

37. *Ibid.*, 55.

38. *Ibid.*, 55.

39. Gillespie, 139.

40. *Ibid.*, 139.

41. *The Gunners,* 75.

42. *Ibid.*, 56.

43. *Ibid.*, 56.

44. *Ibid.*, 56.

45. Third Division Histories Committee, *Pacific Kiwis* (Wellington: A.H. & A.W. Reed, 1947).

46. Horton, 142.

47. Third Marine Division Association *Two Score and Thirteen: Third Marine Division Association History, 1949–2002* (Paducah, Kentucky: Turner Publishing, 2002), 36.

48. Rottman, *WWII Pacific Island Guide,* 128.

49. *Building The Navy's Bases,* 267.

50. U.S. Coast Guard, *The Coast Guard at War,* vol. 7, *Lost Cutters* Washington, DC; Historical Section, Public Information Division, U.S. Coast Guard Headquarters, 1 July 1947, 18–19.

51. Interview Transcript: Denny Frangos: Veterans History Project (Library of Congress), 15 March 2005.

52. U.S. Coast Guard, *The Coastguard at War*, vol. 7, *Lost Cutters*, Washington, DC: Historical Section Public Information Division, U.S. Coast Guard Headquarters, 1 July 1947, 18–19.

53. Brendan O'Carroll, *Khaki Angels: Kiwi Stretcher Bearers in the First and Second World Wars* (Wellington: Ngaio Press, 2009,) 184.

54. 77th Naval Construction Battalion www.history.navy.mil/museums/seabee/unit listpages/NCB/077%20NCBpdf, 37–38.

55. Denny Frangos interview, Veterans History Project.

56. Marine Corps' *Chevron*, 8 January 1944, "Corpsman amputates leg of a Marine in Air Attack," Princeton University Library Historic Newspapers collection.

57. Third Marine Division Association, 32.

58. 77th NCB Cruise Book 38–39.

59. War Diary, Major General Barrowclough, 25 September 1943.

60. *Pacific Pioneers*, 91–93.

61. Historical Record of 37th Bn, September 1943.

62. Archives NZ WAII, 1, DAZ447.33/4. Eyewitness reports Clash at Warambari Bay, Vella Lavella, undated.

63. *A Soldier Remembers*, 29–30.

64. Historical Record of 37th Bn, entry 23, September 1943.

65. The Tanks, 113.

66. *Ibid.*

67. Historical Record of 37th Bn for the month of September 1943, Entry 24 September 1943.

68. Historical Record of 37th Bn for Month of September, 1943. Entry 24 September.

69. Historical Record of 37th Bn—Entry 25 September.

70. *A Soldier Remembers*, 30.

71. Archives NZ, WAII, 1, DAZ 158/1/21 General Summary of Operations, 55B.

72. *Pacific Saga*, 72–73.

73. *Ibid.*, 72.

74. Historical Record of 37th Bn, Entry 27 September 1943.

75. Historical Record of 37th Bn, Entry 28 September 1943.

76. Archives NZ, WAII, 1, DAZ, 37 Bn War Diary, Report 29 September 1943, 46–47.

77. Army Board, 18.

78. Historical Record of 37th Bn, Entry 28 September 1943.

79. *A Soldier Remembers*, 30.

80. Reputedly the craft was called after one of the Battalion's racehorses which had been

a winner in New Caledonia. Archives NZ, WAII, 1, DAZ 158/1/21, Historical Record of 37th Bn, October 1943.

81. *Pacific Saga*, 79.

82. Archives NZ, WAII, 1, DAZ 158/1/22 War Diary Entry, Vella Lavella, 17 October 1943.

83. *Pacific Saga*, 79.

84. Archives NZ, WAII, 1, DAZ 158/1/21, Historical Record of 37th Bn, October 1943, 17 October.

85. Archives NZ, WAII, 1, DAZ War Diary, Entry 17 October 1943.

86. Historical Record of 37th Bn, 13 November 1943.

87. 37 Battalion War diary, entry 15 December 1943.

88. *Pacific Saga*, 79.

89. Archives NZ, WAII, 9, S9 Major General H R Harmon to Major General H E Barrowclough, 23 February 1944.

90. *Ibid.*

91. Archives NZ, WAII, 1, DAZ 158/1/31, 5 December 1943. The danger of using Japanese barges was further made evident the following day—"The old Japanese barge which featured in the strafing incident was set ablaze by a backfire. The engine room was gutted by a fierce blaze and two personnel were fortunate to escape with minor burns."

92. Historical Record of 37th Bn for the month of December.

93. *The 35th*, 113.

94. Archives NZ, WWII, 1, DAZ 157/9/85. Lt. Col Seaward to 14 Brigade HQ, 16 October 1943.

95. Archives NZ, WAII, 1, DAZ Routine Order No 22, 37 Bn 5 December 1943.

96. Lindsay Adams narrative, 146–7, author's collection.

97. War Diary, Barrowclough, entry 25 September 1943, 23.

98. *Headquarters* 197.

99. *Ibid.*

100. Report on Combat Operations, 9.

101. Gillespie 139.

102. *Headquarters*, 236–237.

103. Report on Combat Operations, 10.

104. Gillespie, 139.

105. Historical Record of 37 Bn, Entry 29 September.

106. Historical Record of 37 Bn, Entry 30 September.

107. Archives NZ, WAII, 1, DAZ 447.33/4 Eyewitness Reports "Clash at Warambari Bay, Vella Lavella." Undated.

108. Archives NZ, WAII, I, DAZ, An account of Operations by "A" Coy, 35CT on Vella Lavella, undated.

109. Archives NZ, WAII, 1, 28/15 Vol1 Pacific Operations—14 Brigade Group—3 (NZ) Division Report on Combat Operations—Vella Lavella. Ref: NGOF AG 370.2-W 29 Oct 1943.

110. Archives NZ, WAII, 1, DAZ Report 37 BCT.

111. Australian War Memorial, Combat Intelligence Centre South Pacific Force Translation of Captured Japanese Document, Extract Translation from Notebook belonging to Yoshio Ninoishi, Taken Vella Lavella Oct, 1943.

112. Report on Combat Operations, 13.

113. Larsen, 146.

114. Report on Combat Operations, 16.

115. *Ibid.*

116. *Ibid* 17.

117. Historical Record of 37 Bn, Entry 29 September 1943.

118. Doug Ross interview, 8 November 2006.

119. Hutching, 143.

120. Stout, 42.

121. *The Tanks*, 115.

122. http://www.6thcorpscombatengineers.com/engforum/index. Thurman *Under Enemy Fire—6th Special Seabees, Second Section's Echelon Won at Vella Lavella*: 58th NCB Cruisebook.

123. E-Mail U.S.M.C. Brigadier General Fenwick H. Holmes, Report to John Ratomski, 8 March 2011.

124. Stout.

125. E-Mail Barney L. Quinn, HQ 2nd Section, G.M. 3/C to John Ratomski, 2001.

126. *Taranaki Herald*, "Brave Men," American's Tribute to N.Z. Gunners, November 1943.

127. O'Carroll, 184–185.

128. *The Tanks*, 212.

129. Archives NZ, Air 118 Operational narrative.

130. *The Tanks*, 213.

131. War Diary Major General H.E. Barrowclough, Entry 1 October 1943.

132. Archives NZ, WAII, 9, S9, Barrowclough to Wilkinson, Entry 3 October 1943.

133. Archives NZ, WAII, 9, S9, Wilkinson to Barrowclough, undated.

134. Third Marine Division Association *Two Score and Thirteen*, 31.

135. 77th NCB Seabee Cruise Book, 44.

136. *Ibid.*, 44–45.

137. *Pacific Pioneers*, 93.

138. Archives NZ, Air 118/14. Narratives Section 4, Collapse of Japanese Defense system in the mid Solomons, 2.

139. Miller, 184–186.

Chapter Nine

1. *The 35th Battalion*, 84.

2. *Ibid.*

3. Report of Lt. J.W. Beaumont to Lt. Col. C.F. Seaward, Report on Patrol Marquana Bay area, 26 September to 1 Octiber, 1943, undated, Archives, NZ, WAII, 1, DAZ 158/15/1.

4. *The 35th Battalion*, 85.

5. Gillespie, 134.

6. *The 35th Battalion*, 85.

7. (FN: Beaumont Report).

8. Gillespie, 133.

9. *The 35th Battalion*, .51.

10. Gillespie, 133.

11. Gillespie, 134.

12. Lindsay Adams narrative.

13. *The 35th Battalion*, 86.

14. Recollections of Gordon Graham, 27 April 2007, author's collection.

15. *The 35th*, 86–88.

16. Archives NZ, WAII, 1, Lt. Col. Seaward—Report on Iringila—Timbala-Marquana Bay. Operations 28 September–8 October 1943.

17. *Ibid.*

18. Gordon Graham narrative.

19. Personnel File, NZDF Base Records, Trentham.

20. John Rose narrative.

21. Personnel File, NZDF Base Records, Trentham.

Chapter Ten

1. Doug Ross interview, 8 November 2006.

2. Archives NZ WAII, 1, DAZ 126/1/ 13.

3. Archives NZ WAII, 1, DAZ 121/1/ 1/8 Daily Intelligence Summary No 11, 30 September 1943.

4. Archives NZ WAII, 1, DAZ 157/1/21.

5. *Headquarters*, 201–202

6. *Pacific Saga*, 105.

7. *The Gunners*, 77.

8. *Pacific Saga*, 105.

9. Gillespie, 137.

10. Archives NZ, WAII, 1, DAZ126.1, 1–32 17 Field Regiment September 1942–July 1943.

11. Gillespie, 137.

12. Lindsay Adams narrative, 147.

13. War Diary, Major General H.E. Barrowclough, 7 October 1943.

14. Archives NZ, WAII, 1, 1159 DAZ 158/1/21—DAZ 158/1/31. Translation of leaflet asking Japanese to surrender, 8 October 1943.

15. Archives NZ, WAII, 1, DAZ 158/1/21 Intelligence Report on Jap captured Warambari Bay area at 1640 on 8 October.

16. Miller, 186.

17. War Diary, Barrowclough, Entry 9 October 1943.

18. Gillespie, 138.

19. *The Gunners*, 77.

20. Tameichi Hara *Japanese Destroyer Captain*, New York: Ballantine Books, 1961, 214.

21. *Ibid*.

22. Doscher, *Subchaser in the South Pacific*, 51.

23. S.D. Waters, *The Royal New Zealand Navy* (Wellington, Government Printer, 1956), 330.

24. Dull, 283–286.

25. *Ibid*., 286.

26. Hara, 225.

27. Third Marine Division Association, *Two Score and Thirteen*, 36.

28. Rennie, 47.

29. Archives NZ, Wellington Office, WAII, 1, 151/1/21 Appendix.

30. Rottman, *World War II Pacific Island Guide*, 128.

31. Interview J.T. Humphrey, 19 June 2000.

32. *A Soldier Remembers*, 31.

Chapter Eleven

1. Lt. Col. A.H.L. Sugden, Routine Order 248/43, 5 September 1943.

2. *The 35th Battalion*, 60.

3. Archives NZ, WAII, 1, DAZ 158/1/31, 37 Bn War Diary, 11 October 1943.

4. *Pacific Kiwis*, 78–79.

5. The *Tanks*, 117.

6. *Headquarters*, 201.

7. Archives NZ, WAII, 1, DAZ 158/1/23

Routine Order No 3, Lt Col. A.H.L. Sugden, 16 October 1943.

8. The *Tanks*, 116.

9. Archives NZ, WAII, War Diary 37 Bn Entry, 18 October 1943.

10. *Pacific Kiwis*, 72–73.

11. O'Carroll, 185.

12. War Diary Barrowclough, Entry 20 October 1943.

13. *Pacific Kiwis*, 87.

14. Body of 70771 Pte Corcoran H.G. found and buried. 9 October 1943 War Diary 35Bn.

15. Archives NZ, WAII, 1, DAZ 121/9/18/1 A NZ Prisoner of Japanese, Sgt F. White, 10 October 1943.

16. Ralph Williams, in Megan Hutchings, *Against the Sun*, 204.

17. Historical Record of 37th Bn, Entry 21 December 1943.

18. *Ibid*., Entry 24 December 1943.

19. War Diary, Major General H.E. Barrowclough, 15 October 1943.

20. *Ibid*., 12 November 1943.

21. G.G. Carter *A Family Affair: A Brief Survey of New Zealand Methodism's Involvement in Mission Overseas 1822–1972*, Auckland: Institute Press, 1973, 191.

22. Archives NZ, WAII, 1, DAZ 158/1/21, War Diary 37 Bn Entry 17 October 1943.

23. *The Gunners*, 78.

24. *Ibid*.

25. *Headquarters*, 231.

26. Rennie, 47–48.

27. Gillespie, 141.

28. Archives NZ, WAII, 1, DAZ, Routine Order No 2, Lt. Col. C.F. Seaward, 25 October 1943.

29. Lieutenant-Colonel A.H.L. Sugden routine order 248/43, 5 September 1943.

30. Archives NZ, WAII, 1, DAZ, 158/1/23 Routine Orders by Lt. Col. A.H.L. Sugden, 19 November 1943, Order No. 116.

31. Routine Order No 4, 19 October 1943.

32. Lt. Col. Sugden, 15 October 1943, Routine Order No 2.

33. Routine Orders, Lt. Col. A.H.L. Sugden Order No 3, 16 October 1943.

34. Archives NZ, WAII, 1, DAZ 158/1/21 Entry 27 October 1943. Regular reports of shipping movements came from the Islanders.

35. War Diary, Barrowclough, Entry 20 September 1943.

36. *Pacific Kiwis*, 73–76.

37. Gillespie, 141.

38. Archives NZ, WAII, 1, DAZ 57/9/85,

35 Battalion, No. 2. Combat Team O.O., No 1. 16 October 1943.

39. Operation Order N82.

40. 37 Battalion War Diary Entry, 23 October 1943.

41. Archives NZ, WAII, 1, DAZ 158/1/31 37Bn Routine Orders No1-13 October 1943.

42. Routine Orders, Order No. 1 Lt. Col. A.H.L. Sugden, 13 October 1943.

43. Doug Ross interview 2006.

44. *Pacific Kiwis*, 81.

45. *Pacific Saga*, 83.

46. 37 Battalion War Diary, 7 and 9 December 1943.

47. Rennie, 47.

48. *Ibid*.

49. *Pacific Pioneers*, 67.

50. *Ibid*.

51. *The Tanks*, 213–214.

52. *Ibid*.

53. *Ibid*., 214.

54. War Diary, Barrowclough, Entry 24 October 1943.

55. Archives NZ, AD, 1, 375/1/80 Report on NZASC Operations with 3 Division in South Pacific, Lt. Col. C.A. Blazey, May 1945, 16.

56. Julia Millen *Salute to Service* (Wellington: Victoria University Press, 1997), 268.

57. Archives NZ, WAII, 9, 59 Barrowclough to C.O. 1MAC, Vella Lavella, 25 October 1943.

58. War Diary, Barrowclough, Entry 1 November 1943.

59. Lt. Col. A.H.L. Sugden, Routine Order No. 24.

60. Laurie Barber and Cliff Lord, *Swift and Sure: A History of The Royal New Zealand Corps of Signals and Army Signalling in New Zealand* (Wellington: Wyatt and Wilson, 1996), 199.

61. *Pacific Kiwis*, 99–100.

62. Historical Record, 37th Bn, 25 November 1943.

63. *Headquarterss*, 237.

64. *Pacific Kiwis*, 85.

65. *Pacific Saga*, 83.

66. Archives NZ, WAII, 1, DAZ 156/15/1 30 Battalion Unit History Entry, Sunday, 19 December 1943.

67. War Diary, Barrowclough, Entry 20–27 December 1943.

68. *Headquarters*, 232.

69. *Ibid* 233.

70. Rottman, World War II *Pacific Island Guide*, 130.

71. Duane T. Hove *American Warriors: Five Presidents in the Pacific Theatre of World War II* (Shippensburg, PA: Burd Street Press, 2003), 82.

72. Nigel Hamilton, *JFK: Reckless Youth* (New York: Random House, 1992), 625.

73. Hove, 89–96.

74. Nixon-Gannon interviews, University of Georgia Special collections Libraries, Day 1, Tape 3.

75. *Ibid*.

76. Hove, 113–115.

77. Robert Bulkey, *At Close Quarters: T. boats in the United States Navy* (Washington, DC: Naval History Division, 1962), 137.

78. Archives NZ, WAII, 9, 59 Barrowclough to Commanding General, Forward Area, 27 December 1943.

79. Archives NZ, Air 118, 21, Operational narrative, The Capture of Vila Airfield and Vella Lavella, 2.

80. Eric Bergerud *Fire in the Sky*, 625.

81. Bruce Gamble, *The Black Sheep*, New York: Ballantine Books, 1998, 327.

82. *Ibid*.

83. *Pacific Pioneers*, 31.

84. *Ibid*., 37.

85. *Ibid*., 27.

86. *Ibid*., 25.

87. *Pacific Pioneers*, 50.

88. Lindsay Adams narrative, author's collection.

89. *Pacific Pioneers*, 38.

90. *Ibid*., 78.

91. *Headquarters*, 223.

92. 77th NCB Cruise Book, 48.

93. Ralph Williams in Megan Hutching ed., *Against the Rising Sun*, 210.

94. This also occurred with the New Zealanders stationed on The Green Islands—see *The Tanks*, Chapter 11, "A Cure for Monotony" 53–58.

95. Rob McLean, in Megan Hutching *Against the Rising Sun*, 144–5.

96. *Headquarters*, 223.

97. *The 35th Battalion*, 97.

98. *Pacific Pioneers*, 76–77.

99. Archives NZ, WAII, 1, DAZ 156/15/ 10, 30 Bn Unit History.

100. *Pacific Kiwis*, 99.

101. Archives NZ WAII, 1 DAZ, 30 Bn History.

102. Jennifer Haworth *The Art of War: New Zealand War Artists in the Field 1939–1945*, Christchurch: Hazard Press, 2007.

103. *Ibid*., 157.

104. Lt. Col. A.H.L. Sugden, Routine Order No 1. 13 October 1943.

105. Archives NZ, WAII, 1 DAZ 158/1/21, Historical Record of the 37th Battalion for Month of August 1943, Entry August 16 & 17, 1943.

106. Archives NZ, WAII, 1 DAZ 158/1/31, 37 Bn Routine Order No. 9, 28 October 1943.

107. Archives NZ, WAII, 1 DAZ 182/6/1-6 Report on 35 Bn C.T Area 11 November 1943.

108. 37Bn, Routine Orders, 13 October 1943, No.1, Combat Team.

109. Archives NZ, WAII, 1, DAZ 182/6/1-6 Interim Malaria Report prepared for Lt. Col. Hunter, C.O. 7 FD AMB, 2nd Lt. R.D. Dick, 25 October 1943.

110. 37 BCT Report.

111. Stout 44.

112. *Ibid.*, 44.

113. Stout 46.

114. James F. Christ, *Mission Raise Hell: The U.S. Marines on Choiseul, October–November 1943*, Annapolis: Naval Institute Press, 2006, 82–83.

115. Stout 47.

116. Archives NZ, WAII, DAZ Report on Outbreak of Bacillary Dysentery in No. 1 Combat Team, September & October 1943, 23 October 1943.

117. *Pacific Pioneers*, 62–3.

118. *Headquarters*, 232.

119. Lawrence Baldwin, 15 February 2012.

120. Lt. Col. A.H.L. Sugden, Routine Order No.4, 19 October 1943.

121. *Pacific Kiwis*.

122. Archives NZ, WA II, DAZ, 158/15/1 Historical Record of 37th Bn for the month of October, 1943, Entry 8 October 1943). Sadly, this burden would be borne by the soldiers and their families into the post war years.

123. Archives NZ, WAII, 1, 1553, DAZ 156/15/1 30 Battalion Unit History December 1943.

124. Lt. Col. A.H.L. Sugden Routine Orders 254/43, 11 September 1943.

125. "An Account of Operations by 'A' Company, 35 BCT on Vella Lavella," undated.

126. Gillespie, 139.

127. *Pacific Kiwis*, 101.

128. Gillespie, 142.

129. Archives NZ, EA28, 28/15/4 Barrowclough to Fraser, 31 December 1943. However, casualties continued to occur due to Japanese air attacks and accidents.

130. Gillespie, 138.

131. Stout, 92.

Chapter Twelve

1. *The Gunners*, 118–9.

2. WWII Memorial Plaque dedicated on Vella Lavella Island, Solomon Islands, 31 October 2011. http://www.nzdf.mil.nz/news/mediareleases/2011/20111031-wmpdovlisdi.htm.

3. "Warriors of the Pacific," *Maori Television*, 25 April 2011.

4. *Two Score and Thirteen*, 37–38.

5. Gordon Graham narrative.

6. *Two Score and Thirteen*, 35.

7. *Ibid.*

8. Lindsay Adams narrative, 148.

9. Office of Naval Intelligence *Combat narrative, Solomon Islands Campaign*: XII, 4.

10. Eric Bergerud *Fire in the Sky*, 609.

11. Gillespie, 142.

12. Archives NZ, Air 118/14, 5. Air Combat Intelligence, South Pacific Force, USN September–October 1943. Air H 482/6/6.

13. 35th Battalion, Chapter 11, A Padre in the Pacific, 89.

14. Isley and Crowl 170–174.

15. Harry M. Gailey, *Bougainville 1943–1945: The Forgotten Campaign* (Lexington: University Press of Kentucky, 1991), 2.

16. Prados, 350.

Bibliography

Books

Altobello, Brian. *Into the Shadows Furious: The Brutal Battle for New Georgia.* Novato, CA: Presidio Press, 2000.

Army Board. *Guadalcanal to Nissan: With the Third New Zealand Division through the Solomons.* Wellington: Army Board, 1945.

Barber, Laurie, and Cliff Lord. *Swift and Sure: A History of the Royal New Zealand Corps of Signals and Army Signaling in New Zealand.* Wellington: Wyatt & Wilson, 1996.

Bergerud, Eric. *Fire in the Sky: The Air War in the South Pacific,* Boulder, CO: Westview Press, 2000.

Bergerud, Eric. *Touched with Fire: The Land War in the South Pacific,* New York: Penguin Books, 1996.

Bulkley, Robert J. *At Close Quarters: P.T. Boats in the United States Navy.* Washington, DC: Naval History Division, 1962.

Bull, Stephen. *World War II Jungle Warfare Tactics.* Oxford, UK: Osprey Publishing, 2007.

Carter, G.G. *A Family Affair: A Brief Survey of New Zealand Methodism's Involvement in Mission Overseas 1822–1972.* Auckland: Institute Press, 1973.

Christ, James P. *Mission Raise Hell: The U.S. Marines on Choiseul, October: November, 1943.* Annapolis, MD: Naval Institute Press, 2006.

Collins, John M. *Military Geography for Professionals and the Public.* Washington, DC: Brasseys, 1998.

Colonial Office. *Among Those Present: The Official Story of the Pacific Islands at War Prepared for the Colonial Office by the Central Office of Information.* London: His Majesty's Stationery Office, 1946.

Craven, W.F., and J.L. Cate, eds. *The Army Air Forces in World War II,* vol. 7, *The Pacific: Guadalcanal to Saipan, August 1942: July 1944.* Washington, DC: Office of Air Force History, 1983.

Crawford, J., ed. *Kia Kaha: New Zealand in the Second World War,* Auckland: Oxford University Press, 2000.

Crenshaw, Russell Syndor. *South Pacific Destroyer: The Battle for the Solomons from Savo Island to Vella Gulf.* Annapolis: Naval Institute Press, 1998.

Department of the Navy, Bureau of Yards and Docks. *Building the Navy's Bases in World War II: History of the Bureau of Yards and Docks and Civilian Engineer Corps 1940–1946,* vol. 2. Washington, DC: U.S. Government Printing Office, 1947.

Domagalski, John D. *Sunk in Kula Gulf.* Dulles, VA: Potomac Books, 2012.

Doscher, Henry J. *Subchaser in the South Pacific: A Saga of USS SC-761 During World War II.* Austin, TX: Eakin Press, 1994.

Dower, John. *War Without Mercy: Race and Power in the Pacific War.* London: Faber & Faber, 1986.

Drea, Edward *Japan's Imperial Army: Its Rise and Fall 1853–1945,* Lawrence: University of Kansas, 2009.

Dull, Paul S. *A Battle History of the Imperial Japanese Navy, 1941–1945.* Annapolis: Naval Institute Press, 1978.

Dyer, George C. *The Amphibians Came to Conquer: The Story of Admiral Richmond Kelly Turner*, 2 vols. Washington, DC: U.S. Government Printing Office, 1969.

Gailey, Harry M. *Bougainville: The Forgotten Campaign 1943–1945*. Lexington: University of Kentucky Press, 1991.

Gamble, Bruce. *The Black Sheep*. New York: Ballantine Books, 1998.

Gedeon, Clarence Edward, ed. *History of the 58th Seabees*. Foxcroft Commercial Press, 1950.

Gillespie, Oliver A. *The Pacific*. Wellington: Government Printer, 1952.

Halsey, William F., and Bryan J. Halsey. *Admiral Halsey's Story*. New York: McGraw-Hill, 1947.

Hammel, Eric. *Munda Trail: The New Georgia Campaign June–August 1943,—New Georgia and Bougainville*. Pacifica, CA: Pacifica Military History, 1989.

Hara, Tameichi. *Japanese Destroyer Captain*. New York: Ballantine Books, 1961.

Harper, Glyn, and Joel Hayward, eds. *Born to Lead? Portraits of New Zealand Commanders*. Auckland: Exisle Press, 2003.

Haworth, Jennifer. *The Art of War: New Zealand War Artists in the Field 1939–1945*. Christchurch: Hazard Press, 2007.

Horton, D.C. *New Georgia: Pattern for Victory*. London: Pan/Ballantine, 1972.

Hove, Duane T. *American Warriors: Five Presidents in the Pacific Theater of World War II*. Shippensburg, PA: Burd Street Press, 2003.

Hutching, Megan, ed. *Against the Rising Sun: New Zealanders Remember the Pacific War*. Auckland: HarperCollins, 2006.

Isley, Jeter A., and Philip Crowl. *The U.S. Marines and Amphibious War*. Princeton, PA: Princeton University Press, 1951.

James, Karl. *The Hard Slog: Australians in the Bougainville Campaign 1944–45*. New York: Cambridge University Press, 2012.

Ladd, J.D. *Assault from the Sea 1939–45: The Craft, The Landings, The Men*. New York: Hippocrene Books, 1976.

Larsen, Colin R. *Pacific Commandos: New Zealanders and Fijians in Action: A History of Southern Independent Commando and First Commando Fijian Guerrillas*. Wellington: A.H. & A.W. Reed, 1946.

Lord, Walter. *Lonely Vigil: Coastwatchers of the Solomons*, Annapolis: Naval Institute Press, 2006.

Lorelli, John. *To Foreign Shores: U.S. Amphibious Operations in World War II*. Annapolis: Naval Institute Press, 1995.

McGee, William L. *Amphibious Operations in the South Pacific in WWII, Volume II, The Solomons Campaigns 1942–1943, From Guadalcanal to Bougainville: Pacific War Turning Point*. Santa Barbara, California: BMC Publications, 2002.

McNaughton James C. *Nisei Linguists: Japanese Americans in the American Military Intelligence Service During World War II*, Washington DC: U.S. Government Printing Office, 2006.

Millen, Julia. *Salute to Service: A History of the Royal New Zealand Corps of Transport and Its Predecessors 1860–1996*. Wellington: Victoria University Press, 1997.

Miller, John. *Cartwheel: The Reduction of Rabaul*. Harrisburg, PA: The National Historical Society, 1993.

Morison, Samuel Eliot. *History of United States Naval Operations in World War II*, vol. 6, *Breaking the Bismark's Barrier, 22 July 1942: 1 May 1944*. Edison, NJ: Castle Books, 2001.

Mulligan, Keith. *Kittyhawks and Coconuts*. Otaki, NZ: New Zealand Wings, 1995.

Newell, Reg. *Operation Goodtime and the Battle of the Treasury Islands, 1943: The World War II Invasion by United States and New Zealand Forces*. Jefferson, NC: McFarland, 2012.

Newell, Reg. *Pacific Star: 3 NZ Division in the South Pacific in World War II*. Auckland: Exisle Press, 2015.

O'Carroll, Brendan. *Khaki Angels: Kiwi Stretcher Bearers in the First and Second World Wars*. Wellington: Ngaio Press, 2009.

Office of Naval Intelligence. *U.S. Combat Narratives: Solomon Islands Campaign*. Washington, DC, 1943.

Patrick, Lindsay. *The Coastwatchers*. Sydney: Random House, 2010.

Potter, E.B. *Bull Halsey*. Annapolis: Naval Institute Press, 1985.

Potter, E.B. *Nimitz*. Annapolis: Naval Institute Press, 1976.

Prados, John. *Islands of Destiny: The Solomons Campaign and the Eclipse of the Rising Sun*. New York: New American Library, 2012.

Rennie, Frank. *Regular Soldier: A Life in the New Zealand Army*. Auckland: Endeavour Press, 1986.

Rentz, John N. *Marines in the Central Solomons*. Washington DC: Historical Branch, Headquarters, U.S. Marine Corps, 1952.

Ross, J.M.S. *Royal New Zealand Air Force*. Wellington: Department of Internal Affairs, 1955.

Rottman, Gordon L. *World War II Pacific Island Guide: A Geo: Military Study*. Westport, CT: Greenwood Press, 2002.

Rudge, Chris. *Air to Air: The Story Behind the Air-to-Air Combat Claims of the RNZAF*. Lyttelton: Adventure Air, 2003.

Ruscoe, Theodore. *United States Destroyer Operations in World War II*. Annapolis: United States Naval Institute Press, 1953.

Shaw, Henry I., and Douglas T. Kane. *Isolation of Rabaul: History of U.S. Marine Corps Operations in World War II*, vol. 2. Washington, DC: Historical Branch, H.Q. USMC, 1963.

Spector, Ronald H. *Eagle Against the Sun: the American War with Japan*. New York: Viking Penguin, 1984.

Spurdle, Bob. *The Blue Arena*. London: William Kimber, 1986.

Stille, Mark. *USN Destroyer vs IJN Destroyer, the Pacific 1943*. Oxford: Osprey, 2012.

Stout, T. Duncan. *Medical Services in New Zealand and the Pacific*. Wellington: Historical Publications Branch, 1958.

Styling, Mark. *Corsair Aces of World War II*. Oxford: Osprey Publishing, 1995.

Third Division Histories Committee. *Headquarters: A Brief Outline of the Activities of Headquarters of the Third Division and the 8th and 14th Brigades During Their Service in the Pacific*. Wellington: A.H. & A.W. Reed, 1947.

Third Division Histories Committee. *Pacific Kiwis, Being the Story of the Service in the Pacific of the 30th Battalion, Third Division, Second New Zealand Expeditionary Force*. Wellington: A.H. & A.W. Reed, 1947.

Third Division Histories Committee. *Pacific Pioneers: The Story of the Engineers of the New Zealand Expeditionary Force in the Pacific*. Wellington: A.H. & A.W. Reed, 1947.

Third Division Histories Committee. *Pacific Saga: The Personal Chronicle of the 37th Battalion and Its Part in the Third Division's Campaign*. Wellington: A.H. & A.W. Reed, 1947.

Third Division Histories Committee. *Pacific Service: TheStory of the New Zealand Army Service Units with the Third Division in the Pacific*. Wellington: A.H. & A.W. Reed, 1948.

Third Division Histories Committee. *Shovel, Sword and Scalpel: A Record of Service of Medical Units in the Second New Zealand Expeditionary Force in the Pacific*. Wellington: A.H. & A.W. Reed, 1945.

Third Division Histories Committee. *The 35th Battalion: A Record of Service of the 35th Battalion with the Third Division in the Pacific*. Wellington: A.H. & A.W. Reed, 1947.

Third Division Histories Committee. *The Gunners: An Intimate Record of Units of the 3rd New Zealand Divisional Artillery in the Pacific from 1940 Until 1945*, Wellington: A.H. & A.W. Reed, 1948.

Third Division Histories Committee. *The Tanks (MMGs and Ordnance)*. Wellington: A.H. & A.W. Reed, 1947.

Third Marine Division Association. *Two Score and Thirteen—Third Marine Division Association History*, 1949–2002. Paducah, KY: Turner Publishing, 2002.

U.S. Coast Guard. *The Coast Guard at War*, vol. 7, *Lost Cutters*. Washington, DC: Historical Section, Public Information Division, U.S. Coast Guard Headquarters, 1947.

Waters, S.D. *Royal New Zealand Navy*. Wellington: Government Printer, 1956.

Wolf, William. *13th Fighter Command in World War II: Air Combat Over Guadalcanal and the Solomons*. Atglen, PA: Schiffer Publishing, 2004.

Articles

Allen, W.H. "Action at Vella Lavella." *The Field Artillery Journal*, vol. 40, May–June 1950. Washington, DC: The United States Field Artillery Association, 120–124.

Lord, Walter. "Ordeal at Vella Lavella." *American Heritage*, 1977 vol. 28, Issue 4.

Websites

77th Naval Construction Battalion: http://www.history.navy.mil/museums/seabee
NZ Official War Histories and 3NZ Division Unofficial Histories: http://www.nzvictoria.ac.nz/
    tm/scholarly/tei-corpus-WH2.html
USS *Helena*: http://www.usshelena.org
Dictionary of American Naval Fighting Ships: http://www.hazegray.org/danfs/
United States Navy Combat Narrative Kolombangara and Vella Lavella 6 August–7 October 1943:
    http://www.ibiblio.org/hyperwar/usn-cn-kolombangara/index.html
Military Times Hall of Valor: http://projects.militarytimes.com/citations
35th Infantry (Cacti) Regiment Association: http://www.cacti.org/regiment
Veteran's History Project: http://www.loc.gov/vets

Archives

Australian War Memorial, Canberra, Australia
Archives New Zealand, Wellington, New Zealand
Methodist Church of New Zealand Archives

Interviews and Correspondence

Gordon Graham, 27 April 2006
Doug Ross, interview 8 November 2006
Jack T. Humphrey
Harry Bioletti
Lawrence Baldwin, interview 13 February 2012
Lindsay Adams
Frank Marks
Ross Templeton, 23 June 2012
Terry Hendrick

Narratives

"Hi-S-Tory, a takeoff with two meanings—His Story and History" by Frank L. Marks, F Company,
    2nd Battalion, 35th Infantry Regiment, 25th Infantry Division
Private James C. Cook, 35th Infantry Regiment of the 25th Division Unit Tropic Lightning Divi-
    sion
Lindsay Adams (Author's Collection)
Ross Templeton (Author's Collection)
Jerome J. Hendrick (Author's Collection)
Gordon Graham (Author's Collection)

Other Sources

Interview Transcript, Denny Frangos, 15 March 2005, Veterans History Project
War Diary, Major General Harold E. Barrowclough
Auckland War Memorial Museum Library MS 2006/53 Silvester, Archie Wharton Ellesmere,
    Papers, 1908–1997
Princeton University Library: Historic Newspapers Collection

Index